WORLD WAR I

OPPOSING VIEWPOINTS®

Other Books of Related Interest:

American History Series

African Americans
The American Frontier
The American Revolution
Asian Americans
The Bill of Rights
The Civil Rights Movement
The Civil War
The Cold War
The Creation of the Constitution
The Great Depression
Immigration
The Industrial Revolution
Isolationism
Native Americans
The 1960s
Puritanism
Reconstruction
Slavery
The Vietnam War
The Women's Rights Movement
World War II

Opposing Viewpoints in American History

Volume I: From Colonial Times to Reconstruction
Volume II: From Reconstruction to the Present

WORLD WAR I
OPPOSING VIEWPOINTS®

David L. Bender, *Publisher*
Bruno Leone, *Executive Editor*

William Dudley, *Series Editor*
John C. Chalberg, Ph.D., professor of history,
  Normandale Community College, *Consulting Editor*

William Dudley, *Book Editor*

AMERICAN HISTORY SERIES

Greenhaven Press, Inc.
San Diego, California

Cover photographs, clockwise from top: 1) Women riveters (Library of Congress); 2) President Woodrow Wilson (Library of Congress); 3) U.S. troops in the Argonne Forest, France, 1918 (National Archives); 4) Peace activists Rose Cohn, Dorothy Day, and Charlotte Margolies, February 9, 1917 (UPI/Corbis-Bettmann).

Library of Congress Cataloging-in-Publication Data

World War I : opposing viewpoints / William Dudley,
    book editor.
        p.   cm. — (American history series)
    Includes bibliographical references and index.
    ISBN 1-56510-703-9 (lib. bdg. : alk. paper) —
ISBN 1-56510-702-0 (pbk. : alk. paper)
        1. World War, 1914–1918—United States—Sources.
    2. World War, 1914–1918—Public opinion—Sources.
    3. Public opinion—United States—Sources.
    I. Dudley, William, 1964–   . II. Series: American history series
    (San Diego, Calif.)
    D639.P88W67   1998   97-48281
    940.3'73—dc21   CIP

©1998 by Greenhaven Press, Inc., PO Box 289009,
San Diego, CA 92198-9009

Printed in the U.S.A.

"America was born of revolt, flourished in dissent, became great through experimentation."

Henry Steele Commager, American Historian

Contents

Chapter 6: Woodrow Wilson's Decision to Go to War in Retrospect

Foreword

Aboard the *Arbella* as it lurched across the cold, gray Atlantic, John Winthrop was as calm as the waters surrounding him were wild. With the confidence of a leader, Winthrop gathered his Puritan companions around him. It was time to offer a sermon. England lay behind them, and years of strife and persecution for their religious beliefs were over, he said. But the Puritan abandonment of England, he reminded his followers, did not mean that England was beyond redemption. Winthrop wanted his followers to remember England even as they were leaving it behind. Their goal should be to create a new England, one far removed from the authority of the Anglican church and King Charles I. In Winthrop's words, their settlement in the New World ought to be "a city upon a hill," a just society for corrupt England to emulate.

A Chance to Start Over

One June 8, 1630, John Winthrop and his company of refugees had their first glimpse of what they came to call New England. High on the surrounding hills stood a welcoming band of fir trees whose fragrance drifted to the *Arbella* on a morning breeze. To Winthrop, the "smell off the shore [was] like the smell of a garden." This new world would, in fact, often be compared to the Garden of Eden. Here, John Winthrop would have his opportunity to start life over again. So would his family and his shipmates. So would all those who came after them. These victims of conflict in old England hoped to find peace in New England.

Winthrop, for one, had experienced much conflict in his life. As a Puritan, he was opposed to Catholicism and Anglicanism, both of which, he believed, were burdened by distracting rituals and distant hierarchies. A parliamentarian by conviction, he despised Charles I, who had spurned Parliament and created a private army to do his bidding. Winthrop believed in individual responsibility and fought against the loss of religious and political freedom. A gentleman landowner, he feared the rising economic power of a merchant class that seemed to value only money. Once Winthrop stepped aboard the *Arbella*, he hoped, these conflicts would not be a part of his American future.

Yet his Puritan religion told Winthrop that human beings are fallen creatures and that perfection, whether communal or individual, is unachievable on this earth. Therefore, he faced a paradox: On the one hand, his religion demanded that he attempt to live a perfect life in an imperfect world. On the other hand, it told him that he was destined to fail.

Soon after Winthrop disembarked from the *Arbella*, he came face-to-face with this maddening dilemma. He found himself presiding not over a utopia but over a colony caught up in disputes as troubling as any he had confronted in his English past. John Winthrop, it seems, was not the only Puritan with a dream of a heaven on earth. But others in the community saw the dream differently. They wanted greater political and religious freedom than their leader was prepared to grant. Often, Winthrop was able to handle this conflict diplomatically. For example, he expanded participation in elections and allowed the voters of Massachusetts Bay greater power.

But religious conflict was another matter because it was grounded in competing visions of the Puritan utopia. In Roger Williams and Anne Hutchinson, two of his fellow colonists, John Winthrop faced rivals unprepared to accept his definition of the perfect community. To Williams, perfection demanded that he separate himself from the Puritan institutions in his community and create an even "purer" church. Winthrop, however, disagreed and exiled Williams to Rhode Island. Hutchinson presumed that she could interpret God's will without a minister. Again, Winthrop did not agree. Hutchinson was tried on charges of heresy, convicted, and banished from Massachusetts.

John Winthrop's Massachusetts colony was the first but far from the last American attempt to build a unified, peaceful community that, in the end, only provoked a discord. This glimpse at its history reveals what Winthrop confronted: the unavoidable presence of conflict in American life.

American Assumptions

From America's origins in the early seventeenth century, Americans have often held several interrelated assumptions about their country. First, people believe that to be American is to be free. Second, because Americans did not have to free themselves from feudal lords or an entrenched aristocracy, America has been seen as a perpetual haven from the troubles and disputes that are found in the Old World.

John Winthrop lived his life as though these assumptions were true. But the opposing viewpoints presented in the American History Series should reveal that for many Americans, these assumptions were and are myths. Indeed, for numerous Americans, liberty has not always been guaranteed, and disputes have been an integral, sometimes welcome part of their life.

The American landscape has been torn apart again and again by a great variety of clashes—theological, ideological, political, economic, geographical, and social. But such a landscape is not necessarily a hopelessly divided country. If the editors hope to prove anything during the course of this series, it is not that the United States has been destroyed by conflict but rather that it has been enlivened, enriched, and even strengthened by Americans who have disagreed with one another.

Thomas Jefferson was one of the least confrontational of Americans, but he boldly and irrevocably enriched American life with his individualistic views. Like John Winthrop before him, he had a notion of an American Eden. Like Winthrop, he offered a vision of a harmonious society. And like Winthrop, he not only became enmeshed in conflict but eventually presided over a people beset by it. But unlike Winthrop, Jefferson believed this Eden was not located in a specific community but in each individual American. His Declaration of Independence from Great Britain could also be read as a declaration of independence for each individual in American society.

Jefferson's Ideal

Jefferson's ideal world was composed of "yeoman farmers," each of whom was roughly equal to the others in society's eyes, each of whom was free from the restrictions of both government and fellow citizens. Throughout his life, Jefferson offered a continuing challenge to Americans: Advance individualism and equality or see the death of the American experiment. Jefferson believed that the strength of this experiment depended upon a society of autonomous individuals and a society without great gaps between rich and poor. His challenge to his fellow Americans to create—and sustain—such a society has itself produced both economic and political conflict.

A society whose guiding document is the Declaration of Independence is a society assured of the freedom to dream—and to disagree. We know that Jefferson hated conflict, both personal and political. His tendency was to avoid confrontations of any sort, to squirrel himself away and write rather than to stand up and speak his mind. It is only through his written words that we can grasp Jefferson's utopian dream of a society of independent farmers, all pursuing their private dreams and all leading lives of middling prosperity.

Jefferson, this man of wealth and intellect, lived an essentially happy private life. But his public life was much more troublesome. From the first rumblings of the American Revolution in the 1760s to the North-South skirmishes of the 1820s that ultimately produced the Civil War, Jefferson was at or near the center of American political history. The issues were almost too many—and too crucial—for one lifetime: Jefferson had to choose between sup-

11

porting or rejecting the path of revolution. During and after the ensuing war, he was at the forefront of the battle for religious liberty. After endorsing the Constitution, he opposed the economic plans of Alexander Hamilton. At the end of the century, he fought the infamous Alien and Sedition Acts, which limited civil liberties. As president, he opposed the Federalist court, conspiracies to divide the union, and calls for a new war against England. Throughout his life, Thomas Jefferson, slaveholder, pondered the conflict between American freedom and American slavery. And from retirement at his Monticello retreat, he frowned at the rising spirit of commercialism he feared was dividing Americans and destroying his dream of American harmony.

No matter the issue, however, Thomas Jefferson invariably supported the rights of the individual. Worried as he was about the excesses of commercialism, he accepted them because his main concern was to live in a society where liberty and individualism could flourish. To Jefferson, Americans had to be free to worship as they desired. They also deserved to be free from an over-reaching government. To Jefferson, Americans should also be free to possess slaves.

Harmony, an Elusive Goal

Before reading the articles in this anthology, the editors ask readers to ponder the lives of John Winthrop and Thomas Jefferson. Each held a utopian vision, one based upon the demands of community and the other on the autonomy of the individual. Each dreamed of a country of perpetual new beginnings. Each found himself thrust into a position of leadership and found that conflict could not be avoided. Harmony, whether communal or individual, was a forever elusive goal.

The opposing visions of Winthrop and Jefferson have been at the heart of many differences among Americans from many backgrounds through the whole of American history. Moreover, their visions have provoked important responses that have helped shape American society, the American character, and many an American battle.

The editors of the American History Series have done extensive research to find representative opinions on the issues included in these volumes. They have found numerous outstanding opposing viewpoints from people of all times, classes, and genders in American history. From those, they have selected commentaries that best fit the nature and flavor of the period and topic under consideration. Every attempt was made to include the most important and relevant viewpoints in each chapter. Obviously, not every notable viewpoint could be included. Therefore, a selective, annotated bibliography has been provided at the end of each book to aid readers in seeking additional information.

The editors are confident that as this series reveals past conflicts, it will help revitalize the reader's views of the American present. In that spirit, the American History Series is dedicated to the proposition that American history is more complicated, more fascinating, and more troubling than John Winthrop or Thomas Jefferson ever dared to imagine.

John C. Chalberg
Consulting Editor

Greenhaven Press anthologies primarily consist of previously published material taken from a variety of sources, including periodicals, books, scholarly journals, newspapers, government documents, and position papers from private and public organizations. These original sources are often edited for length and to ensure their accessibility for a young adult audience. The anthology editors also change the original titles of these works in order to clearly present the main thesis of each viewpoint and to explicitly indicate the opinion presented in the viewpoint. These alterations are made in consideration of both the reading and comprehension levels of a young adult audience. Every effort is made to ensure that Greenhaven Press accurately reflects the original intent of the authors included in this anthology.

Introduction

"During World War I, the United States took many actions that indicated a change in how Americans viewed their government and their place in the world."

Early on the morning of September 12, 1918, Eddie Rickenbacker, the most famous American fighter pilot of World War I, flew his airplane above an area of France by the village of St. Mihiel. Beneath him, the First Army of the American Expeditionary Force (AEF), 500,000 strong, was making its first major offensive of the war. It had been more than four years since the "Great War" had started in Europe, and for much of that time a salient, or bulge, in the Allied line in this part of France had been held and fortified by the opposing German army.

It had been seventeen months since the United States entered the conflict on the side of the Allies. From one perspective, the battle unfolding beneath Rickenbacker was the culmination of a long and arduous process in which America first debated whether to intervene in the war in Europe, then struggled to build and train an army to do just that. The offensive was a chance to demonstrate to both the Germans and the Allies what U.S. soldiers under American command could do. In his 1919 book *Fighting the Flying Circus,* Rickenbacker described what he saw that morning from his high vantage point:

> Closely pressing came our eager doughboys fighting along like Indians. They scurried from cover to cover, always crouching low as they ran. Throwing themselves flat to the ground, they would get their rifles into action and spray the Boches [Germans] with more bullets until they withdrew from sight. Then another running advance and another serious pumping of lead from the Yanks.... I flew above this scene for many miles watching the most spectacular free show that ever men gazed upon.

Rickenbacker's description captures the spirit and enthusiasm that many Americans felt about this war. Yet the sense of glorious spectacle was not shared by everyone. Foot soldiers, especially, experienced the chaos and danger of large-scale assaults against fortified positions. Thus, a somewhat different picture of the St. Mihiel campaign emerges from ground level in this excerpt from the diary of Norman Roberts, one of the "doughboys" in the AEF.

> Day had not broke and you could hardly tell where to go. Bullets, millions of them, flying like rain drops. Rockets and flares in all directions. Shrapnel bursting the air and sending down its deadly iron. High explosives bursting in the ground and sending forth bricks, mud and iron to the destruction of man. . . . Dead and wounded all around you. Comrades falling directly in front and you are not allowed to assist them. The command ONWARD. Every minute looking for the next to be gone to the great beyond.

Later that day Roberts would help dress the wounded and witness at close hand the costs of war.

> Some were wounded in the legs, arms, throat, stomach, lungs. Some having their legs blown entirely away, some with the head blown off. Arms missing, some blinded, some became crazy. Oh what a sight to behold that had been inflicted upon innocent men. In this battle our company lost 12 killed, 80 wounded, 2 lieutenants killed and one wounded.

The casualties that Roberts lists were just a few of the seven thousand casualties that America suffered over the next four days in successfully taking the salient. This represented a small fraction of the 318,000 casualties the United States suffered in the war, including 112,432 American soldiers who lost their lives (more than half from disease rather than enemy fire). These numbers in turn were but a minute part of the war's estimated total of 10 million dead and 20 million wounded. The St. Mihiel campaign, as overwhelming as it seemed to Rickenbacker and Roberts, was a relatively minor operation compared with other major engagements of World War I. In the Battle of the Somme in 1916, for instance, Great Britain suffered 60,000 casualties in a single day and 400,000 casualties over the course of that offensive.

The reasons why this war took place, and the factors that led Americans—from President Woodrow Wilson to infantryman Norman Roberts—to cross the ocean and intervene in this great conflict, remain a cause for debate. Although the United States entered the war at a relatively late date, and its casualties were much fewer than those of the major fighting nations, its contribution to the war's final outcome was decisively important. The following discussion will provide a brief overview of the causes and course of World War I and the role the United States played in the war.

Causes of the War

World War I was triggered by the assassination of one man—Archduke Francis Ferdinand, the heir to the throne of Austria-Hungary. Historians have generally pointed to three reasons why the killing of one person could plunge so many nations into war: the competition for colonies and for military and economic might among the major European powers, the ethnic and political conflict between and within the empires in eastern Europe, and the system of military alliances that left Europe divided in two armed and hostile camps.

Beneath all of these contributing causes was nationalism. The belief that people who share ethnic origin, language, and history are part of a national group—and should therefore have their own independent state that they should support above other political loyalties—was an increasingly powerful force in nineteenth-century Europe. Nationalist ambition, for example, helped to create the empire-state of Germany out of smaller kingdoms and principalities in 1871. Soon Germany was a leading industrial and military power of Europe, along with Great Britain and France. It competed with those more established nations for domination of western Europe, military and naval supremacy, and colonies in Africa and other parts of the world.

Nationalism among various ethnic groups also weakened the bonds of the three multiethnic empires of eastern Europe: Austria-Hungary, Ottoman Turkey, and Russia. Many of the distinct national groups within these empires had more allegiance to their ethnic enclaves than to the government that ruled over them. Bosnia, the site of Archduke Francis Ferdinand's 1914 assassination by a Serbian nationalist, was a province of the Austro-Hungarian Empire, but it contained many Serbs who felt greater loyalty to their brethren in the neighboring country of Serbia. The Balkan Peninsula, where Bosnia and Serbia were located, was a tense region where mutually antagonistic ethnic groups had just broken away from the control of the Ottoman Empire; it was also an area where Russia and Austria-Hungary competed with each other for influence.

To enhance their national security, the competing nations and empires of Europe adopted foreign and domestic policies between 1871 and 1914 that made war more likely. Following Germany's example, many nations maintained large standing armies, conscripted all of their able-bodied youth to spend some time in military service, and spent enormous sums on arms and naval development. Nations sought additional protection by entering into political and military agreements, or alliances, with other countries. These diplomatic alliances varied in their terms and commitments, ranging from simple pledges not to enter into war against the treaty partner to mutual promises to come to each other's aid in case of war or threatened attack. By 1914, the major nations of Europe had divided along two opposing camps. The Triple Alliance, consisting of Germany, Austria-Hungary, and Italy, was opposed by the Triple Entente, consisting of Russia, France, and Great Britain (Russia and France were bound by military alliance agreements; Great Britain, while not so bound, was becoming diplomatically and strategically aligned with the other two).

The United States was not immediately affected by these foreign pacts nor by the nationalistic fervor that was pushing Europe toward war. Separated from Europe by the Atlantic Ocean, America had made no military alliances with European powers. The United States was militarily weak in comparison: It had not set up a system of universal military conscription, nor did it possess a large standing army. The nationalist aspirations of its people were bound up in continental expansion, industrial development, and some imperialistic ventures in the Western Hemisphere and in Asia. The concept that the United States would send its soldiers across the Atlantic Ocean to fight in a European war was unthinkable to most Americans.

Assassination and War

Many Americans, if they heard or read about the assassination of Ferdinand in 1914, probably had a reaction similar to that of the editorialist of the *Daily Herald* of Grand Forks, North Dakota, who wrote, "To the world, or to a nation, an archduke more or less makes little difference." However, in the volatile atmosphere of Europe, the shooting set off a train of events that led to World War I.

Austria-Hungary viewed the assassination of its future emperor by a Serbian as a just and opportune reason to punish Serbia. After consulting with its ally, Germany, it declared war on Serbia on July 28, 1914. Russia, which viewed itself as a protector of Serbia and opposed Austro-Hungarian designs on the Balkans, began the cumbersome process of mobilizing its armies—a preparatory step toward war. Germany considered this action threatening and subsequently declared war on Russia on August 1. Two days later, in response to French mobilization, Germany declared war on France.

The German military staff had long planned for a possible two-front war against France and Russia. Their strategy was to quickly attack France with overwhelming force and knock it out of the war before Russia could fully mobilize its armies. The plan required German troops to attack France through Belgium, a small nation whose neutrality in event of war was guaranteed by both Germany and Great Britain. Germany's August 4, 1914, invasion of Belgium initiated the actual fighting of World War I and brought Great Britain into the conflict. By the end of the year, the Ottoman Empire was at war against the Allies and had invaded Russia. Germany, Austria-Hungary, and Ottoman Turkey were called the Central Powers, while France, Great Britain, and Russia became known as the Allies. In 1915, Italy broke with the Triple Alliance and entered the war on the Allied side in the hope of gaining territory from Austria-Hungary.

The Nature of the War

World War I differed greatly from previous wars in Europe. Because of universal conscription, as well as nationalist fervor that translated into mass popular support, countries were able to field huge armies. The Industrial Revolution, which had created competition between Germany, France, and Great Britain for foreign colonies and markets, also led to the mass production of weapons and munitions to equip those armies, while railroads and trucks helped move troops and supplies to the battlefield. New technological inventions were introduced or used to a greater degree during World War I, including the machine gun, the airplane, and poison gas. Technology lent an impersonal nature to the war—a soldier was at least as likely to be killed by an artillery shell fired from miles away as by an enemy he could see.

A World War on Many Fronts

World War I was fought on several fronts. Italy and Austria-Hungary fought over territory on their borders. Serbia defended itself against invaders, and when Bulgaria and Romania entered the war, fighting in the Balkan region intensified. There was conflict in the Near East as Great Britain and France aided Arab peoples in their revolt against Ottoman Turkey. British and German forces also fought over colonies in Africa.

In the opinion of most military leaders of the time, however, these disputes were peripheral. The central question of the war was whether Germany—the dominant nation of the Central Powers—would succeed in becoming the dominant power of Europe. The two most important fronts in this respect were the western front, where Germany opposed France and Great Britain, and the eastern front, along which Germany and Austria-Hungary faced Russia.

On the western front, Germany's initial drive toward Paris, France, was halted at the First Battle of the Marne in September 1914. A subsequent attempt to seize French and Belgian ports on the English Channel was checked by the British in the First Battle of Ypres in November. By the end of 1914, a five-hundred-mile front extended from the Channel across southwestern Belgium and northeastern France to Switzerland.

The line would remain basically unchanged for the next three years as the armies dug in and fortified the entire front, resulting in what became known as trench warfare. Elaborate systems of interconnecting trenches or ditches were created by both sides, between which ran no-man's land. The tactics of trench warfare relied on artillery barrages followed by soldiers going "over the top" from their trenches to charge the enemy—usually to be killed or wounded by machine-gun fire as they crossed no man's-land.

For the common soldier, trench warfare was a nightmare of mud, lice, poison gas attacks, exploding artillery shells that uncovered buried bodies, and the constant threat of sudden and random death. For generals, trench warfare meant a strategic stalemate as both sides launched massive attacks that gained little territory at great cost. In February 1916, Germany took two forts near the French town of Verdun with the purpose of defending them against French counterattacks and inflicting the maximum casualties possible. By June, France had recaptured the two forts, now in ruins; both countries had each suffered about 350,000 casualties. British prime minister David Lloyd George later described the western front struggles as "the most gigantic, tenacious, grim, futile, and bloody fight ever waged in the history of war."

The eastern front was too large for its armies to become bogged down in stationary trench warfare. In 1914, Russian armies thrust deep into the German territories of East Prussia, only to be annihilated by Germany in the Battle of Tannenberg and the Battle of the Masurian Lakes. Russia attempted other offensives in subsequent years, but these accomplished little and cost the Russians millions of casualties. Russia's lack of military success contributed to mounting political tensions at home, where more and more Russians were growing dissatisfied with the rule of Czar Nicholas II.

The United States and the War

While Europeans on the western front fought in their trenches and Russia faced political crisis, Americans tried to determine how the war would impact them. President Wilson's contention that the war was one "with which we have nothing to do, whose causes cannot reach us" did not prevent the conflict from affecting the United States. Both Germany and Great Britain attempted to sway American emotions with propaganda attacking their enemies, an attempt in which Britain was more successful. In reading and hearing about the war, many Americans came to the conclusion that Germany was a ruthless and barbarous nation whose global designs threatened America. These impressions were strengthened in 1915 when the federal government found a cache of secret documents that revealed an espionage and sabotage ring operated in the United States by German diplomats.

Britain was also successful in its naval blockade which effectively ended most American trade with the Central Powers. U.S. exports to the Allies rose from $753 million in 1914 to almost $3 billion in 1916, while during the same period, trade with the Central Powers fell from $345 million to $29 million. American economic prosperity became to some extent dependent on the war trade with the Allies. Germany's efforts to interdict American trade with the Allies only made relations between Germany and the United States worse. Because of British naval supremacy, Germany was forced to rely on surprise submarine attacks. However, when Germany sank passenger and merchant ships on which Americans were traveling, the United States responded with outrage. In response to American protests, Germany restricted its submarine missions for a time. In February 1917, however, German leaders, seeing victory on both the western and eastern fronts within their grasp, decided to unleash submarine warfare on all ships—including American vessels—sailing to Great Britain. German leaders rightly calculated that this step would lead the United States to declare war. Woodrow Wilson asked Congress for such a declaration on April 2, 1917.

1917: A Critical Year

America's decision to enter World War I came at a critical time for the Allies. In 1917, Germany and its allies scored several military successes that appeared to place them on the verge of victory. On the western front, Germany had repositioned its forces to stronger defensive positions and waited for the Allies to attack. Allied attempts to break through this, the Hindenberg Line (called the Siegfried Line by the Germans), proved disastrous. On April 15, France began a major frontal offensive that its new commander, General Robert Nivelle, predicted would smash through the German lines in two days. By the end of the first day it was clear that the offensive, for which the Germans were well prepared, could have no outcome other than the slaughter of French soldiers. But Nivelle continued to order his soldiers onward. Finally, French troops on the front lines mutinied and refused to obey orders to fight. In May 1917, Henri Pétain replaced Nivelle and halted the attacks. He restored troop morale by improving the soldiers' living conditions and by promising that France would not go on the offensive again until the Americans arrived.

Despite some successes in its campaigns against Ottoman Turkey, Great Britain was not faring much better. Germany's submarine attacks had left Great Britain with chronic shortages of coal and food. Its government was bankrupt, and its own attempted grand offensive of 1917 (the Third Battle of Ypres) expended 400,000 casualties while advancing the line only four miles. Great Britain, like France, faced extreme difficulties in replenishing its ranks and rebuilding morale.

Furthermore, the Allies suffered a major blow on the Italian front in the fall of 1917 when Austria-Hungary defeated and expelled an invading Italian force in the Battle of Caporetto. The worst news for the Allies, however, was the withdrawal of Russia from the war. In March 1917, amidst popular unrest, the czar abdicated and was replaced by a provisional government. The new government proved unstable and was overthrown in November 1917 when a faction of the revolutionary movement known as the Bolsheviks seized power. Their leader, Lenin, immediately called for peace talks with Germany. Russian withdrawal was formalized in a March 1918 peace treaty in which Germany was ceded large sections of Russian territory. The Russian Revolution would raise fears of communism in the United States and have worldwide long-term repercussions for the rest of the twentieth century. Its most important immediate effect, however, was that it ended the fighting on the eastern front, thus freeing German troops for use in the west.

Americans at War

With these reinforcements, Germans significantly outnumbered Allied forces on the western front. German military commanders Paul von Hindenberg and Erich Ludendorff knew that this advantage was temporary because American troops had already started arriving in limited numbers by July 1917. Therefore, the German staff planned a final grand offensive in order to end the war before more American soldiers could reach France.

Germany launched three large offensives between March and July 1918. Despite some initial setbacks, the Allies ultimately held with help from the increasing numbers of U.S. reinforcements. Early in June, 27,500 Americans fought alongside French soldiers at Château-Thierry and nearby Belleau Wood. By early July, the number of Americans fighting on the western front had grown to 270,000; they helped prevent Germany from taking Paris in the Second Battle of the Marne. In these defenses against German attack, American divisions and battalions were sent to reinforce French and British armies. General John J. Pershing, commander of the AEF, was insistent that when the Allies launched their own offensives in the fall, U.S. troops would participate as an independent army under American command.

Pershing got his wish with the St. Mihiel operation. Two weeks later, 1.2 million Americans participated in their largest campaign, driving into the Argonne Forest in a forty-seven-day onslaught in which 120,000 Americans were killed or wounded. The AEF slowly drove back the Germans, as did French and British forces in other areas of the western front. Pershing was planning another major offensive when word came that Germany had agreed to an armistice. The fighting ceased on November 11, 1918.

Effects of the War

The effects of World War I were profound. Ten million soldiers and perhaps a similar number of civilians perished. Much of Europe suffered the loss of nearly a generation of young men. The war had cost the belligerents $337 billion and left many nations under heavy war debts they could not repay. Property damage ran into billions of dollars. The war and the subsequent peace settlements also redrew the boundaries of Europe. Old empires, including the Ottoman Empire, Russia, and Austria-Hungary, collapsed. New nations such as Czechoslovakia and Yugoslavia were created.

World War I did not affect the United States to the extent it did other nations. The U.S. government did not fall to revolution, as did the government of Russia. America did not experience defeat, as did Germany, nor did it suffer 73 percent casualties of its armed forces, as did France. However, America's decision to intervene in the war did have several significant ramifications. During World War I, the United States took many actions that indicated a change in how Americans viewed their government and their place in the world. These actions included raising an army through mass conscription, sending American soldiers to fight in a European war, utilizing the government to regulate business and mobilize economic resources, and borrowing money and taxing the American people at unprecedented levels. The viewpoints in this volume focus not so much on the fighting itself, but on the debates surrounding America's decision to intervene in the conflict and the ramifications of implementing that decision.

The chief American contribution to the Allied cause, many have argued, was not its soldiers that went "over there," but hope. American reinforcements gave hope to French and British leaders that war could be won—and extinguished such hope among the German leaders. Furthermore, the United States, especially through the words and ideas of Woodrow Wilson, also raised the hopes of many Americans and Europeans that the war, though destructive, could ultimately lead to a better world where a new diplomatic order would replace the old system of military alliances and nationalistic conflicts that had led to World War I. Sadly, the peace that Wilson and the other Allied leaders managed to fashion after World War I would contain its own seeds of hatred and bitterness, and it would last just a little over twenty years before a second world war would begin.

CHAPTER 1

The War in Europe and American Preparedness

Chapter Preface

When World War I began in 1914, most European nations already possessed large standing armies. To maintain these armies, governments established a peacetime draft under which all able-bodied men were expected to perform a term of active service and then remain available as members of the armed reserves. This was true not only of major powers such as Germany (which in 1914 had a standing army of 700,000 and a reserve force of 2.8 million that could be rapidly mobilized) and France (823,000 regulars and nearly 3 million reservists), but also of smaller countries such as Bulgaria (85,000 regulars and 400,000 reservists). By contrast, the United States did not have universal conscription; the military was composed of volunteers. By June 1916—a time when millions of soldiers were fighting in Europe—the U.S. Army had only 107,641 regulars and 132,000 reservists (in the loosely organized National Guard).

After war broke out in Europe, some Americans worried that the relatively small military of the United States could become a liability. Concerned citizens formed organizations to persuade the general public of the necessity to increase defense spending and to mobilize a larger army. To help mobilization, some advocates proposed a program of compulsory military service or training for all young male Americans. The United States needed to strengthen its military, many argued, in order to prepare for possible conflict. Proponents also asserted that such measures would ensure America's security and bolster its diplomatic strength. Furthermore, some maintained that universal military service would promote patriotism and other desirable character traits in young Americans.

The "preparedness" movement, however, had its detractors. Skeptics viewed war preparations as having the potential to provoke German hostilities against the United States. Others felt that these steps would raise the chances of American military intervention in the war. Some even feared an increase in the influence of the military on U.S. society, arguing that it would jeopardize civil liberties. For many Americans, the small size of the U.S. armed forces was something to be proud of—a national characteristic that, in their view, distinguished the liberty-loving New World of the United States from the militaristic and corrupt Old World of Europe. Believing that large standing armies were a contributing cause of the war in Europe, these individuals formed their own groups, such as the American Union Against Militarism, to build public support for their concerns.

President Woodrow Wilson favored keeping America's military small. As historian William J. Koenig writes, Wilson possessed "a personal distaste for things military" and thus originally resisted calls to strengthen the armed forces or to take other steps promoted by preparedness advocates. However, as the war in Europe persisted and the preparedness movement gained public and congressional support, he eventually backed legislation that would fortify the nation's defense. Although too weak for some and too strong for others, much of Wilson's defense program was passed by Congress in 1916. The National Defense Act authorized an increase in the size of the U.S. Army and the National Guard and placed the latter under stronger federal control. Other measures expanded the navy and raised taxes to pay for the new military expenditures. Nevertheless, when the United States declared war on Germany in April 1917, the army was still composed of volunteers and numbered only 5,791 officers and 121,797 enlisted men, with the National Guard adding only 181,000 more personnel. America was not able to dispatch more than one division of infantry to Europe until February 1918, by which time the ranks of its army had been swelled by the 3 million recruits drafted under the National Selective Service Act of 1917.

VIEWPOINT 1

"The United States has been drifting for years. No real military preparations of an adequate character have been made."

America Must Improve Its Military Preparedness

Leonard Wood (1860–1927)

Following the outbreak of war in Europe in 1914, Americans engaged in a national debate over whether the country needed to build up its military forces. Advocates of military "preparedness" argued that it was the only way of ensuring American neutrality in the conflict in Europe. A leading participant in the preparedness debate was the National Security League, a private organization whose members included prominent military, corporate, and political leaders. The following viewpoint is taken from a 1915 book by one of the league's members, Leonard Wood.

Wood was an army general who had originally joined the Army Medical Corps as a doctor in 1884. During the Spanish-American War, he fought in Cuba as commander of a volunteer regiment known as the Rough Riders. (He shared the command of the regiment with Theodore Roosevelt.) Following the war, Wood served as military governor of Cuba from 1899 until 1902 (when Cuba attained independence from the United States), as commander of U.S. forces in the Philippines from 1906 to 1908, and as chief of staff of the U.S. Army from 1910 to 1914. In 1915, in response to the war in Europe, he helped establish a summer military training program for college students and other civilian volunteers in Plattsburgh, New York. Similar "Plattsburgh Camps" were subsequently established around the country.

In the following viewpoint, Wood argues that the United States is unprepared for modern warfare and that its military forces

Reprinted from Leonard Wood, *The Military Obligations of Citizenship* (Princeton, NJ: Princeton University Press, 1915).

need to be enlarged and reorganized. He contends that military preparedness can be achieved without risking the rise of militarism in the United States, which he defines as a "condition . . . under which the military element dominates that nation's policy." The preservation of peace in the United States, Wood concludes, depends on the state of its military strength and readiness.

The people of the United States are singularly lacking in information concerning both the military history of their country and its military policy. Students in school and college as a rule receive entirely erroneous ideas on both of these subjects. The average young man, unless he has really made a study of the country's history, is firmly convinced that the Revolutionary War was characterized throughout by the highest quality of patriotism and devotion to the best interests of the country on the part of the people as a whole.

He is not at all familiar with the desperate struggle which was made by [George] Washington, various colonial assemblies, and the Confederation of Colonies to keep in the field even a small force of troops. He hears very little of the bickerings, mutinies, desertions, and frequent changes of personnel which made the war a difficult one to conduct and served to bring out into strong relief the remarkable qualities of Washington—those qualities of patience, good judgment, discretion, and again patience, and more patience, which made it possible for him to hold the illy-equipped, disjointed, and discordant elements together, and to have always available some kind of a fighting force, although seldom an effective one.

We have as a nation neglected the lessons of past wars and have learned little from the example of the great military nations. . . . The great nations with policies to uphold and interests to defend have made what they believe to be adequate military preparation.

Military Preparedness

The United States has been drifting for years. No real military preparations of an adequate character have been made. Military preparedness means the organization of all the resources of a nation—men, material, and money—so that the full power of the nation may be promptly applied and continued at maximum strength for a considerable period of time. War today, when initiated by a country prepared for war, comes with great suddenness, because all preparations have been made in advance; plans have been worked out to the last detail, organization completed, and reserve supplies purchased and assembled long in advance, and the whole force of the mighty machine can be applied in a very brief period of time at any designated point.

Back of the machine itself is the railroad service, so organized as to be turned over immediately to the military authorities. Back of this come the civil hospitals, the bakeries, and the supply departments of all sorts, each with its responsibility fixed in case of operations within its area or in case of a demand for supplies in other sections of the theater of war. The capacity of every ship is known and plans completed for her use as a troop ship; and when war threatens, the whereabouts of the shipping is closely watched, and ships are assembled quietly to meet any demand which may be required for oversea operations. These are but an outline of what is meant by military preparedness.

Mere numbers of men and undeveloped military resources are of little value. It has been well said that in the sudden onrush of modern war undeveloped military resources are of no more use than an undeveloped gold mine in Alaska would be in a panic on Wall Street. The comparison is not overdrawn. You must remember, all of you, that this country has never yet engaged in war with a first-class power prepared for war.

You must remember also that once sea power is lost or held in check an enormous force can be landed on these shores within a month—a force sufficient to go where it will and to hold whatever it desires to hold.

Why have we failed to make adequate preparation? Partly because of ignorance of the true facts concerning our utter unpreparedness and partly due to a conceit fostered by the average Fourth of July orator and politician, through statements to the effect that we possess peculiar and remarkable military characteristics which make our soldiers trained and efficient without preparation, and as good as equally brave and equally sound men of other countries who have spent years in training. Again there is the curious Anglo-Saxon prejudice against a large standing army and the feeling that it is always a menace to civil liberty.

Changing Circumstances

In our past wars we were not confronted by great nations with highly organized military machines; steam navigation had not appeared; our possible enemies were without standing armies of any size and lacked entirely that complete military organization which characterizes them today. It took a long time to get troops together and prepare supplies for them and a considerable period of time to cross the ocean.

Our forefathers had more time to prepare. Then, again, they

were more familiar with the use of arms; weapons were of a simple type; they could be made quickly and instruction in their use was a relatively simple matter.

Preparedness Against War

John Grier Hibben, president of Princeton University, maintains in a February 1916 article in American Defense *that the United States should strengthen its military in order to avoid war.*

It is . . . urged by those who would object to any program of preparedness that if we increase our military strength we as a nation will be tempted to use our power in a war of aggression and that our attitude to other nations of the earth will be one of arrogant superiority and irritating challenge. I feel very strongly that preparedness is not at all incompatible with the love of peace and the hatred of war. If we as a people are trained in the essential principles of justice and our ideas of right are grounded in the conviction that there is one ethic for the individual as well as for the nation the ability to defend ourselves will not lead to aggressive and insolent militarism.

Why is it that there is this general movement throughout our land demanding a wise and adequate policy of military preparedness? Because we loathe the very thought of war. Because we have been stirred to the lowest depths of our nature by the cruel catastrophe which has befallen the civilization of Europe. We believe in the policy of adequate preparedness because we hate war and do not propose to have it forced upon us through our conspicuous weakness and widely recognized lack of military resources in men and material. The true pacifist is one whose counsel makes for peace and therefore I hold that he who urges a policy which will leave our nation shorn of her strength and a prey to any envious and covetous people, has no right to call himself a pacifist—a maker of peace. His way is the way of war—war which if resisted means disaster and death; if not resisted means shame and servitude, the loss of liberty and the surrender of our birthright. As I have said in another place and would here repeat with an emphasis intensified by growing conviction, a true and wise preparedness is "preparedness against war and not for war."

Now, highly organized military establishments are the rule among our possible antagonists. Rapid steam transportation in vast amount is available. The arms of war are extremely complicated and costly; it takes a long time to make them and a long time to instruct soldiers in their use. In other words, today everything is in favor of the prepared aggressor and everything against the unready pacific nation. The blow comes more quickly and with greater force, and it is not possible to provide even a semblance of protection against it unless wise measures have been taken long in advance.

Since the foundation of the republic, war has existed as follows: Revolutionary War, 7 years; War of 1812-14, 2½ years; Mexican War, 2 years; Florida War, 7 years; Civil War, 4 years; War with Spain and Philippine Rebellion, 2 years—not to mention numerous Indian wars and internal disturbances requiring the use of troops.

We have struggled through these wars and have emerged generally successfully, but in none of them has there been any evidence of well-thought-out preparations or the application of a sound military policy. Our people remember only the success and forget entirely the great and unnecessary cost in blood and treasure in which our defective method of conducting these wars resulted. By faulty methods I mean that we have generally conducted war as a confederacy instead of as a nation. We have permitted altogether too much interference by states. Too many officers have been appointed by the governors of states. New regiments have been raised oftentimes in order that new officers might be appointed and political patronage increased, whereas the old regiments should have been filled up as they had acquired experience, some traditions and *esprit*, and were much more valuable than new regiments. This is seen in the Civil War in case of the Wisconsin organizations. Wisconsin had the good sense to veteranize her regiments, and the result is seen when one remembers the term "Iron Brigade" applied to a Wisconsin brigade.

The Limits of Volunteers

Then again we have had frequently the intervention of civilians, either through the activities of the secretary of war or of the civil arms of the government. There has been a general lack of a sense of individual responsibility for military service. Reliance on volunteer enlistments has continued and has been one of the gravest sources of danger to the Republic. The experience of the Revolution should have taught us that it is not safe in a real war to depend upon volunteers. There is an enthusiastic response by a certain proportion of the best element in the early days of war, but this response cannot be counted upon to continue throughout a long war involving severe strains upon the population, nor is it right or just to throw the burden of military service upon a portion of the population. It is a universal obligation and the country will never be secure or safe until it is recognized as such and measures are taken to develop military preparation on a basis of universal military obligation. . . .

The voluntary system failed us in the past and will fail us in the future. It is uncertain in operation, prevents organized preparation, tends to destroy that individual sense of obligation for military service which should be found in every citizen, costs excessively in life and treasure, and does not permit that condition of preparedness which must exist if we are to wage war successfully with any great power prepared for war.

The question is: What shall we do to adequately prepare ourselves for war without establishing a huge standing army or bringing about a condition which might be described as one of militarism, which term, as I use it, means the condition under which the military forces of a nation demand and secure special recognition, both socially and officially, and exercise an undue influence in the conduct of the civil affairs of the government, both at home and abroad? In other words, a condition which may be described as one under which the military element dominates the nation's policy. Nothing could be more unfortunate than the establishment of such a condition in this country or elsewhere, so far as development on normal lines is concerned. However, a condition of thorough preparedness can be established without creating a condition of militarism. . . .

We must preserve our ideals, strive for world peace, and do what we can to build up the adjustment of international difficulties through arbitration, but we must not fail to give due heed to the conditions under which we live. Whatever we may hope for in the way of universal peace does not justify us in disregarding the conditions which surround us today.

If we want to hand down to our children the heritage which has come to us from our fathers, we must not place confidence in idle boasting but give serious heed to well-thought-out preparation and adopt a policy for the future with reference to our military establishment very different from that which has existed in the past. We can do this without violating our ideals. If I were to state such a military policy I would say, briefly, have an army sufficient for the peace needs of the nation, a good militia, an adequate navy, and behind them the largest possible number of men trained to be efficient soldiers if needed; but in time of peace following their ordinary civil occupations—ready to come when wanted. A country so prepared will have the largest possible measure of peace.

VIEWPOINT 2

"Our greatest peril is the peril of military preparedness."

Military Preparedness Endangers America

Charles E. Jefferson (1860–1937)

In December 1915, President Woodrow Wilson proposed to Congress and the American people that the United States, while maintaining its ideals of peace and neutrality, should embark on a military rebuilding program that would greatly enlarge the armed and naval forces. His program was strongly opposed by those who decried the rise of militarism. These critics maintained that Wilson's proposal would actually endanger the nation by increasing the probability that the United States would become entangled in war.

The following viewpoint is taken from a 1916 article by Charles E. Jefferson, a religious lecturer and writer whose books included *Christianity and International Peace, The Cause of the War,* and *The Character of Jesus*. Jefferson argues that the United States should concentrate its energies on reforming its social and political institutions rather than on expanding the military. By strengthening the military, he asserts, America risks placing control of its foreign policy into the hands of generals, admirals, and arms manufacturers, thereby increasing the chances of U.S. involvement in the war in Europe—a war Americans do not want or need.

An anti-preparedness man is always constrained to begin his argument with the declaration that he is a stout defender of the virtue of preparedness. In his opinion, so called anti-prepared-

Reprinted from Charles E. Jefferson, "Military Preparedness a Danger to Democracy," *Annals of the American Academy of Political and Social Science*, July 1916.

ness men are the most enthusiastic, consistent, persistent, and thorough-going preparedness people now alive. We place extraordinary emphasis on the absolute necessity of this nation preparing itself to meet coming duties and perils. We all believe in national defense. We all realize the value of security. We all desire to safeguard the nation against invasion. We are second to nobody in devotion to the flag, in desire to keep its folds free from stain, and to maintain the principles for which it was unfurled, and to preserve and perpetuate the institutions over which it waves.

Types of Preparedness

The much derided anti-preparedness men freely admit that we as a nation are not prepared to meet victoriously the strains and storms of the coming years. We know that as a people we are not equipped to fulfill our obligations either to ourselves or to mankind. We realize we are not *politically* prepared. Our governmental machinery in its present shape is not adequate for our expanding needs. Our legal apparatus is not sufficiently developed to grapple with the world's baffling problems. . . . We have a department of the Navy, but no department of International Conciliation, a secretary of war but no secretary of peace. We spend the enormous sum of one quarter of a billion dollars every year on our army and navy and scarcely a dollar for the maintenance of agencies for feeding the fountains of international goodwill. We have erected no safeguards by which a President of the United States can be prevented from plunging us into war. Technically only Congress can declare war, but as our constitution now stands, any President is at liberty in his dealing with foreign governments, to take steps of such a character that Congress is virtually committed to war. To reduce the points of international friction, and to work out a solution for the problems that hang on from year to year and which, because of their confused condition, are thunder clouds out of which lightnings may come: to foster and multiply the forces working for friendly feeling, and to create more effective legal devices by which the nations may live harmoniously together, this is preparedness of the most fundamental and indispensable sort, and of it we have altogether too little. The first charge which we bring against the labelled advocates of preparedness is that they overlook the things which are of primary importance, and lead the nation astray by creating a great hubbub over matters that are superficial, and do not at all touch the heart of the world problem.

There is such a thing as industrial preparedness, and we need it. The great world of the wage-earning masses must be elevated and harmonized, and a better spirit must be created in the hearts both of capital and labor. The idea that a nation's life depends wholly on the courage of its soldiers is an ancient superstition which the present war has exploded. The delusion that generals and admirals are the sole custodians of a nation's honor has been dissipated forever. We now know that mechanics are as necessary for success on the battle field as the men who carry guns, and that without the loyal support of the common day laborer no nation can hope for victory. When Mr. [David] Lloyd George [prime minister of Great Britain] begged the Welsh coal miners to go back to their work, assuring them that the destiny of the British Empire rested on their shoulders, the world caught a glimpse of a fact it will never forget. No nation can any longer be victorious in war unless it has the loyal coöperation of all classes of its people. Unity of spirit, even more than dreadnaughts and howitzers, is the final safeguard of a nation's life. The men who give their days and nights to elaborating fresh schemes for the multiplication of guns, deal too much with the physical, forgetting that at last everything depends on a nation's soul.

There is such a thing as social preparedness, and we ought to think about it. We are an unkempt and undisciplined people. Things run at loose ends in every department of our life. We are extravagant and wasteful beyond belief. We lack social efficiency. . . .

And are we as a nation morally prepared? Read the annual record of our homicides, our divorces, our drunkenness, and our thefts and robberies and defalcations, and all the atrocities of high finance, and you must admit that we are not morally prepared to face triumphantly the searching fires of the coming years. Our criticism of the so-called preparedness crowd is that they think too much of the outside of the cup and the platter and forget to look inside. They think only of the external armor, and pay scant attention to the interior defenses, lacking which a nation inevitably succumbs. . . .

The world-tragedy of the last forty years has been the squandering of brain energy on devising material defenses which in the crucial hour failed to save Europe from the unspeakable havoc which they had been created to ward off. If one tenth of the money spent on defense had been spent in cultivating kindlier feelings and loftier ideals, this war would never have been. The tragedy of the [international] Hague Conferences was that both in 1899 and in 1907, a large part of the time was devoted, not to working out a scheme by which war might be abolished, but to the work of laying down technical rules by which the bloody game of human butchery could still be played. This is the tragedy of America at the present hour. When every sound mind and heart should be brooding over the question: How can we so order the world's life that a recurrence of this tragedy shall never be, there are thousands of Americans thinking of nothing else, talking of nothing else, suggesting nothing else but the old stupid experiment which has again and again soaked our planet with blood. How are we ever going to get out of the heart-breaking predicament in which humanity finds itself unless men who think, dare to break away from the military traditions which have cursed and destroyed so many generations? Cannot we get beyond the ideas of Tiglath Pileser and Ramses II? Cannot we rise above the ideal of the cave man? He always armed for defense. He thought only of his own skin. He was a low-down undeveloped creature, and is to be excused, because he lived in the morning of the world. But what shall we say of men who, living two thousand years after the death of Jesus Christ, cannot advance an inch in their conception of international life beyond that which was regnant in the ancient barbaric world?

But some one asks: Do you not believe in any army or navy at all? Certainly. We all believe in an army and navy for police purposes. That is not now up for discussion. The question before the American people is shall we have *adequate* preparedness—that is, a preparedness which is considered adequate by the military-naval experts? That is a kind which we have never had. From the days of [George] Washington we have been continuously unprepared. All the experts say so. For one hundred and forty years we have lived in a fool's paradise. The specialists are all agreed. We now spend 250 million dollars a year, but this is a mere bagatelle. "This is not preparedness at all. Let us now prepare in earnest!" But a multitude of us shout no! Not now. Not till the end of the war at least. Let us lick into shape the army and navy we already have. Let us learn how to spend a budget of 250 millions before we squander more.

Our Greatest Peril

But somebody says: Is there not danger of a foreign invasion? We think not. No such danger has ever existed, and there is less danger now than at any time in our whole history. Our greatest peril is the peril of military preparedness.

Military preparedness is a peril to democracy, and a menace to the peace of the world. Piling up explosives in a world where so many persons carry matches is perilous. Running races in naval tonnage is exciting, but perilous. Diplomacy which relies on the pressure of guns is sometimes effective, but always perilous. Making other nations afraid of us is perilous. Germany made her neighbors afraid of her, and so she was gradually surrounded by a tightening ring of steel. We shall circle ourselves with a similar ring by a like policy of military efficiency. It is perilous to drill the young men of a nation in the art of shooting human beings. It brings a degradation of the spirit which is blighting. It is perilous in these restless days, to pile additional burdens on the backs of the taxpayers for the support of vast numbers of men in barracks and on battleships. It is perilous to squander on instruments of slaughter the money entrusted to us by the Almighty for the service of mankind. Our nation is a steward, and it must render a strict account for all its gold. This is a fact which political and social science must never fail to take into account. . . . It is perilous to waste the time of our National Congress in interminable discussions over the army and navy. For twenty-five years Congress has shamefully neglected matters of sovereign importance to devote session after session to wrangling over the types and numbers and prices of ships and guns. It is perilous to play with the passion of fear. Fear is the mightiest and most demoralizing of all the passions. Fear paralyzes the nerves of reason. Men no longer think when they are afraid. Militarism flourishes only in an atmosphere of fear. Huge appropriations for ships and guns are possible only when nations are terrorized. The astute men who are at the bottom of all this preparedness movement know that now when the whole world is panic stricken because of long continued bloodshed, is the best possible time for making a desperate effort to swing our republic still farther out into the maelstrom of military preparedness.

Sources of Mischief

Building a huge war machine is perilous again because it plays into the hands of five men who because of the structure of modern civilization are endowed with extraordinary power for working mischief. First comes the military-naval expert. Modern armies and navies are colossal. Officers are numbered by the thousands, 35,000 to every million men. Some of these officers are certain to be . . . Bernhardis. [Friedrich von Bernhardi, a German general, was noted for his book *Germany and the Next War*, translated in 1912, in which he called war a biological necessity.] This is inevitable. You cannot have a gigantic war machine without a military caste. You cannot have a military caste without a war party. You cannot in this republic prevent army and naval officials of a certain type chattering with reporters, talking at banquets, writing for magazines and the Sunday newspapers, publishing books, everlastingly trying to scare the public, and working day and night to increase the size and prestige of the military and naval establishments.

Along with the military naval expert comes the war trader. Vote hundreds of millions of dollars for any purpose whatever, and you raise up at once colossal corporations eager to make the profit which vast contracts bring. Wherever you have great armies and navies, you have the Krupps, and the Armstrongs, and the Vickers, and the Creusots [arms and munitions manufacturers], and in order to keep their costly machinery running, you must always, even in days of profoundest peace, be vigorously preparing for war. You must change your guns every few years, you must scrap heap your ships before they are used and buy new ones. The nations are systematically and continuously and mercilessly fleeced.

Preparedness and Militarism

Oswald Garrison Villard, the grandson of the famous abolitionist William Lloyd Garrison, was editor of the New York Evening Post *from 1897 to 1917. He opposed both war and military preparedness programs. In a 1916 article, written shortly before Congress passed legislation enlarging the navy and army, Villard argued that the United States was forsaking its position as a great nation that had forsworn military power and the "evils of militarism."*

We have all at once, in the midst of a terrifying cataclysm, abjured our faith in many things American. We no longer believe, as for 140 years, in the moral power of an America unarmed and unafraid; we believe suddenly that the influence of the United States is to be measured only by the number of our soldiery and our dreadnoughts—our whole history to the contrary notwithstanding. The ardent efforts of both sides in the present European struggle at the outbreak of the war to win for their cause the enormous prestige of the sympathy and moral support of the United States—although "unprepared"—we overlook as if it were not the most outstanding fact of the year from August 1, 1914, to August 1, 1915. We are to deprive the world of the one great beacon-light of a nation unarmed and unafraid, free from the admitted evils of militarism. We are to complete the vicious military circle of the world, so that, if we do not desist, if the oppressed of the nations do not rise in revolt against the whole accursed military system, the United States will be doing more than any other nation to intensify the race between peoples as to which will be armed most and at the greatest cost, and it will be one of the most hated and dreaded.

Next comes the irresponsible newspaper editor. He fears neither God nor man. He fills his columns day after day with insolent gossip and lying rumors, always poisoning the wells of international good will, always playing on the fears and the prejudices and ignorance of the crowd. Some future Dante who writes the Divine Comedy of America will put this type of scoundrel in the lowest round of hell.

And then comes the Jingo politician, the glowing, effervescing patriot who wants the United States flag to float all the way to the Isthmus, or who is certain that in a hundred years we as a nation will be extinct, or hold in our possession the entire North American continent. Who has power to close the mouths of the dunces? By every increase in your army and navy you add new cubits to the stature of every fool in the land.

And finally there is the commercial exploiter, the money maker who rushes into belated countries and gathers up concessions, and stakes out zones of influence. He invests the millions of powerful corporations and syndicates. By unscrupulous methods he pushes his operations, counting on the government to safeguard his investments by its army and navy. The gold of a few men shall be made safe by the blood of the boys of other men. He is a dangerous man. In every war of the last twenty-five years, he has been at the center of the clique which has brought on the conflict. The bigger the army and navy, the more insolent and ambitious this arch-mischief maker becomes.

The military and naval expert of the Bernhardi type, the covetous and unscrupulous war trader, the irresponsible and diabolical newspaper editor, the hot-headed Jingo politician, and the pushing and rapacious commercial promoter—look at them! These are the five fingers of the hand which is now crushing the world. You cannot increase the size of your war machine without increasing the strength of every one of these fingers. To break the power of that infernal hand, is the first and most imperative duty of all men who love mankind.

Somebody says: "We arm solely for defense. We prepare not for war, but *against* war." Indeed! European nations prepared only against war, and behold! You cannot change a situation by altering a preposition. Things are what they are, no matter what names you give them. Preparing *against* war is identically the same thing as preparing *for* war, and that is why all the military naval experts, and all the war traders, and all the editors of the baser sort are heartily in favor of it. They like the change of the preposition. It hoodwinks innocent people who do not take time to think the subject through.

"We are never going to use our army or our navy for aggression." Who said that? Who has authority to say that? No one. The Secretary of the Navy cannot say it. Poor man, he will be out of office long before the big machine he has planned is ready for use. No congressman can say it. He also is like a flower of the field. In the morning he grows up and flourishes, but in the evening he is cut down and withered. No President of the United States can say it. He is in his office for a brief season, and then the place that once knew him knows him no more. He may possibly be succeeded by a megalomaniac who has a fashion of thinking his own notions synonymous with eternal justice, and who when he wants a thing takes it. Let no one be fooled by all this talk about never using our army and navy except for defense. Create a war machine, and God only knows who will use it!

"Ah, but we are a peace loving people." So we are, and so are all Europeans. There is not a war loving people in Europe. They all love peace. They all hate war. They spent forty billion dollars in trying to ward this war off. They simply prepared for it and so they got it. We live in a universe in which we get not what we want, but what we deserve. Our deserts are determined by our actions. Whatsoever we sow, we reap. The universe pays no attention to what we want. No tipler or guzzler wants delirium tremens. He simply wants the exhilaration which alcohol imparts. But let him drink long and hard enough and delirium tremens comes. We do not want war, but let us make ever increasing preparation for war, and there is no escape. Whatsoever we sow we reap: what we prepare for we get. This is the solemn significance of preparedness, it leads to death! Therefore let us prepare now for peace. It will take the self sacrificing labors of tens of thousands of men, we know not how many years, to work out the machinery of peace. We have got to organize the world. It will cost brain and time and money. Let us spend money for peace, tens of millions, hundreds of millions, billions, tens of billions, whatever is necessary for peace!

Spending for Peace

The preparedness program of the administration makes me sick at heart. Either America is likely to be invaded or she is not. If she is in danger of invasion, this program is a trifling and paltry thing, nothing but a sop to the militaristic Cerberus. It is simply playing with fire. If we are *not* likely to be invaded, then this program is wildly and wickedly wasteful. It would be wicked at any time, but is a hundredfold more wicked just now, when we stand at the gravest crisis in all human history, and when every nation not engaged in the conflict ought to be asking itself, not how it can save its own hide, but how it can minister to the crying and awful needs of a wounded, bleeding world. Tens of thousands of human beings like ourselves—men, women and little children— are on the verge of starvation, and our government officials come forward with a scheme that calls for the expenditure in one department alone of 500 million dollars within five short years for the extension of the machinery of human slaughter. Not one dollar for bread—but every dollar for the dogs of war! "O judgment, thou hast fled to brutish beasts, and men have lost their reason. " Would that we had a secretary of peace, a man who, at an hour like this, would present a scheme for increasing the happiness and well being of our people. Millions for new roads, millions for new buildings, millions for new schools, millions for new farms to be carved out of the deserts and the swamps, millions for fighting disease, millions for preventing accidents, millions for brightening the lives of the poor and the ignorant and the forlorn, millions for the solution of problems which have long vexed us, and millions for forwarding noble enterprises to their coronation. Five hundred million dollars to be spent the next five years in making us a healthier, happier and better people. This is the preparedness which fits us to fulfill our duties. This is the preparedness which fits us to stand before God!

But this would not defend us—some one says—from our foreign enemies. They would be attracted by our increased prosperity and might break in and steal our treasures. Well then, let us build up lines of defense in foreign lands. We have spent one hundred and seventy eight million on coast defenses, and an expert has declared that any foreign army can easily walk around them. Why not build coast defenses which nobody can walk around? Why not build them in the hearts of the nations? O for a secretary who would suggest not 500 million dollars for machinery to sink boys of foreign countries to the bottom of the sea, but who would recommend 500 million dollars for healing the open sore of the world. The price of a dreadnaught to each of the warring nations for the erection, at the close of the war, of asylums and hospitals and orphanages and homes and schools for the service of the great company of those whom the war will have left impoverished and helpless. The price of a battle cruiser and torpedo boat and a submarine to each of those nations for the endowment of these various institutions. Five hundred million dollars for the relief of the nations who are stripped of their raiment, and wounded and half dead. Why should it be thought a thing incredible that a Christian nation should do a Christian deed? Would there then be danger of a foreign invasion? Some men are so hidebound in their materialism they cannot conceive of any defenses except those made of concrete and steel. We Americans are often accused of worshiping the almighty dollar. We are counted money makers, money grabbers. Why not show the world that we can be money givers? Why not cease this shameful shivering and whimpering over the prospect of somebody hurting us, and show the world that we can think of helping others? Spend your 500 millions on war ships, and in less than twenty years they are all on the scrap heap. Spend 500 millions on institutions scattered over Europe for the care of those whom this awful war has maimed and mangled, and they will stand forever as the imperishable monuments of a great republic's love. Do you say this is impracticable? I tell you it is not. A noble deed is always practicable.

VIEWPOINT 3

"Universal military service is the safest, most humane, and worthiest policy for the United States."

America Should Adopt a System of Universal Military Service

Charles W. Eliot (1834–1926)

In the years prior to U.S. entry into World War I, one of the reforms emphasized by advocates of American military preparedness was the creation of mandatory military training and service for all young American men. Proposals made during this time ranged from military training courses in high schools and colleges to a national draft and creation of an armed reserve force.

The following viewpoint is taken from a 1916 article by Charles W. Eliot. A president emeritus of Harvard University (which he led from 1869 to 1909), Eliot was a frequent commentator on public affairs and a leading participant in what became known as the preparedness movement. In the following viewpoint, Eliot advocates a system in which all American men ages eighteen to twenty-one would be subject to military service. Such training would be beneficial both for the young men and for the nation as a whole, he contends. In the course of his argument for universal military service, Eliot also expresses his views toward the war itself, asserting that the United States has a compelling interest in preventing Germany and its allies from becoming the dominant powers in Europe and on the oceans.

Reprinted from Charles W. Eliot, "Shall We Adopt Universal Military Service?" *World's Work*, November 1916.

There is endless talk in these days about "preparedness." Both political parties and both candidates for the Presidency advocate a larger Navy and a larger Army. On preparedness and Americanism the Republican platform uses the braver words; but the Democratic Party has voted—with more or less reluctance—the largest appropriations for the Navy and Army that have ever been voted, and also made the most earnest attempt ever made to convert the state militias into a national force. . . . Under these political conditions at home and in the present fearful state of Europe, it is important that the American people, and particularly the public men who undertake to lead the people, should consider, first, for what uses the United States needs a navy and an army; and secondly, the sort of navy and army which the United States should prepare.

To undertake the maintenance of a great modern navy and a great modern army, always prepared for immediate action, involves the abandonment of a deeply rooted American policy— the ancient reliance for safety on the physical isolation of the country between two great oceans. The maintenance of a larger navy will not require much new legislation, or much change of customs; but the maintenance of a great land force which can be mobilized in a few days—all ready for service in the field—will require much new legislation, great new expenditures, and many changes in the habits and customs of the people. The policy of maintaining only a small professional army, and even that imperfectly equipped, will have to be abandoned.

Necessary Changes

Why should the American people make this formidable change in their national habits and their international policy? First, because the industrial and commercial interests of the Nation have completely changed since the Civil War, and can no longer be preserved and promoted in isolation. The country cannot keep its existing machinery running, or sell its surplus foods and raw materials, unless the foreign markets are open to it, and are freely developed. The United States, having become an industrial and commercial World Power, needs to have all the seas and oceans of the world open for its foreign trade in times of peace, and so far as is practicable in times of war also—open for both its imports and its exports of foods, drinks, drugs, raw materials, and manufactured articles.

So long as the British navy ruled the seas, freedom for American trade with all nations was secure in peaceful times, and with Great Britain and her allies in war times; but the war has demonstrated that Great Britain can no longer secure the freedom of the seas for herself and other nations without assistance. During the present war the combined navies of Great Britain, France, Italy, and Russia have not succeeded in maintaining an effectual blockade of all German, Austrian, Bulgarian, and Turkish ports, or in preventing the destruction of an immense tonnage of merchantmen belonging to the Entente Allies, with their cargoes. Although many German and Austrian submarines have been destroyed, and a few short lines of transportation by water have been made safe against submarines, it cannot be said to-day that adequate means of defending commercial vessels and fishermen against destruction by hostile submarines have been discovered, or that the full power of the submarine to destroy enemies' property, or to maintain some foreign commerce in spite of a blockade, has as yet been developed and exhibited. The world still has much to learn about the functions of the submarine. Hence it follows that the task of keeping the oceans safe for the commerce of the free, manufacturing nations—to which foreign commerce is indispensable—is one in which the United States may reasonably be expected to take its fair part. It is not doing so now. If the United States expects to share the benefits of the resistance the Entente Allies are making to the domination of seas and lands by Germany, should it not also prepare to share the terrible sacrifices that resistance costs?

Secondly, steam and electricity have done away with the physical isolation of the United States. The oceans are not barriers, but highways which invite the passage of fleets, pacific or hostile. The security of America can no longer be trusted to the width of the Atlantic and the Pacific.

If any one says that the risk of an invasion of the United States by a strong naval and military Power is very small, particularly within twenty years of the close of the present terrifying and exhausting war, the answer is that, since the war in Europe has demonstrated how horrible a catastrophe an invasion would be, the American people may wisely insure themselves against even a small risk of invasion. The only available insurance is a Navy powerful in every respect, and an Army in reserve visibly strong in numbers and visibly prepared for immediate service.

If We Had Universal Service

If the principle of universal military service should be accepted and acted on in the United States, several important consequences would immediately follow:

1. The country would always have on call a trained force for all the duties and services which the Regular Army now performs, and this force could be increased by telegraph and telephone to

any desired extent up to the limit of the reserves. Within ten years these reserves would be formidable in number. It would probably be desirable to maintain a special force for a service of two years in the Philippines, the Panama Zone, and other outlying regions; but this force should consist of young men who volunteered for that special service after they had received the universal training at home, or the better part of it.

The Need for Universal Military Training

General Hugh Scott, chief of staff of the U.S. Army, writes in a 1915 report that the United States can no longer rely on volunteers to provide an adequate defense and thus is in need of a system of universal military service and training.

In my judgment, the country will never be prepared for defense until we do as other great nations do that have large interests to guard, like Germany, Japan, and France, where everybody is ready and does perform military service in time of peace as he would pay every other tax and is willing to make sacrifices for the protection he gets and the country gets in return. The volunteer system in this country, in view of the highly organized, trained, and disciplined armies that our possible opponents possess, should be relegated to the past. There is no reason why one woman's son should go out and defend or be trained to defend another woman and her son who refuses to take training or give service. The only democratic method is for every man in his youth to become trained in order that he may render efficient service if called upon in war.

Universal military training has been the corner stone upon which has been built every republic in the history of the world, and its abandonment the signal for decline and obliteration.

---

2. It would no longer be necessary to maintain any state militia; provided the governors were authorized to call on the national War Department for any troops they might need for local service. But if any state preferred to do so, it might maintain a local volunteer force made up of young men who had already served their first period (sixty to ninety days) in the national army.

3. The Nation would be always prepared for defensive combat with any military power which might assail it for purposes of conquest or ransom; and, being prepared, would probably be safe from such attempts.

4. In case of rebellion or outbreak of any sort within the country itself, a national force could be promptly put into the field to subdue it.

5. All the able-bodied young men in the country would receive

a training in the hard work of a soldier which would be of some service to them in any industry in which they might afterward engage. They would have become accustomed to a discipline under which many men coöperate strenuously in the pursuit of common objects. They would have mastered the use of some instruments of precision; and would have learned much about personal and public hygiene, and the means of preserving bodily vigor and utilizing it to advantage.

6. The defense of the country would be always in charge of a Navy and Army neither feudal nor mercenary, neither drafted "for the war" nor professional in the sense that its members mean to spend their active lives in the service, but on the contrary composed of all the able-bodied youth of the Nation, acting under a universal sense of obligation or duty, but also willing to serve the country in a hearty coöperative spirit out of love of freedom, justice, and all that makes "home."

7. In case of war, large or small, long or short, the great waste of lives and money which has taken place at the beginning of every war in which the United States has been engaged since the Government was organized would be avoided; because the country would have at call any desired number of competent officers and well-trained men. In case of war alarms the country would not be obliged to summon untrained militia, or to resort to such crude and unsound methods as Plattsburg camps [unofficial military training camps for civilians] and college regiments.

Moral Advantages

Some moral advantages would result to the United States from maintaining the second navy in the world and a numerous army always ready. A strong democracy, always prepared to defend itself against attacks from without or within, would be less exposed to intentional provocation by critical or jealous governments, and less liable to the occasional internal panics which are apt to cause wastes and other unnecessary evils. Some improvement in the character and efficiency of the American people itself might also be expected, especially in regard to coöperative discipline, self-reliance, and self-control. To be always ready to defend and to maintain American ideals of public justice and liberty would add to the self-respect of the people. If every able-bodied youth were well trained for service in the national army or navy at some serious sacrifice of his ease and earning time, and then held himself constantly in readiness to fight for his country, if it were in peril, until he became too old for soldier's work, the whole people would soon attain to a new sentiment of patriotic duty and self-sacrificing devotion to the country as the groundwork of home, kinship, and friendship, and the representative of public justice and liberty and of progressive hope for mankind. The entire Nation, without distinction of race or class, would be taught to think of itself as a unified and exalted power for good in the world—humane, unselfish, and aspiring.

To protect this country and its productive industries and to exalt the patriotic sentiments of its people are, however, not the only or the strongest motives for abandoning the precious traditional policies of the United States in respect to isolation and the avoidance of foreign entanglements. Durable peace can be maintained after the present war only by a dominant force too strong for Germany, Austria-Hungary, Turkey, and Bulgaria, separately, or in any possible combination, or with any imaginable allies, to attack or to resist. A limited alliance of competent nations—three, four, or five—can promptly provide such a force already trained to concurrent, coöperative action. Federations and parliaments of the world could not do it. They would be too complicated, vast, slow, and unstable. The "Concert of Europe" [a term used to describe the loose agreement among the major European powers in the nineteenth century to preserve peace and coöperate on issues of common interest] is utterly discredited, because it has too often brought about, or permitted, concerted injustice, and perpetuated poisonous wrongs. There is no hope of establishing lasting peace through any treaty-making which should include the Central Monarchies. Their acts since July, 1914, prove beyond a doubt that no reliance is to be placed on any pledges or treaties signed by them. No verbal or written evidence of a change of heart on the part of the German people could be depended on. If such a change shall happily occur, the rest of the world will not trust it until its reality is proved by a long course of rational and honorable conduct. What would be the best group of nations for supplying this dominant force? There might well be two distinct alliances; one for the oceans, the other for the lands. For the oceans, Great Britain, France, and the United States would suffice; but Russia, Italy, Brazil, Argentina, Chile, and Japan would be convenient additions. For continental Europe and the Near East, Great Britain, France, Italy, and Russia would be indispensable, and Spain, Portugal, Belgium, Holland, and Scandinavia would be acceptable additions. . . .

The Navy and the Army

In order to do its part in maintaining a lasting peace throughout the world, this country should possess a navy next to that of Great Britain in size, and as perfect as it can be made in construction, equipment, and appointments, and in the skill of its officers and men. This up-to-date navy should be kept ready for instant service at full strength; so long as it can contribute to prevent war in Europe and the East and to impart that universal confidence in the maintenance of peace which must precede any general reduction of armaments. Such a navy cannot be procured and maintained unless the principle of universal military service is adopted by the American people and put into force. Voluntary enlistment will not furnish in times of peace and industrial prosperity the number of men required for such a navy, nor supply a reserve force of trained men who can be depended on in time of war. Even under the present incitements the American Navy is not fully manned, and it seldom has been except in war time. When war has broken out, there has been no adequate naval reserve. . . .

The United States has found uses, since the [1898] war with Spain, for a fairly equipped army of something less than one hundred thousand men; and a minority of the states have seen reason to maintain a volunteer militia, in the organizing of which no attention has been paid to the married or single state of the volunteers, and but little to their physical fitness for the duties of a soldier. The militia has also been poorly equipped, or sometimes hardly equipped at all for real work. . . .

As a national force to be used in any part of the country, or beyond its borders, and for long periods during which the men are detached from their homes and their employments, the state militias are inappropriate. In war with a strong military Power, the militia would not be available for several months, or until all the units had been converted into national units and re-officered in large part.

Although the Regular Army of the United States is an efficient body of men, well selected, well officered, and possessing a fine esprit de corps, it is not a modern army in the European sense; and it is not the kind of army that a democratic people ought to maintain, having been essentially copied from the English army, which has . . . been . . . an army officered from the upper classes and recruited by voluntary enlistment from the lower. It has never been a popular or national army in the sense of continental Europe, where conscription or universal military service has long prevailed.

If the United States sees reason for maintaining any army at all, it will be wise for it to maintain a democratic army, in which all able-bodied young Americans should serve for several short periods, and then be held in reserve for a long period, its officers being selected from the ranks by their instructors and commanders during the prescribed periods of service, and educated as now at the Military Academy to serve for life as teachers of the successive levies of raw recruits, or held in reserve with liberty to follow civil occupations. A few thousand non-commissioned officers would also be kept in the service permanently, or for considerable periods, to serve as instructors to the raw levies and as non-commissioned officers of any force the country might need for sudden and sustained service.

The Fallacy of Non-Resistance

A few philanthropists believe that the world would get on better if there were no armies and navies and no use of force to resist wrong-doers; but non-resistance seems to almost everybody an impracticable international policy at mankind's actual state of progress. The nations have not yet come into [Ralph Waldo] Emerson's "region of holiness" where passion passes from them. On the contrary, never before was outrageous violence so rife in the world, and resistance to it by force so indispensable. The policy of non-resistance is nowhere applied to burglars, murderers, or maniacs. No more can it be applied to Europe, in full view of invasions of Belgium and Serbia, Armenian massacres, and the sudden sinking of passenger steamers, merchantmen, and fishermen. Non-resistance is an admirable moral goal; but reaching it seems at the present day as far off as when Buddha taught, twenty-five hundred years ago, that the use of force was never justifiable or even expedient.

Since peaceful international relations will need for decades the firm support of a trustworthy protective international force, the United States ought to be in a position to supply part of that force. It is America's clear duty to her inheritance of liberty and to civilization itself to take an effective part in the maintenance of peace and of the freedom of the seas when the present war is over. For the discharge of this duty, and for her own security, America needs a strong navy and a strong potential army, both kept always ready. She can secure neither without adopting the principle of universal service. Such are the lessons of Germany's outbreak in 1914, and of the fifty-years-long Prussian preparation for that outbreak in such secrecy, and with such protestations of innocency, that the other European nations were taken by surprise when the German armies rushed over Belgium bound for Paris. . . .

The Swiss System

Most of the details in the Swiss system of national defense could be copied with appropriate modifications in an American system of national defense. Before the twentieth year—that is, during school life—the Swiss aim at turning out from their schools vigorous and agile youths who can read, write, and cipher, and know something of the history and geography of Switzerland and the neighboring countries, and something about the history of religious toleration and civil liberty. Swiss boys are also encouraged to become, between the ages of sixteen and twenty, members of preparatory semi-military organizations whose chief object is rifle-shooting on Sundays. Saturdays could be substituted for Sundays in the United States. The Swiss regulations for encouraging target practice are elaborate and effectual; and the Swiss practices in this respect might all be copied in the United States with one possible exception. The Swiss soldier, during his period of service, is allowed to retain in his own possession the rifle, uniform, and other equipments which the Federation supplies. He keeps them in good order, and does not use them except for work which the State encourages or orders. It may be doubted whether this method could be safely adopted in the United States—at least, until we have had some years' experience of the discipline appropriate to universal military service. . . .

The Swiss Republic resembles the American Republic in several important respects, although the two territories and situations are strikingly unlike. Switzerland is a federation of distinct political entities called cantons, in which four different languages severally prevail, part of the cantons being Catholic and part Protestant. Industrially the people are agricultural, pastoral, manufacturing, or commercial, but universally democratic in manners and customs. The federal legislation concerning education and taxation is more democratic than that of the United States. The country is annually invaded by large numbers of alien laborers. On the whole the stout little republic is a safe guide for the United States in respect to the organization of a competent modern army. . . .

Many thoughtful Americans believe that nothing but heavy disasters in war can bring the country to adopt the system of universal military service; but others, more sanguine about democratic capacity for wise action in matters which concern nearly the whole people, hope that the horrors of the present war and the example of the national army maintained by Switzerland can bring a majority of the American voters to the conviction that universal military service is the safest, most humane, and worthiest policy for the United States during the next fifty years at least.

The present American Navy can be built up in three or four years into a navy adequate in size, which will embody all the most recent improvements in naval equipment, without much legislation in addition to that recently adopted by Congress in response to the urgency of the present Administration; provided means be found to procure the number of men necessary to keep the whole navy in commission. Universal service would furnish the men.

America's Military Needs

The answer then to the question at the head of this article is— the United States needs a navy modeled on the British navy, and an army modeled on the Swiss army; and in order to procure both it needs to adopt the principle of brief universal service in the army or the navy. The time lost by the young men from the productive industries and the service of the family will be a trifling loss compared with the gain from an increased feeling of devotion to the country in the hearts of multitudes and a quickened sense of responsibility for its welfare. The slight loss of individual liberty will be more than compensated by experience of a strict, coöperative discipline, and by an enlarged sense of comradeship and community interest among the people.

It is a grave conclusion to come to, that a great democracy whose primary object is the promotion of the public welfare and happiness must arm itself to fight, and must teach all its young men how to fight—which means how to kill and wound other men with whom individually they have no quarrel, to destroy public and private property, to disrupt homes and extinguish families, to interrupt commerce, and to waste on a prodigious scale the accumulated savings of generations.

What forces this Republic to so awful a conclusion? The same experience which has compelled civilized Society in general to defend itself by force against lunatics and criminals, and the demonstration given during the last two years that the existing governmental and ecclesiastical institutions of the civilized world afford no adequate protection from a sudden but long-prepared outbreak of primitive savagery which has compelled nearly half the population of the earth to set to work with all their energy and ingenuity to kill each other and to destroy each other's property, and to use in that killing and destruction not only all the new instruments with which modern physics, chemistry, and mechanics have supplied it, but all the old instruments of hand-to-hand fighting, such as the spear—now bayonet—the short sword, and the hand grenade. Neither religion nor popular education has shown any power to prevent this relapse into savagery. The modern means of easy communication by printing press, telegraph, and telephone have not prevented governments from misleading their people by withholding the truth and circulating falsehoods. Censors and martial law have triumphed over the ordinary means of publicity. Never in the whole history of the world has despotic government wrought such immense mischief; because never before have despotisms been able to wield with so much skill such highly organized and accumulated forces.

Like all the other free nations, the United States must be prepared to defend its territory and its ideals. Submission and non-resistance are not safe policies either for the United States or for civilized society. Therefore the United States needs a navy of the best possible sort as regards men, vessels, and equipment, and an army of the most patriotic quality and surest efficiency. To secure this navy and this army it needs to adopt the principle of universal service. To do nothing and run for luck is not good sense, when such vital interests are at stake. Those who think it high time for men to learn war no more, and that all teaching of the military art is to be deplored, can console themselves with the reflections that, whereas many millions of young Americans, on the principle of universal service, would learn how to fight, only a small proportion of the total mass would ever be called on actually to fight, and that the better the teaching the smaller that proportion would probably be. Moreover, that small proportion of the American youth that in the course of years would come to the actual killing of fellow-men would be actuated at the moment by lofty motives, such as love of home and country, and unselfish devotion to the highest interests of humanity.

Uniting America

Despite the heterogeneous character of the people of the United States as respects race or stock the masses of the people worship the same precious ideals of liberty, law and public happiness. At heart they know that these ideals, so dear to them, will have to be protected and furthered by force for many a year to come, the world being what it is. Everybody hopes that the world is going to be very different hereafter from what it is in these grievous days of return to primitive savagery; but the conduct of the liberty-loving nations to-day and to-morrow must be determined by the hard, actual facts. They cannot organize now the perpetual defense of liberty under law; but they can provide promptly, through practicable alliances, securities which will last at least for one generation.

VIEWPOINT 4

"We need greatly a rebirth of true patriotism, just as we need . . . deeper national unity, more self-discipline, but universal military service is not the panacea for these ills."

America Should Not Adopt a System of Universal Military Service

George Nasmyth (1882–1920)

George Nasmyth was a writer and an activist in several peace organizations during World War I, including the League to Enforce Peace, which promoted the elimination of war through the creation of an international peacekeeping organization. Among Nasmyth's writings was the book *Social Progress and the Darwinian Theory; A Study of Force as a Factor in Human Relations.* The following viewpoint is taken from his 1917 pamphlet, which was published by the American Union Against Militarism (AUAM).

Nasmyth argues against the establishment of universal military service or training for Americans, asserting that such programs would be undemocratic and are unnecessary for ensuring America's security. Furthermore, he maintains, these programs are not as helpful in fostering patriotism or national unity as their advocates claim. Establishing a system of compulsory military training, Nasmyth insists, would be a first step toward the creation of a militarized society that would extinguish civil liberties and other principles of democracy.

Reprinted from George Nasmyth, *Universal Military Service and Democracy,* a pamphlet published in 1917 by the American Union Against Militarism.

If any person had predicted two years ago that the people of America would be seriously discussing the adoption of universal military service in 1917 he would have been looked upon as a visionary. But since the outbreak of the war in Europe, the rising tide of reaction which resulted from the international reign of terror; the increasing power of militarism in the world; and the great preparedness campaign which was carried to a successful conclusion in 1915 and 1916, have led, step by step, to an increasing agitation for universal military service, as an essential part of the system of national defense.

Moreover, laws have actually been passed in the closing hours of the session of the legislature in New York State providing for military training in the high school and universal military service for all young men between the ages of 18 and 21. Finally the national defense act passed by the United States Congress in July, 1916, gives to the military authorities the power to "draft" men into the army whenever voluntary enlistments shall be insufficient, so that universal military service or conscription, to use a more convenient term for the same idea, has been established as a legal principle in the Empire State and in the nation.

Universal Military Service and Preparedness

The case for universal military service rests on entirely different grounds than does the general case for preparedness. If we did not have our other five lines of national defense which protect us from any attack from European or Asiatic powers, there might be some justification in this universal military service in America. But with two oceans, one 3,000 and the other 5,000 miles in width; the navy, the second largest in the world; submarines, which make the transport of large bodies of troops across great distances a most hazardous undertaking; automatic and electric contact mines and coast fortifications, such as have made it impossible for the Allies successfully to land troops on the shores of Germany or even Turkey, even when the Allies were backed by a naval force three or four times greater than that of the Central European Powers—with all these first lines of defense, not even the most fearful and extreme of our militarists pretend that an army of seven to ten million men, which the system of universal military service would give us after a few years of building up reserves who had passed through the military machine, would be necessary to repel an actual invasion on American soil.

But the volunteer system will fail, it is argued. Even the standing army of 250,000 men and the militia of 400,000 provided for in the national defense act cannot be raised by the voluntary method.

If this force is needed, it can be raised by the right kind of an appeal to the American people. This involves a fundamental transformation of an army from its old-world character of a machine trained solely for wholesale murder, to a new world army of social service. An army of labor trained in the work of reforestation, of irrigation, of building great highways, instructed in methods of camp sanitation and effective coöperation; from which every man would come out a more useful member of society and a more productive economic unit, would make a far different appeal to American young men than the standing army on the present system, or even a National Guard of the socially elite. With this employment in useful production should go adequate compensation, just as there goes adequate compensation for police work, for the work of firemen and life-savers. Under a really democratic system of social service such as this, there will be no difficulty in finding all the men that are needed, without resort to conscription.

But since the case which can be made out for compulsory service is so weak from the point of view of military necessity, its advocates fall back on other arguments. Universal military service, they claim, will promote democracy; it will unify the nation; it will increase patriotism; it will form greatly needed habits of obedience and discipline. These arguments constitute, in brief, the case for conscription, around which the great debate will rage, and they are so important that they should be subjected to the most searching analysis.

Democracy and Equality

Does universal military service involve equal sacrifice on the part of rich and poor alike? If both are killed, of course, both have made the last great sacrifice, and so far as their individual lives are concerned, it is equal. But for the families of the two men the difference is very great. For the family of the poor man, the loss of the breadwinner means that the widow must go out to work, that the children must be deprived of an opportunity for education, that their whole lives must be limited because they did not have the opportunities they would have had if their father had lived. For the rich man, on the contrary, no such sacrifice on the part of his family is involved. His wife is not compelled to go out and work, his children are not deprived of the opportunity of receiving a liberal education.

Even if sacrifice of life is not involved, the sacrifice of time required for universal military service imposes an unequal burden upon the rich and the poor. For the rich man, Plattsburg [a New York town that was the site of summer volunteer military training camps] is an enjoyable vacation, and a longer period of military service would not be any great hardship, but for the poor man it means a definite interruption of his economic life, the stopping of his earnings, a postponement of the time when he can afford to marry, an interruption of his difficult task of getting a foothold in his trade or small business. No element of equality of sacrifice can be discovered in the two cases.

Army Medical Examiner: "At last a perfect soldier!"

This 1916 cartoon by Robert Minor first appeared in The Masses, *a small radical periodical published in Greenwich Village in New York City. It reflects the views of those who feared the rise of a dehumanizing ideology of militarism in the United States.*

Those who believe that class distinctions can be broken down and democracy created by regimenting men into masses and forcing them to drill together, have missed the central idea of democracy which is based on the principle of voluntary coöperation, of equality of opportunity, and the abolition of caste privileges. Those who believe that democracy can be imposed from without by force and point to the examples of France and Switzerland, should analyze the conditions in those countries more deeply. As soon as we penetrate below the surface, we find in each of them a great conflict between the forces of militarism and democracy. This conflict rages in all countries where universal military service is established. . . .

Switzerland has not had an aggressive militarism of the Pan-German type, it is true, but this is not due to any lack of desire on the part of the Swiss military officers who are like military officers the world over. It has been due to the fact that Switzerland is a small country and any propaganda for a career of "national destiny," or the conquest of the world would render its advocates ludicrous.

Everywhere militarism has been the most formidable enemy of democracy. For every million soldiers you must have at least 30,000 officers, and these 30,000 officers must make the military profession their life work. They must cultivate an iron will and a spirit of domination as essential elements of success, and necessarily they chafe with impatience at the discussions and restraints of democracy and the civil powers of government. Altogether they constitute a source of ever present danger to the peace of a nation which is powerful enough to be a menace to the world.

If the breakdown of civilization in Europe has anything to teach America, surely it is the danger of any increase in the forces or the philosophy of militarism.

Discipline and National Unity

The second argument for universal military service is that it will promote discipline. It will teach obedience and respect for authority, it is urged, and these elements are greatly needed in American life. The trouble here is the kind of discipline which military service provides. It is a discipline enforced from without and breaks down as soon as the restraining force is removed. The whole object of military training is to secure instantaneous obedience without thought, to make a man a part of an automatic military machine so that if he is ordered to sink the Lusitania or destroy the city of Louvain, he will obey instantly and unquestioningly. Such unthinking obedience is far removed from that self-imposed discipline, that respect for laws because they have been enacted by common consent and for the welfare of the people; of freedom of discussion, of speech, of press, of assembly, and of conscience, which are the foundation stones of a self-governing democracy. At first, the German people opposed conscription bitterly, but after a few generations of men had been put through the military machine and taught the right kind of obedience, all opposition ceased. Germany became a servile state.

The third argument is that it will promote Americanism, it will heal all our divisions of race and nationality, eliminate the hyphen and unify the American people.

The experience of European nations which have tried to meet similar problems by this method is in flat contradiction to such an assumption. The history of Poland, of the subject races and nationalities of Russia, and of Turkey is a refutation of the claim that national unity can be secured by universal military service.

America needs unity, a national consciousness, and a national will, but no reactionary, militaristic, obsolete, old world instrument, such as conscription, can unify the American people.

A fourth argument for universal military service is that it will promote patriotism, it will teach a man to be ready to sacrifice himself for others and to lay down his life for his country in the service of a great idea. The difficulty with this plan is that there are various kinds of patriotism and the tendency of militarism is to emphasize the wrong kind—the patriotism which corresponds to a narrow nationalism and to Jingoism and the patriotism which is based upon the hatred of other parts of the human race who happen to live the other side of a boundary line. Patriotism and nationalism of the wrong kind are defeating their own ends in Europe. For the sake of our country, as well as for humanity, we must develop another type of patriotism than universal military service has given us in Germany or any of the European countries, a patriotism which will look upon America as a part of the world and will take pride in the contributions which America can make to the family of nations.

Against Conscription

George Huddleston, a Democratic representative from Alabama, expresses his opposition to universal military service in remarks made before Congress on January 10, 1917.

The militarists having succeeded in committing Congress to a policy of vast increases of Army and Navy, now take the next step and demand conscription. Taking advantage of the world-wide terror inspired by the European debacle, they cause Congress to appropriate for the current year over $650,000,000 for military preparedness, and are now demanding $800,000,000 for next year. Having insisted last year that a standing army of 500,000 was necessary, they now increase the figures to 1,500,000, with a reserve of 1,500,00 additional.

In their new demands the militarists carefully avoid the use of the word "conscription"; they use the euphemisms "universal training" and "universal service." The scheme, however, can not be disguised with agreeable words. Conscription is what they are demanding; conscription in its true and odious form; conscription as real and oppressive as now exists among the embattled nations of Europe; conscription which drags the boy from his mother's side, the father from the bosom of his family, and places them in the ranks as unwilling soldiers in time of peace; conscription with all its crushing weight upon the people, its denial of personal liberty, its espionage, its hateful methods of registration and interference with the freedom of men to come and go, to live their lives, and to seek happiness and well-being in their own way.

We need greatly a rebirth of true patriotism, just as we need a more fundamental democracy, deeper national unity, more self-discipline, but universal military service is not the panacea for these ills. A true American patriotism can be created only by a return to the great principles of the founders of the Republic, a new vision of the mission of America in the world, a great world task such as the establishment of a League to Enforce Peace, calling for the sacrifice of old provincialisms and outworn traditions in the service of humanity, as a whole. In this way, under the great constructive leadership of a world statesman, America can be unified. By these new paths which lead out into a future full of hope and service, it may be that in the coming years the soul of America will be born again into a new and larger life, but never by the path of conscription, of fear and servile obedience, and the mechanical methods of militarism.

A much deeper principle is involved than is usually discussed in connection with universal military service: What kind of a society do we wish to live in? For, if the principle of compulsion is accepted in the case of military service, it must logically be accepted for service in munition factories, on the railroads, in coal mines and in all the industrial and economic life upon which modern wars depend. In other words once having granted the principle of compulsion on the ground of military necessity, all the fundamental principles of democracy must be sacrificed and our country must be "Prussianized" from within. Freedom of speech, freedom of assembly and freedom of the press are all opposed to military effectiveness and must disappear step by step if freedom of conscience, the advance trench of democracy, is carried by the militarists; for in the last analysis, universal military service means conscription of conscience.

America is the only great nation left in the world in which militarism is not enthroned and the principle of conscription established. In order to defend our institutions and our democracy from imaginary dangers from without, we are urged to surrender to this much more real and formidable enemy of militarism and conscription from within.

Sometime in the future, if Europe remains an armed camp after this war, and if militarism is enthroned in the world, it may become inevitable for America to adopt conscription. But if conscription ever does become inevitable let us not add blasphemy to our other crimes by adopting militarism in the name of democracy. No, let us do it with the clear knowledge that we are dealing a death blow to the greatest experiment in democracy the human race has ever tried. Let us do it with the consciousness that we have participated in a great world tragedy, and that, with the triumph of militarism in the New World as well as the Old, we shall have seen government of the people, by the people and for the people, perish from the earth.

CHAPTER 2

The Question of American Neutrality

Chapter Preface

The United States began World War I as a neutral nation. On August 19, 1914, President Woodrow Wilson addressed the American people, asking them to be "impartial in thought as well as in action" concerning the war in Europe. Wilson gave both domestic and foreign policy reasons for his request. Neutrality was necessary to preserve domestic harmony, he argued, because millions of Americans were either foreign-born or children of immigrants from nations involved in the conflict. According to Wilson, the war risked dividing America along ethnic lines, putting its citizens "in camps of hostile opinion, hot against each other." In addition, Wilson asserted that only if the United States remained "neutral in fact as well as in name" could the nation "play a part of impartial mediation and speak the counsels of peace" to the nations at war.

Over the next three years, Wilson would make several attempts at mediating an end to the war. Emphasizing the mounting casualties on all sides, he appealed to the European nations to accept "peace without victory." Meanwhile, he and the American people struggled to determine how and whether American neutrality could be preserved as conflicts developed between the United States and the warring nations.

Between 1914 and 1917, the policy debate over U.S. involvement in the "Great War" was primarily confined to the alternatives of maintaining neutrality or siding with the Allies. The Allied cause encountered opposition from some members of certain ethnic groups, including German Americans sympathetic to Germany, Irish Americans dissatisfied with Britain's rule of Ireland, and Russian immigrants opposed to the oppressive regime of Czar Nicholas II. But the prospect of the United States' entering the war on the side of the Central Powers was never seriously entertained by the government or by most of the American public.

The United States gravitated toward the Allied side for several reasons. Germany and its allies were widely viewed as militaristic dictatorships that compared unfavorably with the more democratic nations of Great Britain and France—countries to which many Americans felt ties of language, culture, and history. Furthermore, Germany's surprise invasion of neutral Belgium in 1914 convinced many of the aggressor's barbarity, as did British propaganda stories of German atrocities. Evidence of German espionage and sabotage in the United States also contributed to anti-German sentiment.

Both Great Britain and Germany took actions to attempt to restrict U.S. trade, but America responded differently to these actions, revealing the nation's sympathies. Prior to the outbreak of World War I, the United States had carried on a substantial trade with many European nations—a trade that America hoped to continue and expand during the war. International maritime law established certain rules for trade and other matters of international conduct in times of war for belligerent and neutral nations. Under these rules, belligerents had the right to search neutral vessels and seize military goods (contraband) destined for their enemies. However, neutrals retained the right to sell nonmilitary goods to all nations. Wilson and many other Americans saw no contradiction between maintaining American neutrality and asserting American rights as a neutral trader.

From the beginning of World War I, Great Britain, possessor of the world's largest navy, sought to impose a broad blockade against Germany and the Central Powers. As part of this blockade, British ships intercepted American shipping and confiscated foodstuffs and other goods that Britain (contrary to established international law) designated as contraband. Between 1914 and 1917, Wilson and the U.S. government issued numerous protests against these British violations of American neutrality. Great Britain responded to America's objections by promising to pay for lost and damaged property and by more than making up for the lost Central Powers markets with its own war orders.

These actions, the extent of Great Britain's trade with the United States, and the fact that Great Britain never sank American ships or took American lives, all helped to prevent a severing of U.S.-British relations. Although Great Britain's blockade reduced U.S.-German trade from $345 million in 1914 to $29 million in 1916, during the same period American trade with the Allied Powers rose from $753 million to almost $3 billion. Moreover, much of this trade was financed by U.S. loans to Allied nations. American goods and loans were therefore effectively propping up the Allied war effort, even as the U.S. government remained officially neutral.

Germany, with a smaller surface fleet, could not impose a blockade. Instead, the German navy chose to use submarines to interdict shipping to Great Britain. The submarine proved itself a powerful weapon for sinking ships, but because it depended on surprise for its effectiveness, German captains were unable to warn merchant ships of attack or otherwise follow international laws designed to protect neutrals and noncombatants.

In February 1915, the German government announced the creation of a war zone around Great Britain, warning that enemy ships entering the zone would be sunk and that neutral ships ran the risk of being attacked by mistake. Wilson responded by declaring that Germany would be held to "strict accountability" if American lives and property were lost in the war zone. Although Germany promised not to attack U.S. ships, some American lives were lost when British vessels and other ships belonging to belligerent nations were sunk. The American public was especially angered when Germany sank the *Lusitania*, a British passenger liner, in 1915, killing 128 Americans. Through stern protests and a threat to break off diplomatic relations, Wilson was able to compel Germany to suspend surprise attacks (effectively all submarine attacks) against passenger ships and later, in May 1916, against all merchant ships. However, in February 1917 Germany, gambling that it could defeat the Allies before America could effectively mobilize for war, resumed unrestricted submarine warfare against all ships (including American vessels) entering the war zone. On March 18, 1917, German submarines sank three American merchant ships.

On April 2, 1917, Wilson asked Congress to declare war on Germany. Blaming Germany's submarine attacks, Wilson maintained that neutrality was no longer possible. America, he stated, must "accept the status of belligerent which has . . . been thrust upon it." During the subsequent debate, most members of Congress agreed with Wilson and voted for a declaration of war. However, some members, recalling Wilson's original plea for neutrality, argued that the submarine crisis could have been avoided had the government remained truly neutral and had not favored Great Britain and the Allies through its foreign policy.

The question of whether U.S. trade policy and Allied sympathies were as much to blame as Germany's actions for America's failure to remain neutral is still a matter of debate among historians. The viewpoints in this chapter provide a sampling of the opinions held in America during this period. They also shed light on the events that led the United States to declare war on Germany.

VIEWPOINT 1

"While . . . such a war as this . . . is a great misfortune, looked at solely from the standpoint of the United States, we have every reason to be happy that we are able to preserve strict neutrality in respect to it."

The United States Should Maintain Neutrality

William Howard Taft (1857–1930)

When World War I began in Europe in August 1914, the initial reaction of many Americans was confusion, shock—and relief that the war was happening three thousand miles away. The following viewpoint by William Howard Taft, first published at the start of the war, is indicative of this public sentiment.

Taft served as president of the United States from 1909 to 1913. After he was defeated for reelection by Democratic candidate Woodrow Wilson in 1912, Taft joined Yale University as a professor of constitutional law, where he remained active in public affairs and in the Republican Party. In this August 1914 article written for the *Independent* magazine, Taft argues that the United States may well be the only great power able to remain neutral in the war. Moreover, he contends, establishing the nation as a neutral power will place it in an advantageous position to eventually mediate an end to the conflict.

As I write, Germany is reported to have declared war against Russia and France, and the participation of England on the one side and of Italy on the other seems imminent. Nothing like it has

Reprinted from William Howard Taft, "A Message to the People of the United States," *Independent*, vol. 79 (1914), pp. 198–99.

occurred since the great Napoleonic wars, and with modern armaments and larger populations nothing has occurred like it since the world began.

It is a cataclysm. It is a retrograde step in Christian civilization. It will be difficult to keep the various countries of the Balkans out of the war, and Greece and Turkey may take part in it. All Europe is to be a battleground. It is reported that the neutrality of Holland has already been ignored and Belgium offers such opportunities in the campaigns certain to follow that her territory, too, will be the scene of struggle.

War and Commerce

Private property and commercial shipping under an enemy's flag are subject to capture and appropriation by prize proceedings and with the formidable navies of England, France, Germany, Russia and Italy active[,] the great carrying trade of the world will be in large part suspended or destroyed or will be burdened with such heavy insurance as greatly to curtail it.

The commerce of the world makes much for the prosperity of the countries with whom it is conducted and its interruption means great inconvenience and economic suffering among all people, whether at peace or war. The capital which the European people have invested by the billions in the United States, Canada, Australia, South Africa and in the Orient must perforce be withdrawn to fill the war chests of the nations engaged in a death grapple, and the enterprises which that capital made possible are likely to be greatly crippled while the hope of any further expansion must be definitely given up.

This general European war will give a feverish activity in a number of branches of our industry, but on the whole we shall suffer with the rest of the world, except that we shall not be destroying or blowing up our existing wealth or sacrificing the lives of our best young men and youth.

It is hard to prophesy the scope of a war like this because history offers no precedent. It is impossible to foresee the limits of a war of any proportions when confined only to two countries. In our own small Spanish war we began it to free Cuba and when the war closed we found ourselves ten thousand miles away with the Philippines on our hands.

The immense waste of life and treasure in a modern war makes the loss to the conqueror only less, if indeed it be less, than the loss to the conquered.

With a high patriotic spirit, people enter upon war with confidence and with the thought of martial glory and success. The sacrifices they have to make, the suffering they have to undergo are generally such that if victory does not rest upon their banners[,] they seek a scapegoat for that which they themselves have brought on in the head of the state, and the king or emperor who begins a war or allows one to begin puts at stake not only the prestige of his nation but also the stability and integrity of his dynasty.

The True Spirit of Neutrality

On August 4, 1914, President Woodrow Wilson issued a proclamation of American neutrality in the war that had erupted in Europe. In Wilson's August 19 speech excerpted below, he asked the American people not to take sides in the war so the United States could be "neutral in fact as well as in name."

The effect of the war upon the United States will depend upon what American citizens say and do. Every man who really loves America will act and speak in the true spirit of neutrality, which is the spirit of impartiality and fairness and friendliness to all concerned. The spirit of the Nation in this critical matter will be determined largely by what individuals and society and those gathered in public meetings do and say, upon what newspapers and magazines contain, upon what ministers utter in their pulpits, and men proclaim as their opinions on the street.

The people of the United States are drawn from many nations, and chiefly from the nations now at war. It is natural and inevitable that there should be the utmost variety of sympathy and desire among them with regard to the issues and circumstances of the conflict. Some will wish one nation, others another, to succeed in the momentous struggle. It will be easy to excite passion and difficult to allay it. Those responsible for exciting it will assume a heavy responsibility, responsibility for no less a thing than that the people of the United States, whose love of their country and whose loyalty to its Government should unite them as Americans all, bound in honor and affection to think first of her and her interests, may be divided in camps of hostile opinion, hot against each other, involved in the war itself in impulse and opinion if not in action.

Such divisions among us would be fatal to our peace of mind and might seriously stand in the way of the proper performance of our duty as the one great nation at peace, the one people holding itself ready to play a part of impartial mediation and speak the counsels of peace and accommodation, not as a partisan, but as a friend.

I venture, therefore, my fellow countrymen, to speak a solemn word of warning to you against that deepest, most subtle, most essential breach of neutrality which may spring out of partisanship, out of passionately taking sides. The United States must be neutral in fact as well as in name during these days that are to try men's souls. We must be impartial in thought as well as in action, must put a curb upon our sentiments as well as upon every transaction that might be construed as a preference of one party to the struggle before another.

65

In such a war as this, therefore, with the universal tendency to popular control in every country, the strain and defeat in war may lead to a state of political flux in those countries which shall suffer defeat, with all the attendant difficulties and disorder that a change of government involves.

U.S. Neutrality

While we can be sure that such a war as this, taking it by and large, will be a burden upon the United States and is a great misfortune, looked at solely from the standpoint of the United States, we have every reason to be happy that we are able to preserve strict neutrality in respect to it. Within our hospitable boundaries we have living prosperous and contented emigrants in large numbers from all the countries who are to take part in the war and the sympathies of these people will of course be with their respective native lands. Were there no other reason this circumstance would tend to keep us free from an entanglement.

We may sincerely hope that Japan will not be involved. She will not be unless the war is carried on to the far Orient, to India or to China. Germany has but a small settlement in the Orient, while France and Russia and England would be allies in this war and it would seem quite unlikely that there would arise any obligation under the English-Japanese alliance for Japan to assist England.

Of the great powers of the world, therefore, the only ones left out are likely to be the United States and Japan, and perhaps only the United States, by reason of the alliance between Japan and England. Japan, if she keeps out of the war, will occupy the same advantageous position, which will be ours, of complete neutrality, of an actually judicial attitude, and therefore, of having an opportunity at some time, we may hope, to mediate between the powers and to help to mitigate this disaster to mankind.

The Future of War

At the time when so many friends of peace have thought that we were making real progress toward the abolition of war this sudden outbreak of the greatest war in history is most discouraging. The future looks dark indeed, but we should not despair.

"God moves in a mysterious way His wonders to perform." Now that the war is a settled fact, we must hope that some good may come from this dreadful scourge. The armaments of Europe had been growing heavier and heavier, bankruptcy has stared many of the nations in the face, conflict between races had begun to develop.

War seemed likely at some stage and the question which each country had to answer for itself was at what time the situation would be most favorable for its success. The immediate participants have decided that the time has come and through their international alliance all Europe is involved.

There has been no real test of the heavy armament on land or water as developed by modern invention and this contest is to show what has been well spent for war purposes and what has been wasted. It is by no means certain that waste will not exceed in cost that which was spent to effective purpose.

One thing I think we can reasonably count on is that with the prostration of industry, with the blows of prosperity, with the state of flux that is likely to follow this titanic struggle, there will be every opportunity for common sense to resume its sway; and after the horrible expenditure of the blood of the best and the savings of the rich and the poor, the opportunity and the motive for a reduction of armament and the taking away of a temptation to further war will be greatly enhanced.

It is an awful remedy, but in the end it may be worth what it costs, if it makes this the last great war. The influence of America can be thrown most effectively for peace when peace is possible and for minimum armaments when disaster and exhaustion shall make the contending peoples and their rulers see things as they are.

VIEWPOINT 2

"If the purpose of our neutrality will have been to give [a victorious] Germany time to recover for her next war, if as its result England shall have been reduced to a third-rate State, the price . . . may come too high."

Neutrality May Harm the United States

Lewis Einstein (1877–1967)

While Americans were divided on whether to sympathize with the Allies or the Central Powers during the first years of World War I, most agreed that the United States should stay out of the conflagration—just as the nation had stayed out of all European conflicts since 1815. Many believed that America was safely isolated from the conflict by the Atlantic Ocean. They also pointed to the Monroe Doctrine—the 1823 policy statement issued by President James Monroe that pledged that America would not become involved in European affairs and that warned European nations not to meddle in the affairs of the Western Hemisphere. To many Americans, the calamitous war in Europe simply reinforced the wisdom of the Monroe Doctrine.

In the following article, published in November 1914 in the British journal *National Review*, American diplomat Lewis Einstein takes issue with these beliefs about U.S. neutrality in the war. Einstein served for many years in the American diplomatic service and wrote numerous books and articles on global affairs. In this viewpoint, he argues that past U.S. success in enforcing the Monroe Doctrine and avoiding involvement in European conflicts was not the result of American strength, wisdom, or geographical location. It was instead the product, he maintains, of the "balance of power" in Europe that prevented one nation from

Reprinted from Lewis Einstein, "The War and American Policy," in Lewis Einstein, *A Prophecy of the War: 1913–1914* (New York: Columbia University Press, 1918).

becoming dominant on the continent. Furthermore, Einstein asserts, the powerful British navy has served as a shield against European interference in the Americas. A German victory in the war would disrupt both of these conditions, he insists, and would therefore have serious implications for the United States. American neutrality, he contends, should not be maintained at the cost of a German victory in the war. He recommends that America must make it a national priority to preserve the integrity and strength of Great Britain—in other words, to "extend the Monroe Doctrine to England."

In the United States we have gazed upon the distant spectacle of war with the keen interest which the greatest event of modern times has warranted. Even as spectators, we have been thrilled by the deeds of heroism, while its train of misery and suffering has awakened our sympathy. We have relieved the plight of our stranded travelers and have watched conscientiously over the obligations of neutrality. We have scanned the situation from its commercial possibilities, and reawakened to the need of a merchant marine. We have studied the crisis from every point save one, though it is the one which most closely touches our interests. In what way will this war affect our future? Surely no graver question has ever loomed on the horizon of American policy.

For ourselves we have hitherto felt little anxiety. There has almost been a smug satisfaction at the three thousand miles of ocean separating America from the main seat of war, coupled with the feeling that we are privileged in being able to lead our life independently of the bloody childishness which has arrested the development of our commercial rivals. While such ideas may not reflect the finer instincts in the country, the consequences of the great struggle have otherwise hardly impressed themselves. The "plague on both your houses" has been a more frequent point of view than the realization of future possibilities in so far as the success of one or the other side may affect our position.

The entire military fabric of continental Europe has been one so alien to our habits of thought, and until lately to our general knowledge, that the conception of the nation in arms, which has for its basis the execution of policy, yet seemed by an odd paradox devoid of all practical wisdom. To the average American it was always a riddle why countries whose high technical skill in other directions we had frequent occasion to appreciate, should yet pay such attention to armaments. There seemed something almost childish connected with this idea which Civil War traditions confirmed rather than dispelled. We remembered with pride our citizen armies raised when danger threatened, and the patriotic determination which, on either side, saw them through to victory or defeat. We had regarded them not without reason as equal to the best professional soldiers. We remembered our great leaders who had risen in the hour of need. But we were inclined to forget that two years elapsed before the Northern armies could be welded into efficient combatant bodies, and that the long-protracted situation was only rendered possible by the disabilities which weighed equally on either side.

Between the Civil and the Spanish War, our military efficiency sank to its lowest ebb. Even afterward, in spite of new problems and responsibilities, in spite of the precariousness of our hold in the Philippines and the burdens assumed in Latin-America, we have done little to improve it. Apart from the fleet which, in the face of German naval increase, could not long keep the second position it had temporarily attained, the army, through no fault of its own, remained inferior in numbers and organization to that of the smallest European State. The armed forces of Bulgaria and Switzerland, nations less in population than New York City, far exceed our own and indeed surpass any army which we could put into the field before probably six months of preparation.

Unrecognized Factors

Such military inferiority has hitherto not proved a handicap nor acted otherwise than to our advantage. The economic prosperity of the nation has been largely built up by a condition of peace which has freed us from the saddling burden of armaments. In continental Europe, in spite of every euphemistic explanation, the years passed with the colors [in the military] are taxes on their youth. From such necessity we have fortunately been dispensed. But we are prone, as a result, to lay undue stress on our insular position in respect to Europe, without realizing the factors of different order which alone have made it possible. It has been far less the distance which allowed our previous weakness than it has been the division of Europe into two camps. Unrealized by the nation at large, the famous balance of power which for centuries has been the basis of European diplomacy, allowed us a freedom from military burdens which we were inclined to ascribe exclusively to our pacifism, our superior wisdom, and our favorable geographical position.

Although lately the Old World has regarded our policy toward Mexico as insolent, it yet confined itself to mere criticism as a result of the intense strain of a situation which allowed no European State to divert any portion of its strength in a secondary enterprise. We have been pleased to consider the consequence as a

A Blockade Proposal

Charles W. Eliot, former president of Harvard University, wrote to President Woodrow Wilson on August 6, 1914, advising that the United States should join forces with the Allies and impose a naval blockade on Germany and Austria-Hungary. He argues that George Washington's venerable advice to remain neutral in European politics is no longer relevant in the face of the threat those two nations pose to world peace and to the United States.

Has not the United States an opportunity at this moment to propose a combination of the British Empire, the United States, France, Japan, Italy, and Russia in offensive and defensive alliance to rebuke and punish Austria-Hungary and Germany for the outrages they are now committing, by enforcing against those two countries non-intercourse with the rest of the world by land and sea? These two Powers have now shown that they are utterly untrustworthy neighbors, and military bullies of the worst sort—Germany being far the worse of the two, because she has already violated neutral territory.

If they are allowed to succeed in their present enterprises, the fear of sudden invasion will constantly hang over all the other European peoples; and the increasing burdens of competitive armaments will have to be borne for another forty years. We shall inevitably share in these losses and miseries. The cost of maintaining immense armaments prevents all the great Powers from spending the money they ought to spend on improving the condition of the people, and promoting the progress of the world in health, human freedom, and industrial productiveness.

In this cause, and under the changed conditions, would not the people of the United States approve of the abandonment of Washington's advice that this country keep out of European complications? . . .

This proposal would involve the taking part by our navy in the blockading process, and, therefore, might entail losses of both life and treasure; but the cause is worthy of heavy sacrifices; and I am inclined to believe that our people would support the Government in taking active part in such an effort to punish international crimes, and to promote future international peace.

In so doing this country would be serving the general cause of peace, liberty, and good will among men.

tribute to our high moral service rather than to the circumstances permitting us to do what we liked, where we liked, and how we liked, with our southern neighbors. So long as a European balance of power continues as before, such liberty will continue to be ours to use or to abuse. But if, as the result of this war, the predominance of one Power is asserted, our own future sphere of action, nay, our own future security, will require for its preservation steps of entirely different order. . . .

American Sympathies

A distinction should be made between the attitude of the Government and the sympathies of the nation in respect to the great war. The first has properly been one of entire neutrality. Our interests remain untouched, and nothing has yet occurred of a nature to affect these. If we now watch over them with vigilance, no cause for apprehension should exist.

American sympathies, on the other hand, if the feelings of the vast majority of the nation are correctly interpreted, have been wholeheartedly with the Allies. Our moral sense has revolted before the ruthlessness of the Prussian doctrine of war, and German attempts to shift the burden of aggression have only encountered a skeptical derision. Certainly, the defeat of Germany promises a moral recasting of the world. The great Liberal wave which had swept over Europe seventy years ago receded when [Otto von] Bismarck introduced the era of force. The battles between Germans and Allies are far less battles between different nations than they represent the contrast between Liberalism and reaction, between the aspirations of democracy and the gospel of iron. In the presence of the great forces locked in battle our feelings cannot remain indifferent. American sympathy would be untrue to its most generous traditions if it expressed any other hope than in the success of the allied cause. The difficulty for our statecraft is to reconcile such feelings with the duties of neutrality and the wish to be of service in ending the war. . . .

[An allied] victory [would mean] the triumph of a combination without other than temporary unity brought about by the common wish to resist German aggression and predominance. Its success would therefore not materially affect our position. While there might be changes in the map of Europe, the rights of neutrals would be vindicated, the balance of power restored, and a relative, if not a general disarmament, most welcome to us would probably ensue. There is certainly nothing in the record of either Great Britain or France in recent years to lead any reasonable person to suppose that their efforts would in case of victory be directed against us, or would not insure a lasting peace.

Consequences of a German Victory

Can the same be said of Germany? Without going so far as to admit the successful invasion of Great Britain, except after another war, it is not impossible to conceive the reality of the Pan-German dream,—to picture Holland, Belgium, and Northeastern France as German provinces; to see the rest of France, Italy, and Spain reduced to the proportions of vassal states, with Russia crushed, her Baltic provinces annexed to Prussia, and Poland forming part of an Austria even more completely dominated by Berlin; the Levant would be controlled through her Turkish satellite, while the possession of the French and Dutch colonies would make German influence paramount in the Far East, and in rivalry with our own through Latin-America. All this may appear to us indifferent: certainly Germany in victory, perhaps more than in defeat, will aim to flatter our opinion and enlist those sympathies which always go to the conqueror. The same German Press Bureau will extend its propaganda, and the same official instructions which caused American flags to be spontaneously waved before our departing tourists will redouble their ordered amiabilities. Though success exceed all German expectations, we still will find ourselves courted, our sagacity praised, our money borrowed until—until the ruins of the war will have made way for new edifices, the gaps in the army filled, the navy rebuilt, the fortresses and arsenals extended, the treasure replenished, and the same patient labor which lifted the Germany of 1870 to the Germany of 1914 has been repeated.

Is this the future to which we must look forward, and is the doctrine of force to be the inevitable accompaniment of progress? Yes and no. The success of modern Germany has been due to its wonderful spirit of disciplined effort in conjunction with high technical efficiency. It has not sought to conquer hearts nor to awaken sympathies. There are millions of Germans, other than Poles and Alsatians and Danes, ill satisfied with their government. The rifts of classes lie deep, with little mutual sympathy to bridge them over. The vigorous remains of Prussian feudalism, all powerful in the army and the administration, have not unfrequently clashed with the democratic aspirations of a new industrial Germany. In the stress of war the sense of discipline, the feeling of danger, and the mendacious presentation of the case have for the time fused the entire population. All parties are now on their mettle, the military aristocracy to maintain its supremacy by qualities of leadership, and the new democracy to prove its patriotism. But for those who look beyond and see peace after the great war, the entire shaping of the German future must depend on the issue. Should she be defeated, it is inconceivable that the anomalous condition under which she has retained a "Samurai" class will not terminate. No unsuccessful adventure could authorize the preservation of a military caste unable to accomplish the purpose of its existence. The new industrial Germany, representing the same Liberal elements as came to the fore in 1848, the German democracy, sincerely peace-loving, would then assert its own, and refuse to accept any longer the inferiority to which they have been relegated by a reactionary Prussian *Junkerdom* [class of aristocrats and military officers]. Without wishing the destruction of the German Empire, it is possible to conceive of a new German régime, republican or monarchical, where an enlightened public opinion breathed nobler aspirations than the crude imperialism and worship of force of the present Hohenzollerns [the reigning royal family of Germany].

A victorious Germany would, on the other hand, provide a definite consecration for the existing pyramid with its dominating military apex. It would inevitably encourage German faith in their actual institutions and incite the spirit of intolerant aggression which now spurs them on to world domination: alone of all national anthems the *Deutschland über Alles* proclaims German superiority over all the world. The instruments of Pan-German propaganda through its different leagues would once more furrow opinion and instill in it new seeds of hatred against whoever dared thwart the Chosen of the Lord. Irritability would again be manifested at any remaining relics of independence elsewhere, and reliance on the army of five million bayonets would once more be invoked on every occasion. Forecasts are hazardous, but from Germany's past record, again confirmed by success, it is obvious that the same all-prevailing spirit of militarism will maintain its ascendancy. The only difference will be, that as former elements of restraint shall have been destroyed or cowed by German victories, an even more emphatic assertion of aggressive policy is to be expected. . . .

America Needs England

If we do not neglect our duty, we must realize that the German triumph cannot but impose on us a military strain which in the interests of self-preservation will have to be as intense as possible. In one form or another the universal service idea will be introduced. If we are convinced of the danger of this impending curse of militarism, our existing neutrality, however sincere, cannot be disinterested with respect to a struggle whose effects on us would vary so greatly. It is well to appreciate this at a point where the issue still remains doubtful. As in the conduct of military operations, a prudent commander maintains his strategic reserve, so we may wisely employ our resources and our influence as a diplomatic reserve, and through preserving neutrality escape the ordeal of war, and at the same time reduce the likelihood of future unwelcome obligations and danger. We are able to do so in a manner easier than is commonly realized. If we wish at least to avoid partially the burdens of militarism, it is evident that we must always keep another Power between Germany and ourselves. For obvious reasons that Power can only be England. In a rough way the calculation of what this would mean to us is simple to make, and may even be mathematically expressed. Just as

England has wisely treated France as her "glacis," and by present assistance is defending her own future, so is Great Britain our bulwark against any foreign foe. For the purposes of security our strength in respect to Germany would have to be equal to the difference between English and German strength. The more Great Britain is crushed, the more her resources are reduced and her strategic position weakened, the greater will be the effort we shall be called upon to make.

Extend the Monroe Doctrine

To guard against this danger, a new conception of our diplomatic policy, or rather an extension of an ancient policy, becomes necessary. We must extend the Monroe Doctrine to England and embrace within its scope the foremost American Power after our own. It must, above all, be made plain that this is done not on grounds of common civilization or race, or tongue, but on grounds of solid interest reinforced by the weight of tradition and sentiment, but not guided thereby. In the presence of a new European danger the integrity of Great Britain has become for us a matter of vital concern. Such conception may astonish by its novelty. It will doubtless be denounced or held in derision by those wiseacres whose vision of the imperial eagle remains blurred by stagnant memories. The weight of our own traditions would seem to conspire against it. But neither our traditions nor our past experience have ever contemplated such a possibility as is now before the world. In the presence of new conditions, new ideas become necessary, and we would do well to borrow a leaf from that German realism which gauges a situation in the cold light of fact without being deviated by other considerations. We should then be able to understand the situation which a German triumph would threaten—of a nation exalted by successful war, imbued with the doctrine of force, persuaded of the destiny impelling it onward to world domination.

If hitherto we have had occasion to complain of a Germany athwart our path in the Philippines, insidiously threatening us in Latin-America, how much more will we have cause to complain when the same restraints as before no more exist; we will see her challenging our policies and chafe at her activity crossing our own, while she will declare the same of us and instill in her people the conviction that we are the enemy. . . .

If the purpose of our neutrality will have been to give Germany time to recover for her next war, if as its result England shall have been reduced to a third-rate State, the price to pay for such obedience to past traditions may come too high. Though our statesmanship be praised for its prudence, though the peaceful intentions of the German people be dinned into our ears, some day when, perhaps, the fate of Louvain [a Belgian city that was largely destroyed by Germany in 1914] has overtaken Boston, when New York will be held up to the ransom of a thousand million dollars, when improved Zeppelins [airships] will have carried, far and wide, proofs of the superiority of Teutonic civilization, there may be those who will regret the sagacity of our traditionalism. . . .

With German success upon the Continent of Europe we could not expect to interfere. Keen as would be our regret at the crushing of France, or the destruction of Belgian independence, we are unable to prevent either misfortune. With regard to England it is otherwise. A warning served on Germany, exhausted even though successful in war, should be adequate to restrain her from further attack upon a nation whose integral preservation after the destruction of other forces would alone separate us from a world-conquering power. The friendly visit of our fleet to British waters might provide another hint. Beyond that it should not now be necessary to go. The Monroe Doctrine would have been extended to Great Britain.

"Nothing in the annals of piracy can, in wanton and cruel ferocity, equal the destruction of the Lusitania."

Germany's Sinking of the *Lusitania* Was an Atrocity

Henry Watterson (1840–1921)

In February 1915, Germany declared the waters of the British Isles to be a war zone, warning that enemy ships would be sunk and that neutral ships entering the zone were at risk of being attacked by mistake. President Woodrow Wilson responded by warning that Germany would be held "to a strict accountability" for American "property endangered or lives lost" in the war zone.

On May 7, 1915, the *Lusitania*, a British passenger liner, was sunk off the coast of Ireland by a torpedo fired by a German submarine. The attack killed 1,198 people, including 128 Americans. The sinking of the *Lusitania* created much anti-German sentiment in the United States. The following viewpoint, taken from an editorial published in the Louisville (Kentucky) *Courier-Journal*, was one of many expressions of outrage printed in American newspapers. It was written by Henry Watterson, a former congressman and long-time editor of the *Courier-Journal*. Watterson condemns Germany for attacking the ocean liner and killing hundreds of noncombatants, including women and children. He asserts that the United States must retaliate against Germany for the *Lusitania* incident, although he stops short of stating that America must declare war.

Reprinted from Henry Watterson, "The Heart of Christ—the Sword of the Lord and Gideon," Louisville (Ky.) *Courier-Journal*, May 11, 1915, in *The Lusitania Case*, compiled by C.L. Droste, edited by W.H. Tantum (Richmond, VA: Dietz, 1916).

That which the *Courier-Journal* has feared—which it has been for weeks forecasting as likely to happen—has come to pass. A great ocean liner, passing peacefully to and from an American port, carrying a harmless ship's company of non-combatants, men, women and children, many of them American citizens, has, without chance of escape or time for prayer, been ruthlessly sent to the bottom of the deep and some thousand or more gone to the death, drowning and mangled by the murderous onset of a German submarine.

Truly, the nation of the Blackhand and the bloody heart has got in its work. It has got in its work, not upon armed antagonists in fair fight on battle front, but upon the unoffending and the helpless, sailing what has always been and should ever remain, to the peaceful and peace-loving, God's free and open sea.

Nothing in the annals of piracy can, in wanton and cruel ferocity, equal the destruction of the *Lusitania.*

But comes the query: What are we going to do about it? Are we at the mercy of the insane Hohenzollern [Wilhelm II of Germany], not only through his emissaries sending his odious system of government and debasing theories of casteism affecting superiority to our doors and proclaiming them, but bringing his war of conquest and murder across the line of our transit and travel over the high seas, which are ours to sail as we list, without let or hindrance from man or monarch, from him or from any one on land or water?

Sovereign or Vassal?

Must we, as a people, sit down like dogs and see our laws defied, our flag flouted and our protests whistled down the wind of this lordling's majestic disdain?

Must we, as a nation, emulate at once the impotence and the docility of China, and before such proof of the contempt in which we are held by him and his, throw up our hands in entreaty and despair, saying to the insistence of autocracy, to the insolence of vanity, "Thy will is law"?

What could the President have meant when he declared that the government of the United States would hold the government of Germany to strict accountability in the event that its war zone pronunciamento resulted in the loss of the life of a single American? How did he intend that his countrymen should understand him when he put forth his supplementary protests? Are we a sovereign or are we a vassal?

Please God, as all men on earth shall behold, we are a nation. Please God, as Europe and all the world shall know, we are Americans.

Too long already have we submitted to the free hand of the foreigner at home and abroad. Months ago should the Pan-German propaganda, issuing from the German Embassy, led by the German Ambassador, erecting in the heart of our country a treasonable organization to support the German foray upon Belgium and France and to control our own domestic politics, have been ended.

Uncle Sam's Problem

—From The New York Times.

"One cannot keep peace longer than his neighbor will let him."

Germany's submarine campaign, which resulted in the sinking of the Lusitania *and other ships, convinced some Americans that peaceful neutrality was impossible, as this 1915* New York Times *cartoon suggests.*

[German ambassador Johann von] Bernstorff should have been severely rebuked and warned to proceed at his peril. For less [Edmond] Genet, the Frenchman, and Crampton, the Englishman, had been ordered away. . . .

Some Good Americans

The poor and honest Germans of the United States—those who came here to better their fortunes and escape despotism and casteism; those who when they took out their naturalization papers, confessing republicanism and democracy, meant it; those who have no interest, part or lot, with Kaiserism, who ceased to be Germans and became Americans should be rescued alike from the teaching and contamination of the newly rich of Germans, whose dearest hope is to go home and build castles on the Rhine, and from the highbrow writers and herr doctors who worship at the shrine of the Hohenzollern, having learned their lesson from the highbrows of Heidelberg, Gottingen and Bonn.

The *Courier-Journal* will not go the length of saying that the President should convene Congress and advise it to declare against these barbarians a state of war. This may yet become necessary. Whilst actual war is not possible—Germany having no fleet we can wipe off the briny deep, nor army near enough to be met face to face and exterminated—yet we are not wholly without reprisal for the murder of our citizens and the destruction of their property. There are many German ships—at least two German men-of-war in the aggregate worth many millions of dollars —within our reach to make our losses, repudiated by Germany, whole again.

We must not act either in haste or passion. This catastrophe is too real, the flashlight it throws upon the methods and purposes of Germany is too appalling, to leave us in any doubt what awaits us as the bloody and brutal work goes on. Civilization should abjure its neutrality. It should rise as one mighty, godlike force, and as far as its moral influence and physical appliance can be made to prevail, forbid the riot of hate and debauch of blood that, like a madman, is running amuck among the innocent and unprotected.

"Much as we regret the staggering loss of life . . . , the facts in the case absolutely justify the action of the Germans."

Germany's Sinking of the *Lusitania* Was Justified

The Fatherland

Many American newspapers strongly condemned the German sinking of the *Lusitania*, a British passenger ship on which Americans were sailing. However, some publications, most of which catered to German American audiences, rejected condemnation of Germany. The following viewpoint is taken from a 1915 editorial by the *Fatherland*, a newspaper published in New York. The writers of the article provide several reasons for their contention that the sinking of the *Lusitania* was a justifiable act of war on Germany's part. They assert that Great Britain's attempt to starve the German people by imposing a naval blockade made necessary Germany's use of submarine warfare "as a measure of retaliation." They further contend that from Germany's perspective, the *Lusitania* was no mere passenger liner; it was an enemy warship that was transporting arms and munitions to Great Britain. These munitions may have accounted for the ship's rapid sinking upon being torpedoed, they surmise. Responsibility for the fatalities of the incident should rest with Great Britain and the shipping company for carrying civilian passengers on a ship of war, the writers conclude. They also argue that the U.S. government bears some blame for failing to warn or prevent Americans from sailing on ships of warring nations passing through declared war zones.

Reprinted from "Why the *Lusitania* Was Sunk," Editorial, *Fatherland*, May 19, 1912, in *The Lusitania Case*, compiled by C.L. Droste, edited by W.H. Tantum (Richmond, VA: Dietz, 1916).

The United States sent three official notes of communication asking Germany to make reparations for the attack and to end its submarine warfare. Seeking to keep the United States out of war, Germany pledged in January 1916 to refrain from surprise attacks on merchant and passenger ships. However, it never offered reparations for the *Lusitania* attack.

Last week we predicted the fate that has overtaken the *Lusitania*. *The Fatherland* did not reach the news-stands till Saturday, but the editorial in question was written several days before publication. To-day we make another prediction. Every large passenger ship bound for England is practically a swimming arsenal, carrying vast quantities of ammunition and explosives of every description. An arsenal, whether on sea or land, is not a safe place for women and children. It is not a safe place for anyone. Every now and then we read of a warship blown up by an explosion caused by spontaneous combustion, in spite of the rigid care exercised to prevent such an accident. Our passenger ships carry more explosives than the ordinary man-of-war. No innocent passenger should be allowed to embark on a vessel carrying explosives. *It stands to reason that a fate not unlike that of the Lusitania will meet before long a passenger ship by an explosion of vast stores of ammunition within.* While Germany is not bound to respect a flag of any ship carrying implements of murder, German submarines may discriminate in favor of a neutral flag. Spontaneous combustion recognizes no international convention.

Much as we regret the staggering loss of life in the disaster that startled the world, the facts in the case absolutely justify the action of the Germans.

No Basis for Protest

Legally and morally there is no basis for any protest on the part of the United States. The *Lusitania* was a British ship. British ships have been instructed by the Admiralty to ram submarines and to take active measures against the enemy. Hence every British ship must be considered in the light of a warship.

The *Lusitania* flew the ensign of the British Naval Reserves before the submarine warfare was initiated. Since that time she has hoisted many a flag, including the Stars and Stripes. According to a statement issued by the advertising manager of the Cunard Line, the *Lusitania* "when torpedoed was entirely out of the control of the Cunard Company and operated under the command of the British Admiralty."

The *Lusitania* carried contraband of war from this country to England. If this contraband had reached its destination it would undoubtedly have killed far more Germans than the total number of passengers lost on the *Lusitania*. As a matter of fact it did actually kill the passengers by precipitating the sinking of the ship. There can be no doubt that the ship would not have sunk for hours, if explosions from within had not hastened its end. *Every passenger on a boat carrying contraband of war takes his life into his hands.* The explosives in the hold of a ship, we repeat, constitutes a graver peril to passengers than the shots of German torpedoes.

On May 1, 1915, the date the Lusitania *was set to depart New York, the German government placed an advertisement in several U.S. newspapers warning of the wartime risks of travel on British ships.*

It cannot be said that the *Lusitania* was torpedoed without warning. Ordinarily a half hour's warning is regarded sufficient. In this case the ship was warned of its fate *four or five days in advance.* We need only turn to the warning notice issued by the German Embassy on the day before the *Lusitania* left the harbor of New York.

Instead of urging the President to take steps against Germany, we should impeach the Secretary of State for his neglect of duty in not warning all Americans of the peril of ocean traffic in the war zone, especially under the flag of a belligerent nation. If the Secretary of State . . . had issued such a warning, not a single American life would have been forfeited.

Germany, provoked by England which established a war zone as early as November [1914] and made the importation of food-stuffs into Germany practically impossible, decided upon submarine warfare as a measure of retaliation. She was forced to do so by the signal failure of the United States to protect the common rights of neutrals. When Germany determines upon a plan of action she means business. The Germans are not a nation of poker players. Germany does not bluff.

The sinking of the *Lusitania* is a terrific lesson, but in order to drive home its force more fully and to safeguard this country from further losses and from the danger of complications with Germany, the State Department should issue at once a formal notice admonishing American citizens to shun all ships flying the flag of a belligerent nation and all ships, *irrespective of nationality,* which carry across the sea the tools of destruction.

The Cunard Line

But if we accuse the State Department of negligence, we should indict the officials of the Cunard Line for murder. They knew that the *Lusitania* was a floating fortress. Yet, for the sake of sordid gain, they jeopardized the lives of more than two thousand people. When the German Embassy issued its warning, the Cunard Line pooh-poohed the danger so as not to forfeit the shekels paid for the passage.

Did the Cunard Line tell its prospective passengers that its crew was short of eighty or ninety stokers?

Did the Cunard Line inform its passengers that the *Lusitania* . . . narrowly escaped an attack by a submarine on a previous voyage?

Did they inform the passengers of the fact that one of its turbines was defective?

How many of the passengers would have remained on the boat if the officials of the Cunard Line had not suppressed the truth?

Those innocent victims believed in the protection of the British Admiralty. The Captain of the *Lusitania* admits that the Admiralty "never seemed to bother" about the *Lusitania.* He knew that England, though she waives the rules, no longer rules the waves. He is a soldier under orders of the Admiralty. He has a right to take chances with his own life. But what right has he to take chances with the lives of his crew and his two thousand passengers?

VIEWPOINT 5

"We enter this war only where we are clearly forced into it because there are no other means of defending our rights."

The United States Must Declare War Against Germany

Woodrow Wilson (1856–1924)

Woodrow Wilson won reelection as president in 1916 on the campaign slogan "He kept us out of war." Trying to maintain official U.S. neutrality, Wilson launched several diplomatic initiatives between 1914 and 1917 in an effort to mediate an end to the European conflict on the basis of "peace without victory" for either side.

On January 31, 1917, however, Germany reversed its previous concessions to U.S. demands and announced that the next day it would resume unrestricted submarine warfare against all vessels destined for Great Britain. Wilson responded to Germany's resumption of submarine warfare by breaking off diplomatic relations and by asking Congress for permission to arm American merchant ships. These actions did not prevent Germany from sinking American ships in February and March. The sinkings led to an increasingly strong public outcry for the country to declare war against Germany. This development was further boosted by the interception, decoding, and publication of the "Zimmerman note" from the German foreign minister to his representative in Mexico, proposing a Mexican-German alliance against the United States.

These events led to Wilson's decision to ask Congress to declare war on Germany. The following viewpoint is taken from his war message delivered to Congress on April 2, 1917. Wilson argues

Reprinted from Woodrow Wilson, war message to Congress, April 2, 1917, 65th Cong., 1st sess., S. Doc. 5.

that Germany's actions have made continued American neutrality impossible. Asserting that "the world must be made safe for democracy," Wilson maintains that the United States must enter the conflict in order to protect its freedoms and to lay the foundations for the creation of a stable international peace.

Within five days of Wilson's speech, Congress voted to declare war on Germany. On December 7, 1917, the United States also declared war on Austria-Hungary.

I have called the Congress into extraordinary session because there are serious, very serious, choices of policy to be made, and made immediately, which it was neither right nor constitutionally permissible that I should assume the responsibility of making.

On the 3rd of February last, I officially laid before you the extraordinary announcement of the Imperial German government that on and after the 1st day of February it was its purpose to put aside all restraints of law or of humanity and use its submarines to sink every vessel that sought to approach either the ports of Great Britain and Ireland or the western coasts of Europe or any of the ports controlled by the enemies of Germany within the Mediterranean.

That had seemed to be the object of the German submarine warfare earlier in the war, but since April of last year the Imperial government had somewhat restrained the commanders of its undersea craft in conformity with its promise then given to us that passenger boats should not be sunk and that due warning would be given to all other vessels which its submarines might seek to destroy, when no resistance was offered or escape attempted, and care taken that their crews were given at least a fair chance to save their lives in their open boats. The precautions taken were meager and haphazard enough, as was proved in distressing instance after instance in the progress of the cruel and unmanly business, but a certain degree of restraint was observed.

Germany's New Submarine Warfare

The new policy has swept every restriction aside. Vessels of every kind, whatever their flag, their character, their cargo, their destination, their errand, have been ruthlessly sent to the bottom without warning and without thought of help or mercy for those on board, the vessels of friendly neutrals along with those of belligerents. Even hospital ships and ships carrying relief to the sorely bereaved and stricken people of Belgium, though the latter were provided with safe conduct through the proscribed areas by the German government itself and were distinguished by unmistakable marks of identity, have been sunk with the same reckless lack of compassion or of principle.

I was for a little while unable to believe that such things would in fact be done by any government that had hitherto subscribed to the humane practices of civilized nations. International law had its origin in the attempt to set up some law which would be respected and observed upon the seas, where no nation had right of dominion and where lay the free highways of the world. By painful stage after stage has that law been built up, with meager enough results, . . . but always with a clear view, at least, of what the heart and conscience of mankind demanded.

This minimum of right the German government has swept aside under the plea of retaliation and necessity and because it had no weapons which it could use at sea except these which it is impossible to employ as it is employing them without throwing to the winds all scruples of humanity or of respect for the understandings that were supposed to underlie the intercourse of the world. I am not now thinking of the loss of property involved, immense and serious as that is, but only of the wanton and wholesale destruction of the lives of noncombatants, men, women, and children, engaged in pursuits which have always, even in the darkest periods of modern history, been deemed innocent and legitimate. Property can be paid for; the lives of peaceful and innocent people cannot be.

The present German submarine warfare against commerce is a warfare against mankind. It is a war against all nations. American ships have been sunk, American lives taken in ways which it has stirred us very deeply to learn of; but the ships and people of other neutral and friendly nations have been sunk and overwhelmed in the waters in the same way. There has been no discrimination. The challenge is to all mankind.

Each nation must decide for itself how it will meet it. The choice we make for ourselves must be made with a moderation of counsel and a temperateness of judgment befitting our character and our motives as a nation. We must put excited feeling away. Our motive will not be revenge or the victorious assertion of the physical might of the nation, but only the vindication of right, of human right, of which we are only a single champion.

Armed Neutrality Will Not Work

When I addressed the Congress on the 26th of February last, I thought that it would suffice to assert our neutral rights with arms, our right to use the seas against unlawful interference, our right to keep our people safe against unlawful violence. But armed neutrality, it now appears, is impracticable. Because submarines are in effect outlaws when used as the German submarines have been used against merchant shipping, it is impossible to defend ships against their attacks as the law of nations has assumed that merchantmen would defend themselves against privateers or cruisers, visible craft giving them chase upon the open sea. It is common prudence in such circumstances, grim necessity indeed, to endeavor to destroy them before they have shown their own intention. They must be dealt with upon sight, if dealt with at all. The German Government denies the right of neutrals to use arms at all within the areas of the sea which it has proscribed, even in the defense of rights which no modern publicist has ever before questioned their right to defend. The intimation is conveyed that the armed guards which we have placed on our merchant ships will be treated as beyond the pale of law and subject to be dealt with as pirates would be. Armed neutrality is ineffectual enough at best; in such circumstances and in the face of such pretensions it is worse than ineffectual; it is likely only to produce what it was meant to prevent; it is practically certain to draw us into the war without either the rights or the effectiveness of belligerents. There is one choice we can not make, we are incapable of making: we will not choose the path of submission and suffer the most sacred rights of our nation and our people to be ignored or violated. The wrongs against which we now array ourselves are no common wrongs; they cut to the very roots of human life.

With a profound sense of the solemn and even tragical character of the step I am taking and of the grave responsibilities which it involves, but in unhesitating obedience to what I deem my constitutional duty, I advise that the Congress declare the recent course of the Imperial German government to be in fact nothing less than war against the government and people of the United States; that it formally accept the status of belligerent which has thus been thrust upon it; and that it take immediate steps, not only to put the country in a more thorough state of defense but also to exert all its power and employ all its resources to bring the government of the German Empire to terms and end the war.

What this will involve is clear. It will involve the utmost practicable cooperation in counsel and action with the governments now at war with Germany and, as incident to that, the extension to those governments of the most liberal financial credits, in order that our resources may so far as possible be added to theirs. It will involve the organization and mobilization of all the material resources of the country to supply the materials of war and serve the incidental needs of the nation in the most abundant and yet the most economical and efficient way possible. It will involve the immediate full equipment of the Navy in all respects but particularly in supplying it with the best means of dealing with the enemy's submarines. It will involve the immediate addition to the armed forces of the United States already provided for by law in case of war at least 500,000 men, who should, in my opinion, be chosen upon the principle of universal liability to service, and also the authorization of subsequent additional increments of equal force so soon as they may be needed and can be handled in training.

A War to Defend American Honor

Senator William E. Borah of Idaho voted to declare war on Germany. However, in his April 4, 1917, speech to the U.S. Senate, Borah took pains to distance himself from some aspects of President Wilson's war message.

If I understand correctly this resolution, not only in its terms but in its import, its meaning is simple and single, and it is not subject in any way to misconstruction. It is the ordinary declaration of a state of war and pledging the resources of this country to prosecute war against those who are waging war against us. In other words . . . it commits this Government to a policy of war in defense of American rights, for the protection of American citizens, and for the security of the American Republic. That being both the import and the express terms of the resolution, I do not find it possible on my part to vote against it. . . .

This is not the time to discuss incidental questions or irrelevant questions; and yet some things have been said in connection with this situation, in the President's message and by Senators, which warrant me in the statement that in voting for this resolution it must be understood that I do not even tacitly indorse some of the propositions with reference to the manner in which this war is to be carried on. . . .

Suffice it to say now that there can, to my mind, be but one sufficient reason for committing this country to war, and that is the honor and security of our own people and our own Nation. . . . I hold fast and firmly to the doctrine that our own national security, our own national honor, the rights of our own people, and the lives of our own citizens are alone, when challenged and assailed, sufficient to justify me in voting for a declaration of war. I join no crusade; I seek or accept no alliances; I obligate this Government to no other power. I make war alone for my countrymen and their rights, for my country and its honor.

It will involve also, of course, the granting of adequate credits to the government, sustained, I hope, so far as they can equitably be sustained by the present generation, by well-conceived taxation. . . .

While we do these things, these deeply momentous things, let us be very clear, and make very clear to all the world what our motives and our objects are. My own thought has not been driven from its habitual and normal course by the unhappy events of the last two months, and I do not believe that the thought of the nation has been altered or clouded by them. I have exactly the same things in mind now that I had in mind when I addressed the Senate on the twenty-second of January last, the same that I had in mind when I addressed the Congress on the third of February and on the twenty-sixth of February. Our object now, as then, is to vindicate the principles of peace and justice in the life of the world as against selfish and autocratic power and to set up amongst the really free and self-governed peoples of the world such a concert of purpose and of action as will henceforth ensure the observance of those principles. Neutrality is no longer feasible or desirable where the peace of the world is involved and the freedom of its peoples, and the menace to that peace and freedom lies in the existence of autocratic governments backed by organized force which is controlled wholly by their will, not by the will of their people. We have seen the last of neutrality in such circumstances. We are at the beginning of an age in which it will be insisted that the same standards of conduct and of responsibility for wrong done shall be observed among nations and their governments that are observed among the individual citizens of civilized states.

We have no quarrel with the German people. We have no feeling toward them but one of sympathy and friendship. It was not upon their impulse that their government acted in entering this war. It was not with their previous knowledge or approval. It was a war determined upon as wars used to be determined upon in the old, unhappy days when peoples were nowhere consulted by their rulers and wars were provoked and waged in the interest of dynasties or of little groups of ambitious men who were accustomed to use their fellowmen as pawns and tools.

Self-governed nations do not fill their neighbor states with spies or set the course of intrigue to bring about some critical posture of affairs which will give them an opportunity to strike and make conquest. Such designs can be successfully worked out only under cover and where no one has the right to ask questions. Cunningly contrived plans of deception or aggression, carried, it may be, from generation to generation, can be worked out and kept from the light only within the privacy of courts or behind the carefully guarded confidences of a narrow and privileged class. They are happily impossible where public opinion commands and insists upon full information concerning all the nation's affairs.

A steadfast concert for peace can never be maintained except by a partnership of democratic nations. No autocratic government could be trusted to keep faith within it or observe its covenants. It must be a league of honor, a partnership of opinion. Intrigue would eat its vitals away; the plottings of inner circles who could plan what they would and render account to no one would be a corruption seated at its very heart. Only free peoples can hold their purpose and their honor steady to a common end and prefer the interests of mankind to any narrow interest of their own. . . .

German Intrigues

One of the things that has served to convince us that the Prussian autocracy was not and could never be our friend is that from the very outset of the present war it has filled our unsuspecting communities and even our offices of government with spies and set criminal intrigues everywhere afoot against our national unity of counsel, our peace within and without, our industries and our commerce. Indeed, it is now evident that its spies were here even before the war began; and it is unhappily not a matter of conjecture but a fact proved in our courts of justice that the intrigues which have more than once come perilously near to disturbing the peace and dislocating the industries of the country have been carried on at the instigation, with the support, and even under the personal direction of official agents of the Imperial government accredited to the government of the United States.

Even in checking these things and trying to extirpate them, we have sought to put the most generous interpretation possible upon them because we knew that their source lay, not in any hostile feeling or purpose of the German people toward us (who were no doubt as ignorant of them as we ourselves were) but only in the selfish designs of a government that did what it pleased and told its people nothing. But they have played their part in serving to convince us at last that that government entertains no real friendship for us and means to act against our peace and security at its convenience. That it means to stir up enemies against us at our very doors the intercepted note to the German minister at Mexico City is eloquent evidence.

We are accepting this challenge of hostile purpose because we know that in such a government, following such methods, we can never have a friend; and that in the presence of its organized power, always lying in wait to accomplish we know not what purpose, there can be no assured security for the democratic governments of the world. We are now about to accept gage of battle with this natural foe to liberty and shall, if necessary, spend the whole force of the nation to check and nullify its pretensions and its power. We are glad, now that we see the facts with no veil of false pretense about them, to fight thus for the ultimate peace of the world and for the liberation of its peoples, the German peoples included: for the rights of nations great and small and the privilege of men everywhere to choose their way of life and of obedience.

American Goals

The world must be made safe for democracy. Its peace must be planted upon the tested foundations of political liberty. We have no selfish ends to serve. We desire no conquest, no dominion. We seek no indemnities for ourselves, no material compensation for the sacrifices we shall freely make. We are but one of the champions of the rights of mankind. We shall be satisfied when those rights have been made as secure as the faith and the freedom of nations can make them.

Just because we fight without rancor and without selfish object, seeking nothing for ourselves but what we shall wish to share with all free peoples, we shall, I feel confident, conduct our operations as belligerents without passion and ourselves observe with proud punctilio the principles of right and of fair play we profess to be fighting for.

I have said nothing of the governments allied with the Imperial Government of Germany because they have not made war upon us or challenged us to defend our right and our honour. The Austro-Hungarian Government has, indeed, avowed its unqualified endorsement and acceptance of the reckless and lawless submarine warfare adopted now without disguise by the Imperial German Government, . . . but that Government has not actually engaged in warfare against citizens of the United States on the seas, and I take the liberty, for the present at least, of postponing a discussion of our relations with the authorities at Vienna. We enter this war only where we are clearly forced into it because there are no other means of defending our rights.

It will be all the easier for us to conduct ourselves as belligerents in a high spirit of right and fairness because we act without animus, not in enmity toward a people or with the desire to bring any injury or disadvantage upon them, but only in armed opposition to an irresponsible government which has thrown aside all considerations of humanity and of right and is running amuck. We are, let me say again, the sincere friends of the German people, and shall desire nothing so much as the early reestablishment of intimate relations of mutual advantage between us—however hard it may be for them, for the time being, to believe that this is spoken from our hearts.

We have borne with their present government through all these bitter months because of that friendship—exercising a patience and forbearance which would otherwise have been impossible. We shall, happily, still have an opportunity to prove that friendship in our daily attitude and actions toward the millions of men and women of German birth and native sympathy who live among us and share our life, and we shall be proud to prove it toward all who are in fact loyal to their neighbors and to the government in the hour of test. They are, most of them, as true and loyal Americans as if they had never known any other fealty or allegiance. They will be prompt to stand with us in rebuking and restraining the few who may be of a different mind and purpose. If there should be disloyalty, it will be dealt with with a firm hand of stern repression; but, if it lifts its head at all, it will lift it only here and there and without countenance except from a lawless and malignant few.

It is a distressing and oppressive duty, gentlemen of the Congress, which I have performed in thus addressing you. There are, it may be, many months of fiery trial and sacrifice ahead of us. It is a fearful thing to lead this great peaceful people into war, into the most terrible and disastrous of all wars, civilization itself seeming to be in the balance. But the right is more precious than peace, and we shall fight for the things which we have always carried nearest our hearts—for democracy, for the right of those who submit to authority to have a voice in their own governments, for the rights and liberties of small nations, for a universal dominion of right by such a concert of free peoples as shall bring peace and safety to all nations and make the world itself at last free.

To such a task we can dedicate our lives and our fortunes, everything that we are and everything that we have, with the pride of those who know that the day has come when America is privileged to spend her blood and her might for the principles that gave her birth and happiness and the peace which she has treasured. God helping her, she can do no other.

VIEWPOINT 6

"We are asked to . . . destroy one belligerent, which the President designates as Prussian militarism, a menace to the world; but English navalism, which is surely as great a menace, we enter into partnership with."

The United States Should Not Declare War Against Germany

William La Follette (1860–1934)

Woodrow Wilson's April 2, 1917, request to Congress for a declaration of war against Germany was debated for several days. Among those who opposed Wilson's call for war against Germany was William La Follette, a progressive Republican from Washington who served as a member of Congress from 1911 to 1919. Excerpts of his April 5, 1917, remarks to the U.S. House of Representatives are presented in the following viewpoint.

La Follette argues that the United States has failed to remain neutral in World War I not because of Germany's actions but because America has from the beginning favored Great Britain and its allies. Although La Follette condemns German submarine warfare, he asserts that Great Britain has also committed acts that violate American rights and international law, such as mining the North Sea, attempting to starve Germany's population through a naval blockade, and violating U.S. neutral rights by seizing American ships and cargoes. The reasons President Wilson gave for going to war against Germany, he contends, could easily be applied to Great Britain as well. He concludes that the United

Reprinted from William La Follette, address to the U.S. House of Representatives, *Congressional Record*, vol. 55, part 1, 65th Cong., 1st sess., pp. 371–72, 1917.

States should stay out of the conflict and not sacrifice American lives for a "war of commercialism."

La Follette was joined by forty-nine other representatives and six U.S. senators in voting against the war resolution—the largest number of dissenting votes in a war declaration in America's history.

Mr. Chairman, when history records the truth about this awful act we are about to commit here, which means the maiming and dismembering of thousands of our noble boys and the deaths of thousands more, it will record that the Congress of the United States made this declaration of war under a misapprehension of the facts inexcusable in itself and that the people at large acquiesced in it on the theory that the Congress should have the facts, and would not make a declaration of war not justified by every rule of equity and fair dealing between nations, impartially applied by this country to all belligerents, and that after our following that course one of these contesting nations, despite our impartial action, had wantonly destroyed our legitimate commerce and destroyed the lives of some of our people.

We Have Favored Great Britain

I say the people acquiesce in our actions here to-day on exactly that false assumption of the facts. We have not treated, as a Government, these belligerents with any degree of impartiality; but, on the contrary, have demanded of one of them absolute obedience to our ideas and interpretations of international law, and have allowed at least one of the other belligerents to override at will the established rules and practice of all the civilized nations of the world for a hundred years with but feeble protest, and, in many cases, with no protest at all.

We surrendered to Great Britain practically all we contested for in the War of 1812. It is true, as far as we know, that she has not impressed our seamen, but she has seized and appropriated to her own use entire cargoes and the ships that carried them. Not carriers in European trade, but carriers to South America.

One of the underlying causes of the awful holocaust in Europe was because Germany had by her systematized reductions in cost of manufacturing, by subsidization of transportation lines and methods of credits made such serious inroads on Great Britain's trade in South America as to seriously disturb her equanimity and threaten her prestige as well as attendant profits.

Mr. Chairman, this war now devastating Europe so ruthlessly is not a war of humanity, but a war of commercialism, and there is not a student of economic conditions within the sound of my voice but knows that to be the fundamental cause of that war, although there are many primary and intermediate questions entering into it. But I digress, Mr. Chairman. I have said that Great Britain has seized our ships engaged in peaceful commerce on the Western Hemisphere, surrounded by all the hallowed shades of the Monroe doctrine, which we are about to abrogate; has taken them to England and impressed them into her own service, and apparently without protest from our Government now demanding a strict accounting by Germany.

Mr. Chairman, there is no doubt in my mind but that Germany's action in regard to her submarine warfare is reprehensible, is wrong, and would merit punishment; but, Mr. Chairman, can we consistently declare war on Germany and enter into an alliance with "perfidious Albion [England]," who, without regard to international law, laid down a prescribed zone in the Atlantic Ocean and the North Sea sowing those waters with deadly contact mines. Three of our vessels were sunk in this prescribed zone with attendant loss of life; many other vessels were likewise destroyed without protest by our Government, which by indisputable evidence has, to some extent at least, suppressed the facts in regard to the matter.

Mr. Chairman, is a life lost by the destruction of a vessel coming in contact with a floating mine less dear than one lost on a vessel sunk by a torpedo fired by a submarine? Is the water less cold or wet?

Mr. Chairman, the highwayman who holds you up is less culpable than the coward who sends you a bomb by express or through the mail or sets a spring gun. The floating mine, in my judgment, is more despicable than the submarine, whose operators are at least taking some chances of losing their own lives. We are asked to go into partnership with the belligerent who prescribed a zone and sowed it full of mines to help it destroy the belligerent who prescribed a zone and in that zone uses submarines. Oh, consistency, thou art a jewel! . . .

The President's Message

Mr. Chairman, the President of the United States in his message to Congress intimated that Germany had maintained a spy system in the United States, even to the extent of having spies in some of our departments. Mr. Chairman, that declaration was made no doubt for what it was worth, as far as affecting the judgment of Congress was concerned, but it was really meant for the consumption of the people at large, who are mostly unaware that the State Department of the United States Government has a secret fund for paying our own secret spies throughout the world, maintained in time of peace as well as in war time. Are our boys to be sent to punish Germany for doing that which, to some extent at least, we practice ourselves? . . .

The American People Do Not Want War

Among the opponents of U.S. entry into World War I was Senator Robert La Follette of Wisconsin (no relation to William La Follette). Speaking before Congress on April 4, 1917, the outspoken senator (whose constituency included a large German American population) asserted that the majority of the American people did not want the nation to go to war.

Will the President and the supporters of this war bill submit it to a vote of the people before the declaration of war goes into effect? Until we are willing to do that, it illy becomes us to offer as an excuse for our entry into the war the unsupported claim that this war was forced upon the German people by their government "without their previous knowledge or approval."

Who has registered the knowledge or approval of the American people of the course this Congress is called upon to take in declaring war upon Germany? Submit the question to the people, you who support it. You who support it dare not do it, for you know that by a vote of more than ten to one the American people as a body would register their declaration against it.

In the sense that this war is being forced upon our people without their knowing why and without their approval, and that wars are usually forced upon all peoples in the same way, there is some truth in the statement; but I venture to say that the response which the German people have made to the demands of this war shows that it has a degree of popular support which the war upon which we are entering has not and never will have among our people. The espionage bills, the conscription bills, and other forcible military measures which we understand are being ground out of the war machine in this country is the complete proof that those responsible for this war fear that it has no popular support and that armies sufficient to satisfy the demand of the Entente Allies cannot be recruited by voluntary enlistments.

The President of the United States in his message of the 2d of April said that the European war was brought on by Germany's rulers without the sanction or will of the people. For God's sake, what are we doing now? Does the President of the United States feel that the will of the American people is being consulted in regard to this declaration of war? The people of Germany surely had as much consideration as he has given the people of the

United States. He has heard the cry of the Shylocks calling for their pound of flesh; later on he will hear the cry of Rachel weeping for her children and mourning because they are not, sacrificed to make good the pound of flesh in the name of liberty. The exclamation "O Liberty! Liberty! how many crimes are committed in thy name! " was well made.

Ours is the greatest Nation on the face of the globe. We have had a chance, if we had maintained a strict neutrality, to have bound up the wounds of the oppressed and to have upheld the tenets of the highest civilization throughout the world. But, no; we are asked to go into partnership with the country that has never allowed justice and right to have any weight with her when conquest and gold were placed in the balance. In India, which she held by right of conquest, as a punishment to those natives of that country who desired to be free of England's yoke and rebelled, even as did we in our Revolutionary period, she mercifully tied many of the rebels to the mouths of her cannon and humanely blew them to atoms as a sample of English Christianity. She destroyed the Boer Republic by intrigue and force of arms; she forced, for love of gold, the opium trade on China. Christian England, our would-be partner! In the Napoleonic wars she, by force of arms, confiscated the entire shipping of small but neutral nations to her own use, just as she has in a smaller degree appropriated ships of our citizens to her own use within the past two years. During the Civil War she fell over herself to recognize the Confederacy, and gave it every encouragement possible. Now we are asked to become her faithful ally against a country that, whatever her faults, surely has no blacker record than that of Christian England; to contribute our money and our people in the holy name of liberty to destroy one belligerent, which the President designates as Prussian militarism, a menace to the world; but English navalism, which is surely as great a menace, we enter into partnership with. George Washington said, "Avoid European entanglements," but we are recklessly entering a path to the end of which no man can foresee or comprehend, at the behest of, in many cases, a venal press and of a pacifist President.

God pity our country, gentlemen of the House of Representatives, if you desire that this cup be placed to our country's lips to quaff for crimes committed by a country for unneutral actions and that we enter into an alliance with another country which has been much less neutral. You may do so; I can not so vote at this time. . . .

A Suggested Resolution

Mr. Chairman, throughout the country patriotic meetings are being held to encourage enlistments of our young men and boys into the Army to engage in this war in advance of our declaration.

Mr. Chairman, I suggest a resolution, which should be passed and adhered to by the young men of our country and by our soldiers who are asked to enter the trenches of Europe:

"I hereby pledge myself to the service of my country and will guarantee to go and uphold its honor and its flag as soon as the sons of all the newspaper editors who have stood out for our entering the war, and who are of age for enlistment, have enlisted for the cause and the proprietors and editors themselves have patriotically enlisted, on the theory that they should feel it their duty to do so as instigators of the act."

Likewise, Mr. Chairman, the sons of manufacturers of ammunition and war supplies, and all stockholders making profits from such trade. They should freely offer their sons on the altar of their country and, in case of their being under military age, go themselves. Likewise, Mr. Chairman, the J. Pierpont Morgans and their associates, who have floated war loans running into millions which they now want the United States to guarantee by entering the European war; after they and all the holders of such securities have offered their sons and themselves, when of military age, on the altar of their country, and, Mr. Chairman, when the above-mentioned persons have no sons and are too old themselves to accept military service, then they shall, to make good their desire for the upholding of American honor and American rights, donate in lieu of such service of selves or sons one-half of all their worldly goods to make good their patriotic desire for our entering the European war in the name of liberty and patriotism.

Mr. Chairman, it will be fitting for those who have really nothing at stake in this war but death to enter into it and give their lives in the name of liberty and patriotism, after the persons covered by the above resolution have done their part as above suggested and many thousands of our citizens will see it that way ere long.

Mr. Chairman, I have voted since I have been a Member of Congress at all times for the largest supply bills offered to take care of and build up our Army and Navy and put ourselves into a state of reasonable preparedness for any difficulties which may arise, and I shall, while I am a Member of the House, in case this cup is put to our country's lips, vote for everything which in my judgment is essential to her success, keeping in mind always the fundamentals of our liberties; but, Mr. Chairman, while I am a Member I shall claim the same right to free speech and expression I am willing to accord to my compeers.

May God guide us and keep us.

CHAPTER 3

The Decision to Go to War: Criticisms and Defenses

Chapter Preface

President Woodrow Wilson asked Congress to declare war on Germany on April 2, 1917. Congress voted to support Wilson's petition despite the fact that not all Americans were in favor of intervening in a European war. The national debate over U.S. involvement continued in the months following the declaration of war. Advocates of intervention sought to rally public support behind the war effort, while many opponents maintained their efforts to convince the American public of the rightness of their cause.

Opposition to World War I was not uniform; diverse sectors of the public objected to the war for different reasons. Those who were dedicated pacifists, both within and outside religious groups, maintained their stance of opposition to all war. In addition, many German Americans remained less than enthusiastic at the prospect of going to war against Germany, and some Irish Americans did not favor aiding Britain because England's Parliament refused to grant independence to Ireland. Even some black Americans questioned whether they could support their country's crusade for democracy abroad when they were denied citizenship rights at home. Socialists, communists, and others from the political left asserted that this war was fostered by the economic elite who were using the common people as cannon fodder. Although some opponents of American intervention ceased their criticism after Congress voted to declare war, others continued to protest American involvement through political demonstrations and civil disobedience.

Those who actively supported U.S. intervention in World War I were equally diverse in their arguments and motives. Some simply asserted that President Wilson and Congress had made their decision, that the time for debate was over, and that it was the patriotic duty of all Americans to support the war effort. Others emphasized the belief that Germany was a tyrannical nation whose aggressive actions would eventually affect American freedoms, both personal and economic. Woodrow Wilson's characterization of the war as a general crusade to make the world "safe for democracy" attracted the support of many Americans. Noted black leader W.E.B. Du Bois, for example, argued in an editorial that whatever problems blacks faced in the United States, they would be worse off if Germany emerged victorious. Blacks, Du

Bois concluded, must "close ranks," put their special grievances temporarily behind them, and support the war effort.

Moreover, the leaders of certain organizations supported the war not only for patriotic reasons but also because they saw in the war effort an opportunity to influence changes in American society. For instance, labor leader Samuel Gompers, hoping to increase union membership and gain government support for union policies, gave a no-strike pledge for the duration of the war to the Wilson administration. Gompers also served on several wartime government agencies and made speeches around the nation urging laborers to support the war and reject the arguments of those who saw the war as of no concern to workers. His efforts were rewarded when union membership rose from 2.7 million in 1916 to more than 4 million in 1919, in part due to the boom in war industries and in part due to policies enacted by the National War Labor Board that gave unions greater government recognition. Similarly, leaders in the feminist movement actively contributed to the war effort and argued that an Allied victory would help women attain equal rights around the world. They publicized the contributions women were making to the war in order to win the political support of voters and elected officials. With this leverage, feminists were successful in obtaining the passage of the women's suffrage amendment to the Constitution in 1920.

The viewpoints in this chapter include some of the arguments used by both proponents and opponents of U.S. involvement in World War I in the months following America's entry into that conflict. They present sharply differing visions of what effects the war would have on America and the world.

VIEWPOINT 1

*"To me it is a subject of such obscurity how it is . . .
possible for any man who loves liberty, who is a . . .
citizen of the United States, to make even the slightest
. . . objection to the prosecution of this war."*

The American People
Should Support the War

Samuel Gompers (1850–1924)

Following America's official entry into World War I in April
1917, both public and private organizations sponsored speeches
and rallies designed to raise public support for the war effort. An
example of such speechmaking is found in the following viewpoint, which is excerpted from a September 1917 address by labor
leader Samuel Gompers. The speech was given in Chicago at a
rally held under the auspices of the National Security League, a
private organization that prior to April 1917 had supported measures to increase America's military forces.

Gompers was a founder and longtime president of the American
Federation of Labor (AFL), which he helped build into one of the
nation's most prominent and politically active labor organizations.
He worked with President Woodrow Wilson during Wilson's first
term in promoting the cause of organized labor, and that record as
well as Gompers's endorsement of the war resulted in a presidential appointment to the Advisory Commission of the Council of
National Defense. During the war he sought to maintain and improve the wages and working standards of American workers.

While building up the AFL, Gompers had often clashed with
more radical elements of the labor movement—such as members
of the Industrial Workers of the World (IWW) and the Socialist
Party—who regarded him as too conservative. During World War

Excerpted from Samuel Gompers, *Address by Samuel Gompers*, Patriotism Through Education
Series, no. 19 (New York: National Security League, 1917).

I both of these organizations opposed American entry into the war, charging that it was a capitalist struggle in which the workers of all nations had no stake. In his address, Gompers takes an opposite position, arguing that all Americans have a stake in the conflict and that the United States must defend its ideals of peace and freedom against enemies that threaten both. Citing the German sinking of the *Lusitania*, he maintains that Germany has subjected the United States to "repeated insults and assaults upon the character and upon the lives of our people." The United States must fight until the militaristic regimes of Germany and its allies are thoroughly defeated and discredited, he asserts. Gompers calls for Americans to temporarily put aside their political differences in order to build a united effort to successfully prosecute the war.

Mr. Chairman and Friends:

I am more gratified this evening at having had the opportunity of listening to that magnificent oration, that wonderful presentation of America's cause in this great struggle, presented by that eminent American, Elihu Root, than I can find words to express. And I beg to assure you that my task has been made much easier by reason of that address. It was my intention to in part trace the developments of this struggle until we were literally dragged into it. It seemed to me that the policy of the German Imperial Government was so set, that do what we would, we could not escape the responsibility of entering into this war.

There is such a thing as humility. There is such a thing as patience. But when some bully will undertake to make an assault upon an innocent, peace-loving man or woman, then patience ceases to be a virtue and humility brings on the brand of cowardice. That was the position in which the United States found itself as a nation by the repeated insults and assaults upon the character and upon the lives of our people, our men, our women and our innocent children.

The Lusitania Sinking

There is one thought in connection with the atrocious murder of our people in the case of our torpedoed boats. I ask you, my friends, to consider for a moment the fact that the German Ambassador, Count [Johann] von Bernstorff, a few days before the sailing of the Lusitania, had an advertisement in the newspapers of our country, warning the people of the United States against taking passage on the Lusitania, and advising them that there was danger in their taking passage on that vessel. The impudence of the whole transaction caused a smile to spread over the countenances of the people of the United States. They thought it a hoax, a jest of a very, very somber character, and many of them took passage and then within a few days the great ship went on her way, where she had a perfect right to go.

Supporters of the American war effort often argued that Germany posed a threat to the entire world. Such a view is expressed in "The Python," a 1917 Jay N. (Ding) Darling cartoon first published in the Des Moines Register.

Nearly 2,000 souls boarded that vessel before her departure. More than 150 American men and women and children were on that vessel when she went; she was torpedoed without a moment's warning, and all of them sent to the waters and more than 1,500 human souls, of which more than 100 were American men and women and children, were sent to a watery grave.

I ask you, my friends, to reverse the position for a moment. Supposing our Ambassador at Berlin, Mr. Gerard, had placed an advertisement in the newspapers of Germany advising the German people against taking passage on a steamer to go to any port that that steamer and her master had a right to go, and supposing further that some American steamer, some American U-boat, had sent a torpedo into that merchant ship, and supposing that there had been 100 or more German men, women and children sent to

105

an untimely grave, what do you think the treatment of Gerard would have been at the hands of the Kaiser? Do you think for a moment that there would have been any further parley with Gerard or the Government of the United States? Is it possible to imagine that with Germany's mental attitude Gerard would have been given his passports? Or is it in keeping with the whole policy of "Kultur" that Gerard would have been given his passports? Or is it not in keeping with the whole policy of "Kultur" that Gerard would have paid the penalty with his life?

Surely, it would be untimely and inappropriate did I attempt or did any one attempt to interject any political issue in this campaign of education and Americanism in our country. But I ask you, my friends, whether it is not true that considerable of the opposition to the re-election of Mr. Wilson to the Presidency was based on the accusation that he had too long kept us out of war? It is doubtful if there has been in history a more patient yet courageous man to meet a great emergency than is Woodrow Wilson. It was for more than two years that President Wilson pursued his policy, basing his position upon the belief that there was some honor at the core, possibly to be discovered, of the German Imperial Government. He was misled into the belief that there was some honor in German diplomacy. He finally discovered that there comes a time, and that the time did come, when men would be too proud not to fight. . . .

Entrance Delayed

To me it seemed that the entrance of our republic into this conflict had been too long delayed, but as a loyal citizen I yielded to the judgment of the Commander-in-chief of the army and navy of the United States. I felt that the time was near at hand when the outrages would increase in such numbers and in such horror that in self respect we would take advantage of the current as it served or we would lose our ventures.

We have entered into this struggle, and there can be no let-up from the time of our declaration of war until either Imperial Germany, with her militarism, shall surrender to the democracies of the world or the democracies shall crush Germany.

We have heard the cries of a few of our people echoing the wishes and the hope of defeated Germany today. I say defeated Germany, although she is not conquered by any means. But Germany is defeated in the objects for which she has entered into the war. We have heard an element here and they are crying out in the wilderness, for it finds no lodgment in the conscience or the hearts of red-blooded men, "Peace! Peace!" Yes, I have seen it printed in newspapers, taken up by other pacifists, so-called, masking under the name of pacifists, but, through ignorance or pro-Germanism, I do not know which, they have declared: "Why not now?"...

Let us bear this fact in mind, that Germany and Austria are still fighting on land invaded by them. If we were to consent to peace today, without the surrender of Kaiserism, for all history written now in the future the Teutonic forces will be given the credit and the prestige of being the conqueror in this war. There can be no peace, not while there is a Teuton on the soil of glorious France. There can be no peace, and there must not be any peace, until the Teutons are driven back, back, from outraged Belgium.

There cannot be any peace until the people of the world who love peace, who love liberty, and who love peace and liberty more than their own lives, until they are assured that never again shall it be possible for Germany or Austria, or any other country for that matter, to make such a bloody war upon the freedom of the people. To me it is a subject of such obscurity how it is physically or mentally possible for any man who loves liberty, who is a native or a naturalized citizen of the United States, to make even the slightest manifestation of objection to the prosecution of this war until the final end.

I grieve that many of our poor boys may fall, and God grant that but few shall fall or be hurt, but I ask you, my friends, to think back whether there is any one among you who can trace some distant ancestor who fought in the Revolution to establish this republic and give to the world not only a new nation, but a new meaning of the rights of man. Is there anyone among you who begrudges the sacrifice of any man who gave his life in order that that great privilege should be established? Who among our men, who among our women, regrets even the sacrifices that were made during our Civil War to abolish human slavery and to maintain the Union? Who among us regrets the sacrifices that were made to rescue Cuba from the domination of Spain and make her an independent republic? Why, all our hearts throb and our whole beings thrill when we can trace one who gave some contributory effort or sacrifice in order that these great achievements should lie as the successes of our country. And so the wonderful achievement of our great Revolution, the tremendous advance to maintain the Union and abolish human slavery, the independence of Cuba, all of them, great and glorious as they are, today the time and the opportunity means the overthrow of Torryism the world over and the establishment of universal democracy among all peoples on the face of the earth.

Fight for Principles

That which we call freedom, that which we call liberty, are not tangible things. They are not handed to any people on a silver platter. They are principles, they are questions of the spirit, and people must have a consciousness that they not only have the term liberty and freedom, but they must have the power and the right to exercise these great attributes of life.

War and Efficiency

During World War I, Samuel Gompers devoted his energies both to marshaling workers behind the American war effort and to improving and maintaining their economic and political standing. In an article written for the Independent *at the onset of American entry into World War I, he contends that newly established labor benchmarks such as the eight-hour day should not be abandoned because of the war.*

We have heard the claim that democracy is not and cannot be efficient.

With the people of the United States rests the responsibility of demonstrating that democracy, as exemplified in America, can—in war as well as in peace—prove itself to be efficient.

To make this country efficient in the highest degree cooperation between the agencies of the Government and particular units is necessary. That cooperation is dependent very largely upon the men and women who handle the tools. . . . Cooperation in the form of good results cannot be got from underfed workingmen and women. They must be paid enough to permit them to live decently. They must not be asked to work over eight hours a day, six days a week. They must not be asked to work unnecessarily in unhealthful conditions. . . .

In a word, good working conditions are as essential to high production as high production in this time of stress is essential to the maintenance of a battlefront. It would seem to be treason to the best interests of this country to desert such principles now. Now more than at any time in our national history we do not want production to fall off; rather, we want to accentuate it. Now more than ever we want the army in the factories and fields to be an army of strength, fighting for democracy; we don't want a nation of working people with hearts and bodies weakened. We need, rather to strengthen our men and women for the war and for the reconstruction after the war.

And if liberty, freedom, justice and democracy are not meaningless terms, they are worth something to us. They are worth anything. They are too priceless to surrender without a struggle, and he who is unwilling to fight for freedom is undeserving to enjoy that freedom. . . .

May I suggest this: . . . that so far as possible let every controversial question be laid on the table until after the war is closed. Of course, my friends, I would not have you or anyone else interpret that statement to mean that the human aspiration for a better life can be or will be suppressed; that ought to be encouraged; but shall we array church against church, party against party, religion against religion, politics against politics, nationality against nationality, aye, even the question of raising funds to carry on the war, the bonds that are to be issued? Let us do our share to see to it that Uncle Sam has the fighting men and the men to produce at home and the money with which to carry on the war. Let us defer questions which can be deferred, questions that are likely to divide us in this war, divide any appreciable element of our people in this war; let us remain united and fight it out, no matter how long we fight, until America and America's allies shall prove victorious in the struggle. . . .

Sacrifices to Come

We do not know now just exactly what sacrifices we may be called upon to make. Let us pray and hope and work that they may be few, if any at all; but this we feel assured of, from the President down to everyone aiding him and his in the great work of carrying on the war, it is the purpose that the home shall be maintained, that the standard of American life shall not go down, but shall be maintained throughout the war.

We must make it possible that our fighting force shall be provided with every necessity to fight and every means contributing to their subsistence and comfort, and that the American people shall go on in their economic, industrial, social and spiritual life just as well as it is possible to do, and only when it is necessary to make additional sacrifices we shall—you, and you, and you—the people of Chicago, the people of Illinois, the people of the United States, standing as one solid phalanx of the manhood and the womanhood of the people of our country, of our republic, united, determined to stand by our cause and our gallant allies until the world has been made safe for freedom, for justice, for democracy, for humanity.

"We brand the declaration of war by our government as a crime against the people of the United States and against the nations of the world."

The American People Should Oppose the War

Socialist Party

Founded in 1901 by a merger of several organizations, the Socialist Party achieved modest political success in the early years of the twentieth century. Hundreds of Socialist candidates were elected as state and local officials across the country, and the party drew nine hundred thousand votes for its presidential candidate (labor leader Eugene V. Debs) in the 1912 election. In 1917 it claimed an active membership of seventy thousand. Many of its members were immigrants from Germany and other European countries.

In April 1917, following the decision of the U.S. Congress to declare war on Germany, the Socialist Party held an emergency convention in St. Louis, Missouri, where the delegates adopted a position of opposition to the war. Their "majority report," reprinted here, condemns the war as an unjustifiable conflict forced upon the American people by the capitalist class. The working people of the United States have no cause for war against the working people of Germany or of other nations, the report asserts, and the United States does not need to enter the war in order to protect American rights or the cause of democracy. The statement concludes with a suggested "course of action" for party members to take, including public demonstrations against the war, resistance to military conscription, and campaigns to educate the American public on the "true relation between capitalism and war."

The Socialist Party became one of the largest organized centers of opposition to the American war effort. However, the party suf-

Reprinted from *The American Socialists and the War*, edited by Alexander Trachtenberg (New York: Rand School of Social Science, 1917).

fered from internal divisions as many prominent Socialists disassociated themselves from the St. Louis manifesto and supported the war. In addition, the federal government responded to the party's stance by arresting many of its members—including Debs—and banning mail circulation of its publications. Weakened by these events, the Socialist Party never again reached the political and electoral success it had attained prior to World War I.

The Socialist Party of the United States in the present grave crisis, solemnly reaffirms its allegiance to the principle of internationalism and working-class solidarity the world over, and proclaims its unalterable opposition to the war just declared by the government of the United States.

Modern wars as a rule have been caused by the commercial and financial rivalry and intrigues of the capitalist interests in the different countries. Whether they have been frankly waged as wars of aggression or have been hypocritically represented as wars of "defense," they have always been made by the classes and fought by the masses. Wars bring wealth and power to the ruling classes, and suffering, death and demoralization to the workers.

They breed a sinister spirit of passion, unreason, race hatred and false patriotism. They obscure the struggles of the workers for life, liberty and social justice. They tend to sever the vital bonds of solidarity between them and their brothers in other countries, to destroy their organizations and to curtail their civic and political rights and liberties.

We Call Upon the Workers

The Socialist Party of the United States is unalterably opposed to the system of exploitation and class rule which is upheld and strengthened by military power and sham national patriotism. We, therefore, call upon the workers of all countries to refuse support to their governments in their wars. The wars of the contending national groups of capitalists are not the concern of the workers. The only struggle which would justify the workers in taking up arms is the great struggle of the working class of the world to free itself from economic exploitation and political oppression, and we particularly warn the workers against the snare and delusion of so-called defensive warfare. As against the false doctrine of national patriotism we uphold the ideal of international working-class solidarity. In support of capitalism, we will not willingly give a single life or a single dollar; in support of the struggle of the workers for freedom we pledge our all.

The mad orgy of death and destruction which is now convulsing unfortunate Europe was caused by the conflict of capitalist interests in the European countries.

In each of these countries, the workers were oppressed and exploited. They produced enormous wealth but the bulk of it was withheld from them by the owners of the industries. The workers were thus deprived of the means to repurchase the wealth which they themselves had created.

Not a War for Democracy

Max Eastman, editor of the Masses, *a radical periodical published in New York City, wrote the following passage for its June 1917 issue. The publication was later barred from the mail by the U.S. Postal Service because of its antiwar views.*

It is not a war for democracy. It did not originate in a dispute about democracy, and it is unlikely to terminate in a democratic settlement. There is a bare possibility that a victory of the Allies will hasten the fall of the autocracies in central Europe but there is a practical certainty that in trimming for such a victory the Allies will throw out most of the essence of their own democracy. We will Prussianize ourselves and will probably not democratize Prussia.

The capitalist class of each country was forced to look for foreign markets to dispose of the accumulated "surplus" wealth. The huge profits made by the capitalists could no longer be profitably reinvested in their own countries, hence, they were driven to look for foreign fields of investment. The geographical boundaries of each modern capitalist country thus became too narrow for the industrial and commercial operations of its capitalist class.

The efforts of the capitalists of all leading nations were therefore centered upon the domination of the world markets. Imperialism became the dominant note in the politics of Europe. The acquisition of colonial possessions and the extension of spheres of commercial and political influence became the object of diplomatic intrigues and the cause of constant clashes between nations.

The acute competition between the capitalist powers of the earth, their jealousies and distrusts of one another and the fear of the rising power of the working class forced each of them to arm to the teeth. This led to the mad rivalry of armament, which, years before the outbreak of the present war, had turned the leading countries of Europe into armed camps with standing armies of many millions, drilled and equipped for war in times of peace.

Capitalism, imperialism and militarism had thus laid the foundation of an inevitable general conflict in Europe. The ghastly war in Europe was not caused by an accidental event, nor by the policy or institutions of any single nation. It was the logical outcome of the competitive capitalist system.

The six million men of all countries and races who have been ruthlessly slain in the first thirty months of this war, the millions of others who have been crippled and maimed, the vast treasures of wealth that have been destroyed, the untold misery and sufferings of Europe, have not been sacrifices exacted in a struggle for principles or ideals, but wanton offerings upon the altar of private profit.

The forces of capitalism which have led to the war in Europe are even more hideously transparent in the war recently provoked by the ruling class of this country.

When Belgium was invaded, the government enjoined upon the people of this country the duty of remaining neutral, thus clearly demonstrating that the "dictates of humanity," and the fate of small nations and of democratic institutions were matters that did not concern it. But when our enormous war traffic was seriously threatened, our government calls upon us to rally to the "defense of democracy and civilization."

Predatory Capitalists

Our entrance into the European war was instigated by the predatory capitalists in the United States who boast of the enormous profit of seven billion dollars from the manufacture and sale of munitions and war supplies and from the exportation of American food stuffs and other necessaries. They are also deeply interested in the continuance of war and the success of the allied arms through their huge loans to the governments of the allied powers and through other commercial ties. It is the same interests which strive for imperialistic domination of the Western Hemisphere.

The war of the United States against Germany cannot be justified even on the plea that it is a war in defense of American rights or American "honor." Ruthless as the unrestricted submarine war policy of the German government was and is, it is not an invasion of the rights of the American people, as such, but only an interference with the opportunity of certain groups of American capitalists to coin cold profits out of the blood and sufferings of our fellow men in the warring countries of Europe.

It is not a war against the militarist regime of the Central Powers. Militarism can never be abolished by militarism.

It is not a war to advance the cause of democracy in Europe. Democracy can never be imposed upon any country by a foreign power by force of arms.

It is cant and hypocrisy to say that the war is not directed against the German people, but against the Imperial Government of Germany. If we send an armed force to the battlefields of Europe, its cannon will mow down the masses of the German people and not the Imperial German Government.

Our entrance into the European conflict at this time will serve only to multiply the horrors of the war, to increase the toll of death and destruction and to prolong the fiendish slaughter. It will bring death, suffering and destitution to the people of the United States and particularly to the working class. It will give the powers of reaction in this country, the pretext for an attempt to throttle our rights and to crush our democratic institutions, and to fasten upon this country a permanent militarism.

No Quarrel with the People of Germany

The working class of the United States has no quarrel with the working class of Germany or of any other country. The people of the United States have no quarrel with the people of Germany or any other country. The American people did not want and do not want this war. They have not been consulted about the war and have had no part in declaring war. They have been plunged into this war by the trickery and treachery of the ruling class of the country through its representatives in the National Administration and National Congress, its demagogic agitators, its subsidized press, and other servile instruments of public expression.

We brand the declaration of war by our government as a crime against the people of the United States and against the nations of the world.

In all modern history there has been no war more unjustifiable than the war in which we are about to engage.

No greater dishonor has ever been forced upon a people than that which the capitalist class is forcing upon this nation against its will.

A Course of Action

In harmony with these principles, the Socialist Party emphatically rejects the proposal that in time of war the workers should suspend their struggle for better conditions. On the contrary, the acute situation created by war calls for an even more vigorous prosecution of the class struggle, and we recommend to the workers and pledge ourselves to the following course of action:

1. Continuous, active, and public opposition to the war through demonstrations, mass petitions, and all other means within our power.

2. Unyielding opposition to all proposed legislation for military or industrial conscription. Should such conscription be forced upon the people, we pledge ourselves to continuous efforts for

the repeal of such laws and to the support of all mass movements in opposition to conscription. We pledge ourselves to oppose with all our strength any attempt to raise money for payment of war expense by taxing the necessaries of life or issuing bonds which will put the burden upon future generations. We demand that the capitalist class, which is responsible for the war, pay its cost. Let those who kindled the fire furnish the fuel.

3. Vigorous resistance to all reactionary measures, such as censorship of press and mails, restriction of the rights of free speech, assemblage, and organization, or compulsory arbitration and limitation of the right to strike.

4. Consistent propaganda against military training and militaristic teaching in the public schools.

5. Extension of the campaign of education among the workers to organize them into strong, class-conscious, and closely unified political and industrial organizations to enable them by concerted and harmonious mass action to shorten this war and to establish lasting peace.

6. Widespread educational propaganda to enlighten the masses as to the true relation between capitalism and war, and to rouse and organize them for action, not only against present war evils, but for the prevention of future wars and for the destruction of the causes of war.

7. To protect the masses of the American people from the pressing danger of starvation which the war in Europe has brought upon them, and which the entry of the United States has already accentuated, we demand—

(a) The restriction of food exports so long as the present shortage continues, the fixing of maximum prices and whatever measures may be necessary to prevent the food speculators from holding back the supplies now in their hands;

(b) The socialization and democratic management of the great industries concerned with the production, transportation, storage, and the marketing of food and other necessaries of life;

(c) The socialization and democratic management of all land and other natural resources now held out of use for monopolistic or speculative profit.

These measures are presented as means of protecting the workers against the evil results of the present war. The danger of recurrence of war will exist as long as the capitalist system of industry remains in existence. The end of wars will come with the establishment of socialized industry and industrial democracy the world over. The Socialist Party calls upon all the workers to join it in its struggle to reach this goal, and thus bring into the world a new society in which peace, fraternity, and human brotherhood will be the dominant ideals.

VIEWPOINT 3

"The American nation is entering this war under the influence of a moral verdict reached after the utmost deliberation by the more thoughtful members of the community."

Intellectuals' Support for the War Has Been Crucial and Beneficial

The New Republic

The following viewpoint is taken from an editorial in the *New Republic*, a magazine founded in 1914 to provide a forum for reform-minded progressives to present their views on American public and cultural affairs. During its first years of operation, the magazine's founding editors (who included Herbert C. Croly, Walter Lippmann, and Walter Weyl) sometimes criticized Woodrow Wilson for being too cautious in his foreign policy, but they strongly supported his decision in April 1917 to ask Congress to declare war on Germany. The *New Republic* published numerous articles and editorials that supported American involvement in the war in Europe and criticized war opponents. Among them was a notable series of articles by philosopher John Dewey, who argued that the advent of the war presented "social possibilities" for reshaping American society and the global community. The United States, Dewey and other *New Republic* writers believed, could through its participation in World War I transform that conflict into a worldwide crusade for democracy. They also maintained that the increased power and scope of the federal government that inevitably occurs during wartime could later be channeled into domestic reform programs.

Reprinted from "Who Willed American Participation?" Editorial, *New Republic*, April 14, 1917.

In the following viewpoint, published shortly after the United States entered the war, the editors of the *New Republic* take issue with the argument that the primary instigators of American involvement in the war were capitalists seeking wartime profit. Rather, the editors assert, the main force behind the U.S. decision was the intellectual class of Americans, including college professors, newspaper editors, ministers, and other leaders of local communities. Over a period of time, the editors state, these people convinced the American public that the United States should support the Allies and defeat Germany—a conviction the authors of this viewpoint fully share. The editors also praise Wilson (himself a former college professor) for guiding America into war at this particular juncture when the danger of German militarism has been demonstrated beyond all doubt, the American public has been educated on the need for war, and a firm link has been established between American intervention and the creation of a postwar liberal international order (a "community of nations") to prevent future wars.

Pacifist agitators who have been so courageously opposing, against such heavy odds, American participation in the war have been the victims of one natural but considerable mistake. They have insisted that the chief beneficiaries of American participation would be the munition-makers, bankers and in general the capitalist class, that the chief sufferers would be the petty business men and the wage-earners. They have consequently considered the former classes to be conspiring in favor of war, and now that war has come, they condemn it as the work of a small but powerful group of profiteers. Senator [George W.] Norris had some such meaning in his head when he asserted that a declaration of war would be equivalent to stamping "the dollar mark on the American flag."

This explanation of the great decision is an absurd mistake, but the pacifists have had some excuses for making it. They have seen a great democratic nation gradually forced into war, in spite of the manifest indifference or reluctance of the majority of its population; and they have rightly attributed the successful pressure to the ability of a small but influential minority to impose its will on the rest of the country. But the numerically insignificant class whose influence has been successfully exerted in favor of American participation does not consist of the bankers and the capitalists. Neither will they be the chief beneficiaries of American participation. The bankers and the capitalists have favored war, but they have favored it without realizing the extent to which it would injure their own interests, and their support has been one of the most formidable political obstacles to American participation. The effective and decisive work on behalf of war has been accomplished by an entirely different class—a class which must be comprehensively but loosely described as the "intellectuals."

War and Social Progress

In articles for the New Republic *and other publications, noted educator and philosopher John Dewey wrote that the war could serve as a catalyst for continuing public and social reform in the United States and other nations. The following is excerpted from Dewey's "The Social Possibilities of War," a 1918 article published in the* Independent *magazine.*

The immediate urgency [of war] has in a short time brought into existence [government] agencies for executing the supremacy of the public and social interest over the private and possessive interest which might otherwise have taken a long time to construct. In this sense, no matter how many among the special agencies for public control decay with the disappearance of war stress, the movement will never go backward. Peoples who have learned that billions are available for public needs when the occasion presses will not forget the lesson, and having seen that portions of these billions are necessarily diverted into physical training, industrial education, better housing, and the setting up of agencies for securing a public service and function from private industries will ask why in the future the main stream should not be directed in the same channels.

In short, we shall have a better organized world internally as well as externally, a more integrated, less anarchic, system.

The American nation is entering this war under the influence of a moral verdict reached after the utmost deliberation by the more thoughtful members of the community. They gradually came to a decision that the attack made by Germany on the international order was sufficiently flagrant and dangerous to justify this country in abandoning its cherished isolation and in using its resources to bring about German defeat. But these thoughtful people were always a small minority. They were able to impose their will upon a reluctant or indifferent majority partly because the increasingly offensive nature of German military and diplomatic policy made plausible opposition to American participation very difficult, but still more because of the overwhelming preponderance of pro-Allies conviction in the intellectual life of the country. If the several important professional and social groups could have voted separately on the question of war and peace, the list of college professors would probably have yielded the largest majority in favor of war, except perhaps that contained in the Social Register. A fighting anti-German spirit was more general among physicians, lawyers and clergymen than it was among business men— except those with Wall Street and banking connections. Finally, it was not less general among writers on magazines and in the newspapers. They popularized what the college professors had been thinking. Owing to this consensus of influences opposition to pro-Allies orthodoxy became intellectually somewhat disreputable, and when a final decision had to be made this factor counted with unprecedented and overwhelming force. College professors headed by a President who had himself been a college professor contributed more effectively to the decision in favor of war than did the farmers, the business men or the politicians.

America's Reasons for Entering the War

When one considers the obstacles to American entrance into the war, the more remarkable and unprecedented does the final decision become. Every other belligerent had something immediate and tangible to gain by participating and to lose by not participating. Either they were invaded or were threatened with invasion. Either they dreaded the loss of prestige or territory or coveted some kind or degree of national aggrandizement. Even Australia and Canada, who had little or nothing to gain from fighting, could not have refused to fight without severing their connection with the British Empire, and behaving in a manner which would have been considered treacherous by their fellow Britons. But the American people were not forced into the war either by fears or hopes or previously recognized obligations. On the contrary, the ponderable and tangible realities of the immediate situation counseled neutrality. They were revolted by the hideous brutality of the war and its colossal waste. Participation must be purchased with a similarly colossal diversion of American energy from constructive to destructive work, the imposition of a similarly heavy burden upon the future production of American labor. It implied the voluntary surrender of many of those advantages which had tempted our ancestors to cross the Atlantic and settle in the New World. As against these certain costs there were no equally tangible compensations. The legal rights of American citizens were, it is true, being violated, and the structure of international law with which American security was traditionally associated was being shivered, but the nation had weathered a similar storm during the Napoleonic Wars and at that time participation in the conflict had been wholly unprofitable. By spending a small portion of the money which will have to be spent in helping the Allies to beat

Germany, upon preparations exclusively for defense, the American nation could have protected for the time being the inviolability of its own territory and its necessary communications with the Panama Canal. Many considerations of national egotism counselled such a policy. But although the Hearst newspapers argued most persuasively on behalf of this course, it did not prevail. The American nation allowed itself to be captured by those upon whom the more remote and less tangible reasons for participation acted with compelling authority. For the first time in history a wholly independent nation has entered a great and costly war under the influence of ideas rather than immediate interests and without any expectation of gains, except those which can be shared with all liberal and inoffensive nations.

Imaginative Leadership

The United States might have blundered into the war at any time during the past two years, but to have entered, as it is now doing, at the right time and in the clear interest of a purely international program required the exercise of an intellectualized and imaginative leadership. And in supplying the country with this leadership Mr. [Woodrow] Wilson was interpreting the ideas of thoughtful Americans who wished their country to be fighting on the side of international right, but not until the righteousness of the Allied cause was unequivocally established. It has taken some time to reach this assurance. The war originated in conflicting national ambitions among European Powers for privileged economic and political positions in Africa and Asia, and if it had continued to be a war of this kind there never could have been a question of American intervention. Germany, however, had been dreaming of a more glorious goal than Baghdad and a mightier heritage than that of Turkey. She betrayed her dream by attacking France through Belgium and by threatening the foundations of European order. The crucifying of Belgium established a strong presumption against Germany, but the case was not complete. There still remained the dubious origin of the war. There still remained a doubt whether the defeat of German militarism might not mean a dangerous triumph of Russian autocracy. Above all there remained a more serious doubt whether the United States in aiding the Allies to beat Germany might not be contributing merely to the establishment of a new and equally unstable and demoralizing Balance of Power in Europe. It was well, consequently, to wait and see whether the development of the war would not do away with some of the ambiguities and misgivings, while at the same time to avoid doing anything to embarrass the Allies. The waiting policy has served. Germany was driven by the logic of her original aggression to threaten the security of all neutrals connected with the rest of the world by maritime communications. The Russian autocracy was overthrown, because it betrayed its furtive kinship with German autocracy. Finally, President Wilson used the waiting period for the education of American public opinion. His campaign speeches prophesied the abandonment of American isolation in the interest of a League of Peace. His note of last December [1916] to the belligerents [asking for possible terms of peace] brought out the sinister secrecy of German peace terms and the comparative frankness of that of the Allies. His [January 22, 1917] address to the Senate [in which Wilson called for a "peace without victory" and outlined his ideas for a League of Nations] clearly enunciated the only program on behalf of which America could intervene in European affairs. Never was there a purer and more successful example of Fabian political strategy, for Fabianism [belief in gradual social reform] consists not merely in waiting but in preparing during the meantime for the successful application of a plan to a confused and dangerous situation.

Wilson's Achievement

What Mr. Wilson did was to apply patience and brains to a complicated and difficult but developing political situation. He was distinguished from his morally indignant pro-Allies countrymen, who a few months ago were abusing him for seeking to make a specifically American contribution to the issues of the war, just as Lincoln was distinguished from the abolitionists, not so much by difference in purposes as by greater political wisdom and intelligence. It is because of his Fabianism, because he insisted upon waiting until he had established a clear connection between American intervention and an attempt to create a community of nations, that he can command and secure for American intervention the full allegiance of the American national conscience. His achievement is a great personal triumph, but it is more than that. It is an illustration and a prophecy of the part which intelligence and in general the "intellectual" class have an opportunity of playing in shaping American policy and in moulding American life. The intimate association between action and ideas, characteristic of American political practice at its best has been vindicated once more. The association was started at the foundation of the Republic and was embodied in the work of the Fathers, but particularly in that of [Alexander] Hamilton. It was carried on during the period of the Civil War and was embodied chiefly in the patient and penetrating intelligence which Abraham Lincoln brought to his task. It has just been established in the region of foreign policy by Mr. Wilson's discriminating effort to keep the United States out of the war until it could go in as the instrument of an exclusively international program and with a fair prospect of getting its program accepted. In holding to this policy Mr. Wilson was interpreting with fidelity and imagination the ideas and the aspirations of the more thoughtful Americans. His success should give them increasing confidence in the contribution which they as men of intelligence are capable of making to the fulfilment of the better American national purposes.

"An intellectual class that was wholly rational would have called insistently for peace and not for war."

Intellectuals' Support for the War Has Been Misguided

Randolph Bourne (1886–1918)

Randolph Bourne, a writer and social critic, was a pacifist opponent of both World War I and American involvement in it. He was an early and frequent contributor to the *New Republic*, a progressive political journal, but disagreed with the magazine's support of American entry into the war.

On April 14, 1917, the *New Republic*'s editors published an article in which they commended President Woodrow Wilson's leadership in taking the nation into war and argued that intellectuals had provided crucial support for Wilson's decision (see previous viewpoint). The following viewpoint, excerpted from a June 1917 article that was published in the short-lived radical journal *Seven Arts*, was Bourne's response to that and similar articles in the *New Republic* as well as to the endorsement many progressive intellectuals gave to the war. Bourne faults the nation's intellectuals for aligning themselves with the least democratic elements of American society, for not formulating a viable alternative to military intervention in Europe, and for believing that war can be channeled for good ends. War, not the state of Germany, is the true enemy of American ideals, he maintains. Bourne died in 1918, but his writings on the war and other subjects became influential in the 1920s and after.

Reprinted from Randolph Bourne, "The War and the Intellectuals," *Seven Arts*, vol. 2, June 1917, pp. 133–46.

To those of us who still retain an irreconcilable animus against war, it has been a bitter experience to see the unanimity with which the American intellectuals have thrown their support to the use of war-technique in the crisis in which America found herself. Socialists, college professors, publicists, new-republicans, practitioners of literature, have vied with each other in confirming with their intellectual faith the collapse of neutrality and the riveting of the war-mind on a hundred million more of the world's people. And the intellectuals are not content with confirming our belligerent gesture. They are now complacently asserting that it was they who effectively willed it, against the hesitation and dim perceptions of the American democratic masses. A war made deliberately by the intellectuals! A calm moral verdict, arrived at after a penetrating study of inexorable facts! Sluggish masses, too remote from the world-conflict to be stirred, too lacking in intellect to perceive their danger! An alert intellectual class, saving the people in spite of themselves, biding their time with Fabian strategy until the nation could be moved into war without serious resistance! An intellectual class, gently guiding a nation through sheer force of ideas into what the other nations entered only through predatory craft or popular hysteria or militarist madness! A war free from any taint of self-seeking, a war that will secure the triumph of democracy and internationalize the world! This is the picture which the more self-conscious intellectuals have formed of themselves, and which they are slowly impressing upon a population which is being led no man knows whither by an indubitably intellectualized President. And they are right, in that the war certainly did not spring from either the ideals or the prejudices, from the national ambitions or hysterias, of the American people, however acquiescent the masses prove to be, and however clearly the intellectuals prove their putative intuition.

Those intellectuals who have felt themselves totally out of sympathy with this drag toward war will seek some explanation for this joyful leadership. They will want to understand this willingness of the American intellect to open the sluices and flood us with the sewage of the war spirit. We cannot forget the virtuous horror and stupefaction which filled our college professors when they read the famous manifesto of their ninety-three German colleagues in defence of their war. To the American academic mind of 1914 defence of war was inconceivable. . . . They would have thought anyone mad who talked of shipping American men by the hundreds of thousands—conscripts—to die on the fields of France. Such a spiritual change seems catastrophic when we shoot our minds back to those days when neutrality was a proud thing. But the intellectual progress has been so gradual that the country retains little sense of the irony. The war sentiment, begun so gradually but so perseveringly by the preparedness advocates who came from the ranks of big business, caught hold of one after another of the intellectual groups. With the aid of [Theodore] Roosevelt, the murmurs became a monotonous chant, and finally a chorus so mighty that to be out of it was at first to be disreputable and finally almost obscene. And slowly a strident rant was worked up against Germany which compared very creditably with the German fulminations against the greedy power of England. The nerve of the war-feeling centred, of course, in the richer and older classes of the Atlantic seaboard, and was keenest where there were French or English business and particularly social connections. The sentiment then spread over the country as a class-phenomenon, touching everywhere those upper-class elements in each section who identified themselves with this Eastern ruling group. It must never be forgotten that in every community it was the least liberal and least democratic elements among whom the preparedness and later the war sentiment was found. The farmers were apathetic, the small business men and workingmen are still apathetic towards the war. The [1916] election was a vote of confidence of these latter classes in a President who would keep the faith of neutrality. The intellectuals, in other words, have identified themselves with the least democratic forces in American life. They have assumed the leadership for war of those very classes whom the American democracy has been immemorially fighting. Only in a world where irony was dead could an intellectual class enter war at the head of such illiberal cohorts in the avowed cause of world-liberalism and world-democracy. No one is left to point out the undemocratic nature of this war-liberalism. In a time of faith, skepticism is the most intolerable of all insults.

What Intellectuals Have Accomplished

Our intellectual class might have been occupied, during the last two years of war, in studying and clarifying the ideals and aspirations of the American democracy, in discovering a true Americanism which would not have been merely nebulous but might have federated the different ethnic groups and traditions. They might have spent the time in endeavoring to clear the public mind of the cant of war, to get rid of old mystical notions that clog our thinking. We might have used the time for a great wave of education, for setting our house in spiritual order. We could at least have set the problem before ourselves. If our intellectuals were going to lead the administration, they might conceivably have tried to find some way of securing peace by making neutrality effective. They might have turned their intellectual energy not to the problem of jockeying the nation into war, but to the problem of using our vast neutral power to attain democratic ends for the rest of the world and ourselves without the use of the malevolent technique of war. They might have failed. The point is that they scarcely tried. The time was spent not in clarification and education, but in a mulling over of nebulous ideals of democracy and liberalism and civilization which had never meant anything fruitful to those ruling classes who now so glibly used them, and in giving free rein to the elementary instinct of self-defence. The whole era has been spiritually wasted. . . .

The Shock of War

The sterile results of such an intellectual policy are inevitable. During the war the American intellectual class has produced almost nothing in the way of original and illuminating interpretation. . . . It is true that the shock of war put the American intellectual to an unusual strain. He had to sit idle and think as spectator not as actor. There was no government to which he could docilely and loyally tender his mind as did the Oxford professors to justify England in her own eyes. The American's training was such as to make the fact of war almost incredible. Both in his reading of history and in his lack of economic perspective he was badly prepared for it. He had to explain to himself something which was too colossal for the modern mind, which outran any language or terms which we had to interpret it in. He had to expand his sympathies to the breaking-point, while pulling the past and present into some sort of interpretative order. The intellectuals in the fighting countries had only to rationalize and justify what their country was already doing. Their task was easy. A neutral, however, had really to search out the truth. Perhaps perspective was too much to ask of any mind. Certainly the older colonials among our college professors let their prejudices at once dictate their thought. They have been comfortable ever since. The war has taught them nothing and will teach them nothing. . . .

We have had to watch, therefore, in this country the same process which so shocked us abroad,—the coalescence of the intellectual classes in support of the military programme. . . . We go to war to save the world from subjugation! But the German intellectuals went to war to save their culture from barbarization! And the French went to war to save their beautiful France! And the English to save international honor! And Russia, most altruistic and self-sacrificing of all, to save a small State [Serbia] from destruction! Whence is our miraculous intuition of our moral spotlessness? Whence our confidence that history will not unravel huge economic and imperialist forces upon which our rationalizations float like bubbles? The Jew often marvels that his race alone should have been chosen as the true people of the cosmic God. Are not our intellectuals equally fatuous when they tell us that our war of all wars is stainless and thrillingly achieving for good?

An intellectual class that was wholly rational would have called insistently for peace and not for war. For months the crying need has been for a negotiated peace, in order to avoid the ruin of a deadlock. Would not the same amount of resolute statesmanship thrown into intervention have secured a peace that would have been a subjugation for neither side? Was the terrific bargaining power of a great neutral ever really used? Our war followed, as all wars follow, a monstrous failure of diplomacy. Shamefacedness should now be our intellectuals' attitude, because the American play for peace was made so little more than a polite play. The intellectuals have still to explain why, willing as they now are to use force to continue the war to absolute exhaustion, they were not willing to use force to coerce the world to a speedy peace.

War and Social Change

In an essay published in the October 1917 issue of Seven Arts, *Randolph Bourne directly criticizes John Dewey and his followers for their failure to recognize or appreciate the negative social changes war would bring to the United States.*

How could the pragmatist mind accept war without more violent protest, without a greater wrench? Either Professor Dewey and his friends felt that the forces were too strong for them, that the war had to be, and it was better to take it up intelligently than to drift blindly in; or else they really expected a gallant war, conducted with jealous regard for democratic values at home and a captivating vision of international democracy as the end of all the toil and pain. If their motive was the first, they would seem to have reduced the scope of possible control of events to the vanishing point. If the war is too strong for you to prevent, how is it going to be weak enough for you to control and mould to your liberal purposes? And if their motive was to shape the war firmly for good, they seem to have seriously miscalculated the fierce urgencies of it. Are they to be content, as the materialization of their hopes, with a doubtful League of Nations and the suppression of the I.W.W. [Industrial Workers of the World, a radical labor organization]? Yet the numbing power of the war-situation seems to have kept them from realizing what has happened to their philosophy.

Their forward vision is no more convincing than their past rationality. We go to war now to internationalize the world! But surely their League to Enforce Peace [a group that supported creation of a league of nations to prevent war] is only a palpable apocalyptic myth, like the syndicalists' myth of the "general strike." It is not a rational programme so much as a glowing symbol for the purpose of focusing belief, of setting enthusiasm on fire for international order. As far as it does this it has pragmatic value, but as far as it provides a certain radiant mirage of idealism for this war and for a world-order founded on mutual fear, it is dangerous and obnoxious. Idealism should be kept for what is ideal. It is depressing to think that the prospect of a world so strong that none dare challenge it should be the immediate ideal of the American intellectual. If the League is only a makeshift, a coalition into which we enter to restore order, then it is only a description of existing fact, and the idea should be treated as such. But if it is an actually prospective outcome of the settlement, the keystone of American policy, it is neither realizable nor desirable. For the programme of such a League contains no provision for dynamic national growth or for international economic justice. In a world which requires recognition of economic internationalism far more than of political internationalism, an idea is reactionary which proposes to petrify and federate the nations as political and economic units. Such a scheme for international order is a dubious justification for American policy. And if American policy had been sincere in its belief that our participation would achieve international beatitude, would we not have made our entrance into the war conditional upon a solemn general agreement to respect in the final settlement these principles of international order? Could we have afforded, if our war was to end war by the establishment of a league of honor, to risk the defeat of our vision and our betrayal in the settlement? Yet we are in the war, and no such solemn agreement was made, nor has it even been suggested.

Emotion Trumps Rationality

The case of the intellectuals seems, therefore, only very speciously rational. They could have used their energy to force a just peace or at least to devise other means than war for carrying through American policy. They could have used their intellectual energy to ensure that our participation in the war meant the international order which they wish. Intellect was not so used. It was used to lead an apathetic nation into an irresponsible war, without guarantees from those belligerents whose cause we were saving. The American intellectual, therefore, has been rational neither in his hindsight nor his foresight. To explain him we must look beneath the intellectual reasons to the emotional disposition. It is not so much what they thought as how they felt that explains our intellectual class. Allowing for colonial sympathy, there was still the personal shock in a world-war which outraged all our preconceived notions of the way the world was tending. It reduced to rubbish most of the humanitarian internationalism and democratic nationalism which had been the emotional thread of our intellectuals' life. We had suddenly to make a new orientation. There were mental conflicts. Our latent colonialism strove with our longing for American unity. Our desire for peace strove with our desire for national responsibility in the world. That first lofty and remote and not altogether unsound feeling of our spiritual isolation from the conflict could not last. There was the itch to be in the great experience which the rest of the world was having. Numbers of intelligent people who had never been stirred by the horrors of capitalistic peace at home were shaken out of their slumber by the horrors of war in Belgium. Never having felt responsibility for labor wars and oppressed masses and excluded races at home, they had a large fund of idle emotional capital to invest in the oppressed nationalities and ravaged villages of Europe. Hearts that had felt only ugly contempt for democratic strivings at home beat in tune with the struggle for freedom abroad. All this was natural, but it tended to over-emphasize our responsibility. And it threw our thinking out of gear. The task of making our own country detailedly fit for peace was abandoned in favor of a feverish concern for the management of the war, advice to the fighting governments on all matters, military, social and political, and a gradual working up of the conviction that we were ordained as a nation to lead all erring brothers towards the light of liberty and democracy. The failure of the American intellectual class to erect a creative attitude toward the war can be explained by these sterile mental conflicts which the shock to our ideals sent raging through us. . . .

The Results of War

The results of war on the intellectual class are already apparent. Their thought becomes little more than a description and justification of what is going on. They turn upon any rash one who continues idly to speculate. Once the war is on, the conviction spreads that individual thought is helpless, that the only way one can count is as a cog in the great wheel. There is no good holding back. We are told to dry our unnoticed and ineffective tears and plunge into the great work. . . .

The intellectuals whom the crisis has crystallized into an acceptance of war have put themselves into a terrifyingly strategic position. It is only on the craft, in the stream, they say, that one has any chance of controlling the current forces for liberal purposes. If we obstruct, we surrender all power for influence. If we responsibly approve, we then retain our power for guiding. We will be listened to as responsible thinkers, while those who obstructed the coming of war have committed intellectual suicide and shall be cast into outer darkness. Criticism by the ruling powers will only be accepted from those intellectuals who are in sympathy with the general tendency of the war. Well, it is true that they may guide, but if their stream leads to disaster and the frustration of national life, is their guiding any more than a preference whether they shall go over the right-hand or the left-hand side of the precipice? Meanwhile, however, there is comfort on board. Be with us, they call, or be negligible, irrelevant. Dissenters are already excommunicated. Irreconcilable radicals, wringing their hands among the debris, become the most despicable and impotent of men. There seems no choice for the intellectual but to join the mass of acceptance. But again the terrible dilemma arises,— either support what is going on, in which case you count for nothing because you are swallowed in the mass and great incalculable forces bear you on; or remain aloof, passively resistant, in which case you count for nothing because you are outside the machinery of reality. . . .

War Is the Real Enemy

The American intellectuals, in their preoccupation with reality, seem to have forgotten that the real enemy is War rather than imperial Germany. There is work to be done to prevent this war of ours from passing into popular mythology as a holy crusade. What shall we do with leaders who tell us that we go to war in moral spotlessness, or who make "democracy" synonymous with a republican form of government? There is work to be done in still shouting that all the revolutionary by-products will not justify the war, or make war anything else than the most noxious complex of all the evils that afflict men. There must be some to find no consolation whatever, and some to sneer at those who buy the cheap emotion of sacrifice. There must be some irreconcilables left who will not even accept the war with walrus tears. There must be some to call unceasingly for peace, and some to insist that the terms of settlement shall be not only liberal but democratic. There must be some intellectuals who are not willing to use the old discredited counters again and to support a peace which would leave all the old inflammable materials of armament lying about the world. There must still be opposition to any contemplated "liberal" world-order founded on military coalitions. The "irreconcilable" need not be disloyal. He need not even be "impossibilist." His apathy towards war should take the form of a heightened energy and enthusiasm for the education, the art, the interpretation that make for life in the midst of the world of death. The intellectual who retains his animus against war will push out more boldly than ever to make his case solid against it.

The old ideals crumble; new ideals must be forged. His mind will continue to roam widely and ceaselessly. The thing he will fear most is premature crystallization. If the American intellectual class rivets itself to a "liberal" philosophy that perpetuates the old errors, there will then be need for "democrats" whose task will be to divide, confuse, disturb, keep the intellectual waters constantly in motion to prevent any such ice from ever forming.

"Complete service to their country in this crisis may lead women to that economic freedom which will change a political possession into a political power."

American Women Should Support the War

Harriot Stanton Blatch (1856–1940)

The issue of whether the nation should go to war proved to be divisive among women, including those active in the feminist movement. From 1914 to 1917 many women, including prominent ones such as social reformer Jane Addams and feminist leaders Fanny Garrison Villard and Carrie Chapman Catt, participated in pacifist activities in opposition to war and the militarization of American society. However, both before and after Congress declared war on Germany in April 1917, some feminist leaders, including Catt and Anna Howard Shaw, came to support the war effort. They believed that such a position would lead to greater public support for their goals of equality and opportunity for women—and that continued opposition to war would jeopardize the feminist cause.

Among those who supported the American war effort was Harriot Stanton Blatch, a noted activist for woman suffrage and the daughter of the famous feminist Elizabeth Cady Stanton. During the war Blatch headed the Speaker's Bureau of the Food Administration, where she promoted food conservation and recruited volunteers for the Woman's Land Army to replace male farmworkers who had been drafted. The following viewpoint consists of excerpts from her 1918 book *Mobilizing Woman-Power*. Blatch argues that American women can support the war effort against Germany without reservation because of the actions of that nation's ruling class, both against other countries and against its

Reprinted from Harriot Stanton Blatch, *Mobilizing Woman-Power* (New York: Woman's Press, 1918).

own female population. She also contends the war has brought American women the unique opportunity to work in war industries and other fields usually dominated by men. Blatch concludes that the war will hasten progress in the struggle for woman suffrage.

The nations in which women have influenced national aims face the nation that glorifies brute force. America opposes the exaltation of the glittering sword; opposes the determination of one nation to dominate the world; opposes the claim that the head of one ruling family is the direct and only representative of the Creator; and, above all, America opposes the idea that might makes right.

Let us admit the full weight of the paradox that a people in the name of peace turns to force of arms. The tragedy for us lay in there being no choice of ways, since pacific groups had failed to create machinery to adjust vital international differences, and since the Allies each in turn, we the last, had been struck by a foe determined to settle disagreements by force.

Never did a nation make a crusade more just than this of ours. We were patient, too long patient, perhaps, with challenges. We seek no conquest. We fight to protect the freedom of our citizens. On America's standard is written democracy, on that of Germany autocracy. Without reservation women can give their all to attain our end.

German Society and Values

There may be a cleavage between the German people and the ruling class. It may be that our foe is merely the military caste, though I am inclined to believe that we have the entire German nation on our hands. The supremacy of might may be a doctrine merely instilled in the minds of the people by its rulers. Perhaps the weed is not indigenous, but it flourishes, nevertheless. . . .

The overbearing spirit of the Prussian military caste has drilled a race to worship might; men are overbearing towards women, women towards children, and the laws reflect the cruelties of the strong towards the weak.

As the recent petition of German suffragists to the Reichstag [the lower house of the legislature] states, their country stands "in the lowest rank of nations as regards women's rights." It is a platitude just now worth repeating that the civilization of a people is indicated by the position accorded to its women. On that head, then, the Teutonic Kultur stands challenged. . . .

I hate the system that has so bent and crippled a great race. Revenge we must not feel, that would be to innoculate ourselves with the enemy's virus. But let us be awake to the fact that might making right cuts athwart our ideals. German Kultur, through worship of efficiency, cramps originality and initiative, while our aim—why not be frank about it?— is the protection of inefficiency, which means sympathy with childhood, and opportunity for the spirit of art. German Kultur fixes an inflexible limit to the aspirations of women, while our goal is complete freedom for the mothers of men.

The women of the Allies can fight for all that their men fight for—for national self-respect, for protection of citizens, for the sacredness of international agreements, for the rights of small nations, for the security of democracy, and then our women can be inspired by one thing more—the safety and development of all those things which they have won for human welfare in a long and bloodless battle.

Women fight for a place in the sun for those who hold right above might. . . .

Women Must Contribute

To win the war we must have man-power in the trenches sufficient to win it with. To win, every soldier, every sailor, must be well fed, well clothed, well equipped. To win, behind the armed forces must stand determined peoples. To win, the people of America and her Allies must be heartened by care and food.

The sun shines on the fertile land, the earth teems with forests, with coal, with every necessary mineral and food, but labor, labor alone can transform all to meet our necessities. Man-power unaided cannot supply the demand. Women in America must shoulder as nobly as have the women of Europe, this duty. They must answer their country's call. Let them see clearly that the desire of their men to shield them from possible injury exposes the nation and the world to actual danger.

Our winning of the war depends upon the full use of the energy of our entire people. Every muscle, every brain, must be mobilized if the national aim is to be achieved. . . .

Working Women in America

American women have begun to go over the top. They are going up the scaling-ladder and out into All Man's Land. Perhaps love of adventure tempts them, perhaps love of money, or a fine spirit of service, but whatever the propelling motive, we are seeing them make the venture.

There is nothing new in our day in a woman's being paid for her work—some of it. But she has never before been seen in

America employed, for instance, as a section hand on a railway. The gangs are few and small as yet, but there the women are big and strong specimens of foreign birth. They "trim" the ballast and wield the heavy "tamping" tool with zest. They certainly have muscles, and are tempted to use them vigorously at three dollars a day.

In the machine shops where more skill than strength is called for, the American element with its quick wits and deft fingers predominates. Young women are working at the lathe with so much precision and accuracy that solicitude as to what would become of the world if all its men marched off to war is in a measure assuaged. In the push and drive of the industrial world, women are handling dangerous chemicals in making flash lights, and T.N.T. for high explosive shells. The American college girl is not as yet transmuting her prowess of the athletic field into work on the anvil, as is the university woman in England, but she has demonstrated her manual strength and skill on the farm with plough and harrow. . . .

The Beginnings of Great Change

In short, America is witnessing the beginning of a great industrial and social change, and even those who regard the situation as temporary cannot doubt that the experience will have important reactions. The development is more advanced than it was in Great Britain at a corresponding time, for even before the United States entered the conflict women were being recruited in war industries. They have opened up every line of service. There is not an occupation in which a woman is not found.

When men go a-warring, women go to work.

A distinguished general at the end of the Cuban War, enlarging upon the poet's idea of woman's weeping rôle in wartime, said in a public speech: "When the country called, women put guns in the hands of their soldier boys and bravely sent them away. After the good-byes were said there was nothing for these women to do but to go back and wait, wait, wait. The excitement of battle was not for them. It was simply a season of anxiety and heart-rending inactivity." Now the fact is, when a great call to arms is sounded for the men of a nation, women enlist in the industrial army. If women did indeed sit at home and weep, the enemy would soon conquer. . . .

War compels women to work. That is one of its merits. Women are forced to use body and mind, they are not, cannot be idlers. Perhaps that is the reason military nations hold sway so long; their reign continues, not because they draw strength from the conquered nation, but because their women are roused to exertion. Active mothers ensure a virile race.

The peaceful nation, if its women fall victims to the luxury which rapidly increasing wealth brings, will decay. If there come no spiritual awakening, no sense of responsibility of service, then perhaps war alone can save it. The routing of idleness and ease by compulsory labor is the good counterbalancing some of the evil. . . .

World War I provided new working opportunities for women, including these two electric welders who were among the first women to take part in ship construction.

Whether approved or not, the American woman is going over the top. Four hundred and more are busy on aeroplanes at the Curtiss works. The manager of a munition shop where to-day but fifty women are employed, is putting up a dormitory to accommodate five hundred. An index of expectation! Five thousand are employed by the Remington Arms Company at Bridgeport. At the International Arms and Fuse Company at Bloomfield, New Jersey, two thousand, eight hundred are employed. The day I visited the place, in one of the largest shops women had only just been put on the work, but it was expected that in less than a month they would be found handling all of the twelve hundred machines under that one roof alone.

The skill of the women staggers one. After a week or two they master the operations on the "turret," gauging and routing machines. The best worker on the "facing" machine is a woman. She is a piece worker, as many of the women are, and is paid at the same rate as men. This woman earned, the day I saw her, five dollars and forty cents. She tossed about the fuse parts, and played with that machine, as I would with a baby. Perhaps it was in somewhat the same spirit—she seemed to love her toy. . . .

As to how many women have supplanted men, or poured into the new war industries, no figures are available. One guess has put it at a million. But that is merely a guess. I have seen them by the tens, the hundreds, the thousands. The number is large and rapidly increasing. We may know that something important is happening when even the government takes note. The United States Labor Department has recognized the new-comers by establishing a Division of Women's Work with branches in every State. It looks as if these bureaus of employment would not be idle, with a showing of one thousand, five hundred applicants the first week the New York office was opened. It is to be hoped that this government effort will save the round pegs from getting into the square holes. . . .

The Professional Woman

The professional woman is going over the top, and with a good opinion of herself. "I can do this work better than any man," was the announcement made by a young woman from the Pacific Coast as she descended upon the city hall in an eastern town, credentials in her hand, and asked for the position of city chemist. There was not a microbe she did not know to its undoing, or a deadly poison she could not bring from its hiding place. The town had suffered from graft, and the mayor, thinking a woman might scare the thieves as well as the bacteria, appointed the chemist who believed in herself. And she is just one of many who have been taking up such work.

Formerly two-thirds of the positions filled by the New York Intercollegiate Bureau of Occupations were secretarial or teaching positions; now three-fourths of its applicants have been placed as physicists, chemists, office managers, sanitary experts, exhibit secretaries, and the like. The temporary positions used to outnumber the permanent placements; at present the reverse is true. Of the women placed, four times as many as formerly get salaries ranging above eighteen hundred dollars a year.

The story told at the employment bureaus in connection with professional societies and clubs such as the Chemists' Club is the same. Women are being placed not merely as teachers of chemistry or as routine laboratory workers in hospitals, but also as experimental and control chemists in industrial plants. In the great rolling mills they are testing steel, at the copper smelters they are found in the laboratories. The government has thrown doors wide open to college-trained women. They are physicists and chemists in the United States Bureaus of Standards, Mines, and Soils, sanitary experts in military camps, research chemists in animal nutrition and fertilizers at state experiment stations.

But the industrial barrier is the one most recently scaled.

War and Woman Suffrage

World War I helped American feminists achieve their longtime goal of the right to vote. An important convert to their cause was President Woodrow Wilson, who before the war had declined to endorse woman suffrage. The following passage is an excerpt from Wilson's September 30, 1918, speech to the Senate in which the president called on that body to pass a constitutional amendment extending the vote for women. The amendment was passed by Congress in 1919 and ratified by the states in 1920.

We have made partners of the women in this war; shall we admit them only to a partnership of suffering and sacrifice and toil and not to a partnership of privilege and right? This war could not have been fought, either by the other nations engaged or by America, if it had not been for the services of the women—services rendered in every sphere—not merely in the fields of effort in which we have been accustomed to see them work, but wherever men have worked and upon the very skirts and edges of the battle itself. We shall not only be distrusted but shall deserve to be distrusted if we do not enfranchise them with the fullest possible enfranchisement, as it is now certain that the other great free nations will enfranchise them. We cannot isolate our thought and action in such a matter from the thought of the rest of the world. We must either conform or deliberately reject what they propose and resign the leadership of liberal minds to others. . . .

Have I said that the passage of this amendment is a vitally necessary war measure, and do you need further proof? Do you stand in need of the trust of other peoples and of the trust of our own women? Is that trust an asset or is it not? I tell you plainly, as the commander-in-chief of our armies and of the gallant men in our fleets, as the present spokesman of this people in our dealings with the men and women throughout the world who are now our partners, as the responsible head of a great government which stands and is questioned day by day as to its purposes, its principles, its hopes, whether they be serviceable to men everywhere or only to itself, and who must himself answer these questionings or be shamed, as the guide and director of forces caught in the grip of war and by the same token in need of every material and spiritual resource this great nation possesses—I tell you plainly that this measure which I urge upon you is vital to the winning of the war and to the energies alike of preparation and of battle.

Women are now found as analytical, research or control chemists in the canneries, in dye and electrical works, in flour and paper mills, in insecticide companies, and cement works. They test the steel that will carry us safely on our journeys, they pass upon the chemical composition of the flavor in our cake, as heads of departments in metal refining companies they determine the kind of copper battery we shall use, and they have a finger in our liquid glues, household oils and polishes. . . .

And so we see on all hands women breaking through the old accustomed bounds.

War and Suffrage

Not only as workers but as voters, the war has called women over the top. Since that fateful August, 1914, four provinces of Canada and the Dominion itself have raised the banner of votes for women. Nevada and Montana declared for suffrage before the war was four months old, and Denmark enfranchised its women before the year was out. And when America went forth to fight for democracy abroad, Arkansas, Michigan, Vermont, Nebraska, North Dakota, Rhode Island, began to lay the foundations of freedom at home, and New York in no faltering voice proclaimed full liberty for all its people. Lastly Great Britain has enfranchised its women, and surely the Congress of the United States will not lag behind the Mother of Parliaments!

The world is facing changes as great as the breaking up of the feudal system. Causes as fundamental, more wide-spread, and more cataclysmic are at work than at the end of the Middle Ages. Among the changes none is more marked than the intensified development in what one may call, for lack of a better term, the woman movement. The advance in political freedom has moved steadily forward during the past quarter of a century, but in the last three years progress has been intense and striking.

The peculiarity in attainment of political democracy for women has lain in the fact that while for men economic freedom invariably preceded political enfranchisement, in the case of women the conferring of the vote in no single case was related to the stage which the enfranchised group had attained in the matter of economic independence. Nowhere were even those women who were entirely lacking in economic freedom, excluded on that account from any extension of suffrage. Even in discussions of the right of suffrage no reference has ever been made, in dealing with women's claim, to the relation, universally recognized in the case of men, of political enfranchisement to economic status. Serfdom gave way to the wage system before democracy developed for men, and the colored man was emancipated before he was enfranchised. For this reason the coming of women as paid workers over the top may be regarded as epoch-making.

In any case, self-determination is certainly a strong element in attaining any real political freedom.

Service to the Nation

Complete service to their country in this crisis may lead women to that economic freedom which will change a political possession into a political power. But the requirement is readiness to do, and to do well, the task which offers. Man-power must give itself unreservedly at the front. Women must show not only eagerness but fitness to substitute for man-power. It will hearten the nation, help to make the path clear, if individual women declare that though the call to them has not yet come for a definite service, the time of waiting will not be spent in complaint, nor yet in foolish busyness, but in careful and conscientious training for useful work.

Each woman must prepare so that when the nation's need arises, she can stand at salute and say, "Here is your servant, trained and ready." Women are not driven over the top. Through self-discipline, they go over it of their own accord.

VIEWPOINT 6

"What we hope . . . to accomplish . . . is to bring . . . thousands of women . . . to dedicate their new political power, not to local reforms or personal ambitions, . . . but to ridding the world of war."

American Women Should Support Pacifism

Crystal Eastman (1881–1928)

Crystal Eastman was a political activist and writer whose causes included feminism, socialism, and pacifism. A law school graduate who spent much of her life in the emerging radical community of Greenwich Village in New York City, Eastman first gained public notoriety in the early 1900s as the secretary and the only female member of New York's Employer's Liability Commission, where she helped draft the state's first workers' compensation law. When World War I began in 1914, she concentrated her efforts on organizing opposition against the possibility of America's participation in the war. She founded and led the radical Woman's Peace Party of New York and was also involved in the creation of two national peace organizations: the national Woman's Peace Party and the American Union Against Militarism.

Unlike some feminist and pacifist leaders who eventually came to support or acquiesce to the American decision to enter the war in 1917, Eastman remained steadfastly pacifist in her beliefs throughout the war. The following viewpoint consists of two pamphlets written in 1918 for the Woman's Peace Party of New York City. In the first, published on January 1, 1918, Eastman reviews that group's positions both before and after Congress declared war on Germany in April 1917; of these, two fundamental points are that war is not a necessary recourse of nations and that

Reprinted from Crystal Eastman, *Our War Record: A Plea for Tolerance* (New York: Woman's Peace Party, 1918) and *A Program for Voting Women* (New York: Woman's Peace Party, 1918).

the people should have a direct say in important foreign policy decisions. In addition, she argues that although the group has not wavered from its pacifist beliefs, it has not engaged in illegal or unpatriotic activities. In the second pamphlet, published in March 1918, Eastman maintains that women in general—and activists in the Woman's Peace Party in particular—have a special role in guiding American policy and actions toward a course of lasting world peace.

I

It is true that we opposed the entrance of this country into the war and used every honorable means at our command to prevent it. We believed that cooperation with other neutrals would have furnished a method of maintaining our joint rights without recourse to war, and at the same time a means with which to hasten peace negotiations in Europe. We especially urged that if a democracy is to go to war it should go by direct mandate of the people through a referendum. After war had become a fact, we further urged that conscription was no fit weapon for a democracy to fight its wars with, that forcing men to kill and to be killed against their will does violence to the vital spirit and essence of democracy.

However, once the war and conscription became the law of this land, our agitation against them ceased. Common sense as well as loyalty and the habit of obedience to law counseled this course. We have never in the slightest degree urged or suggested resistance to the selective service law nor followed any other policy of obstruction.

What then has been our position, what have we asked of our government during these critical months? Briefly this:

To begin with, we have insisted not merely upon the right, but upon the need for a full, free and continuous discussion in the press and on the platform of America's war aims and peace terms. We have urged this that the militarists and imperialists might be exposed, that ignorance might be destroyed, that we might be faithful to the declared ideals for which our armed forces are fighting, and that the whole world might know us as the enemies of German aggression but no less the friends of a German democracy.

We have at no time demanded an immediate peace or a separate peace. But, when revolutionary Russia first pronounced its simple, generous, practical peace formula—no forcible annexations, no punitive indemnities, free development for all nations,—we urged that our government should respond, stating its willingness to make peace on this formula. When the German Reichstag [legislature (lower house)] passed a resolution substantially endorsing this formula, we asked our government to welcome the resolution officially, and thus strengthen the hands of the German liberals who were struggling to make it the avowed policy of their government. When the President replied to the Pope, we rejoiced to find him clearly standing for the Russian formula and we advocated a further step, i.e., that our government should support the long unheeded request of Russia for a restatement of the Allied aims,—a policy now supported by [the former British minister] the Marquis of Lansdowne.

Today we are still urging this step. But we also look ahead to the inevitable cessation of hostilities, to the peace conference which must come. We are urging that the ultimate agreement to be reached by the nations at that conference shall include Free Markets and Free Seas, Universal Disarmament, and A League of Nations, the obvious essentials of an enduring peace. And since we are wise enough to know that these ends cannot be achieved at a gathering of military personages and appointed diplomats, we are demanding direct democratic representation of the people of all countries at the peace conference.

What We Are Asking For

This is our complete war record. We hold that there is nothing treasonable or unpatriotic or even emotional about it. On the basis of that record we ask protection from the government for our propaganda no matter how unpopular it may become. We ask tolerance from those who think our ideas are wrong. And from those who think our ideas are fundamentally right, whether they agreed with us about the question of entering the war or not, we ask friendship and loyalty and support.

II

Why a *Woman's* Peace Party?, I am often asked. Is peace any more a concern of women than of men? Is it not of universal human concern? For a feminist—one who believes in breaking down sex barriers so that women and men can work and play and build the world together—it is not an easy question to answer. Yet the answer, when I finally worked it out in my own mind, convinced me that we should be proud and glad, even as feminists, to work for the Woman's Peace Party.

To begin with, there is a great and unique tradition behind our movement which would be lost if we merged our Woman's Peace

Party in the general revolutionary international movement of the time. Do not forget that it was women who gathered at The Hague, a thousand strong, in the early months of the war, women from all the great belligerent and neutral countries, who conferred there together in friendship and sorrow and sanity while the mad war raged around them. Their great conference, despite its soundness and constructive statesmanship, failed of its purpose, failed of its hope. But from the beginning of the war down to the [1917] Russo-German armistice there was no world step of such daring and directness, nor of such honest, unfaltering international spirit and purpose, as the organization of the International Committee of Women for Permanent Peace at The Hague in April, 1915. This Committee has branches in twenty-two countries. The Woman's Peace Party is the American section of the Committee, and our party, organized February 1 and 2, is the New York State Branch.

Women and War

Aletta Jacobs was a Dutch physician who organized an international gathering of women in The Hague, Holland, in February 1915, for the purposes of promoting peace. Crystal Eastman interviewed her for the Survey *magazine; the following is excerpted from the interview, published on October 9, 1915.*

[Dr. Jacobs] believes the coming—and staying—of world peace will depend largely on women. When I asked her if she thought we might see the end of war in a generation or two or if it would take centuries of education to bring it about, she said: "Oh, no. Women will soon have political power. Woman suffrage and permanent peace will go together. When the women of a country are eagerly asking for the vote, and a country is in the state of mind to grant the vote to its women, it is a sign that that country is ripe for permanent peace.

"Yes, the women will do it. They don't feel as men do about war. They are the mothers of the race. Men think of the economic results; women think of the grief and pain, and the damage to the race. If we can bring women to feel that internationalism is higher than nationalism, then they won't stand by governments, they'll stay by humanity."

When the great peace conference comes, a Congress of Women made up of groups from these twenty-two countries will meet in the same city to demand that the deliberate intelligent organization of the world for lasting peace shall be the outcome of that conference.

These established international connections make it important to keep this a woman's movement.

But there is an added reason. We women of New York State, politically speaking, have just been born. We have been born into a world at war, and this fact cannot fail to color greatly the whole field of our political thinking and to determine largely the emphasis of our political action. What we hope, then, to accomplish by keeping our movement distinct is to bring thousands upon thousands of women—women of the international mind—to dedicate their new political power, not to local reforms or personal ambitions, not to discovering the difference between the Democratic and Republican parties, but to *ridding the world of war.*

A Practical Program

For this great purpose we have an immediate, practical program. We shall organize by congressional districts and throw all our spirit and enthusiasm and the political strength of our organization to the support of those candidates who stand for our international program. If the candidate is a Socialist, all right. If the candidate here and there is a woman, so much the better.

To be concrete, we shall go before each candidate in each district of this state with the following definite propositions:

As a candidate for the Congress, which will be in session while the problems incident to the settlement of the war are before the world, *we ask you to indorse the following proposals:*

A democratic league of all nations, based upon: Free seas,—Free markets,—Universal disarmament,—The right of peoples to determine their own destiny.

The development of an international parliament and tribunal as the governing bodies of such a league.

Daylight diplomacy, with democratic control of foreign policy.

Legislation whereby American delegates to the end-of-the-war conference shall be elected directly by the people.

Furthermore, that America's championship of the principle of reduced armaments may appeal to the rest of the world as disinterested and sincere, *we ask you to oppose* legislation committing this country to the adoption of universal compulsory military training.

As the candidate stands or falls by this test, so he will win or lose our support; and we believe that by next fall our support will be something to be reckoned with. There are thousands of radical women in this state, whose energies, whose passion for humanity, have been released by the suffrage victory [New York State granted suffrage to women] of last November [1917]. Among them are experienced workers, speakers, organizers, writers. Every day more of these women leaders come forward and reveal themselves as eager, thinking internationalists. They are caught and held by the intellectual content of our program and its great world purpose. They will work with us, and I may say seriously that we expect to measure the effects of our campaign in the character of New York State's representatives in the next United States Congress.

Thus we shall play a part in building the new world that is to come—a great part; for, unless the peoples rise up and rid themselves of this old intolerable burden of war, they cannot progress far toward liberty.

CHAPTER 4

The War at Home

Chapter Preface

When the United States entered World War I in April 1917, the country was not ready to assume a major role in the conflict. Its armed forces were small and underequipped, the economy was already straining to meet Allied demands for food and war materials, and the American people were still divided over the nation's involvement in a European war. The U.S. government intervened in American life in unprecedented ways over the ensuing months as it sought to create a large military force, mobilize economic resources for war, and garner public support for the war effort. The means used to attain these objectives frequently restricted the freedoms of individuals and were often the subject of debate.

To provide manpower to the Allied cause, the United States faced the task of raising, equipping, training, and transporting a sizable military force. In the two years following America's declaration of war, the army grew from 200,000 to 4 million men (two million of whom would be sent to France). To raise such numbers of troops, the United States resorted to a military draft—a measure that had not been taken since the Civil War. Approximately 24 million men between eighteen and forty-five registered for conscription, of which 5 million received draft notices. To enforce draft compliance, the federal government passed laws making it a crime to obstruct army recruitment or to counsel people to resist or evade conscription. Both draft resisters and their supporters risked imprisonment in military or civilian jails. These laws led some Americans to question whether the conscription system, although successful in raising an army, harmed civil liberties.

Each soldier sent to France required approximately fifty pounds of supplies and equipment daily. Millions of tons of munitions, food, fuel, vehicles, and equipment were shipped from America to the western front. The expense of raising, equipping, and transporting such a force, coupled with other wartime costs (including U.S. treasury loans to the Allies) eventually totaled $34 billion. To raise this sum, the federal government both increased taxes and borrowed money from Americans through the sale of Liberty Bonds and Liberty Stamps.

To support its army and the Allies' war effort—and to effectively deploy the billions of dollars it was raising in loans and taxes—the federal government created several new agencies to activate and manage the nation's resources. The Food Administration, led by Herbert Hoover, launched massive publicity campaigns to persuade Americans to plant gardens and implement "meatless" and "wheatless" days to conserve food. The United States Railways Administration took over the nation's entire private railway network, standardizing rates and schedules and limiting passenger travel and nonessential freight to give priority to war needs. The War Industries Board, under the leadership of Bernard Baruch, allocated raw materials, set prices, and imposed standardization of products and manufacturing processes. The War Labor Policies Board prohibited strikes, forced management to negotiate with unions, and attempted to foster favorable working conditions.

In addition to mobilizing the nation's economic resources, the U.S. government sought to enlist popular support as well. One of the first wartime government agencies President Wilson created was the Committee on Public Information (CPI). The CPI was established on April 13, 1917, by executive order to "mobilize the mind of the world." Under the leadership of journalist George Creel, the CPI organized an army of "four-minute men" to deliver brief lectures in movie theaters and other public places; the speeches bore such titles as "Why We Are Fighting," and "The Meaning of America."

In addition to CPI propaganda efforts, the federal government passed laws aimed at curbing dissent from opponents of U.S. intervention. The Espionage Act, passed in 1917, authorized fines of $10,000 and prison terms of up to twenty years for people who obstructed military operations in wartime. The Sedition Act, passed in 1918, made it a federal crime to voice almost any criticism of government policy or the war effort. The U.S. Postal Service even removed mailing privileges from German American magazines and publications that openly opposed the war.

The federal government was not alone in enforcing conformity. State and local governments banned the speaking or teaching of German, dismissed schoolteachers who questioned the war, and refused to allow antiwar organizations to hold meetings. In addition, private vigilante groups harassed suspected socialists, pacifists, draft evaders ("slackers"), and others who did not conform to the proper spirit of patriotism.

World War I affected the lives of all Americans, not just the soldiers sent to France. The viewpoints in this chapter present a sampling of some of the divisive issues the United States faced in mobilizing for war.

Viewpoint 1

"Our Government, above all others, is founded on the right of the people freely to discuss all matters pertaining to their Government, in war not less than in peace."

War Dissenters' Freedoms of Speech and Assembly Must Be Preserved

Robert La Follette (1855–1925)

Robert La Follette, a senator representing Wisconsin from 1906 to 1925, was one of six members of the U.S. Senate who voted against President Woodrow Wilson's request for a declaration of war against Germany in April 1917. Following his dissenting vote, the former Wisconsin governor (1901–1906), previously best known for his oratorical skills and his leadership in bringing progressive reforms to fruition, was vilified in many parts of the nation. Theodore Roosevelt and other critics called for his expulsion from the Senate. A judge in Texas went so far as to suggest that La Follette and his dissenting colleagues should be shot as traitors, expressing the wish that he himself could pull the trigger.

The following viewpoint is excerpted from an October 1917 speech La Follette made to the Senate in response to the criticism he and other dissenters had received for their views. La Follette argues that many Americans who oppose sending soldiers to fight in Europe have been unlawfully jailed or have otherwise had their constitutional rights of free speech and assembly violated by overzealous supporters of the war. He contends that the country must ensure that freedom of speech, of the press, and of assembly are not disregarded during this time of war.

Reprinted from Robert La Follette, address to the U.S. Senate, *Congressional Record*, October 6, 1917, 65th Cong., 1st sess., pp. 7878–79.

Six Members of the Senate and 50 Members of the House voted against the declaration of war. Immediately there was let loose upon those Senators and Representatives a flood of invective and abuse from newspapers and individuals who had been clamoring for war, unequaled, I believe, in the history of civilized society.

Prior to the declaration of war every man who had ventured to oppose our entrance into it had been condemned as a coward or worse, and even the President had by no means been immune from these attacks.

Since the declaration of war the triumphant war press has pursued those Senators and Representatives who voted against war with malicious falsehood and recklessly libelous attacks, going to the extreme limit of charging them with treason against their country.

This campaign of libel and character assassination directed against the Members of Congress who opposed our entrance into the war has been continued down to the present hour, and I have upon my desk newspaper clippings, some of them libels upon me alone, some directed as well against other Senators who voted in opposition to the declaration of war. . . .

If I alone had been made the victim of these attacks, I should not take one moment of the Senate's time for their consideration, and I believe that other Senators who have been unjustly and unfairly assailed, as I have been, hold the same attitude upon this that I do. *Neither the clamor of the mob nor the voice of power will ever turn me by the breadth of a hair from the course I mark out for myself, guided by such knowledge as I can obtain and controlled and directed by a solemn connection of right and duty. . . .*

But, sir, it is not alone Members of Congress that the war party in this country has sought to intimidate. The mandate seems to have gone forth to the sovereign people of this country that they must be silent while those things are being done by their Government which most vitally concern their well-being, their happiness, and their lives.

Today—for weeks past—honest and law-abiding citizens of this country are being terrorized and outraged in their rights by those sworn to uphold the laws and protect the rights of the people. I have in my possession numerous affidavits establishing the fact that people are being unlawfully arrested, thrown into jail, held incommunicado for days, only to be eventually discharged without ever having been taken into court, because they have committed no crime. Private residences are being invaded, loyal citizens of undoubted integrity and probity arrested, cross-examined, and the most sacred constitutional rights guaranteed to every American citizen are being violated.

It appears to be the purpose of those conducting this campaign to throw the country into a state of terror, to coerce public opinion, to stifle criticism, and suppress discussion of the great issues involved in this war.

We Chain Our Own People

In a June 1917 antiwar speech, Tom Watson, a populist leader and former congressman from Georgia, decried such wartime measures as compulsory military conscription and the silencing of war dissenters. In the following excerpt from the speech, Watson maintains that in an attempt to defeat repressive "Prussianism" in Europe, the United States is imposing similar restrictions on its people. Watson himself was not arrested for giving this speech, but David T. Blodgett, an Iowan who printed and distributed it, was tried for interference in "enlistment and recruiting" and sentenced to twenty years in prison.

Upon the pretext of waging war against Prussianism in Europe, the purpose of Prussianizing this country has been avowed in Congress, with brutal frankness, by a spokesman of the administration.

On the pretext of sending armies to Europe, to crush militarism there, we first enthrone it here.

On the pretext of carrying to all the nations of the world the liberties won by the heroic lifeblood of our forefathers, we first deprive our own people of liberties they inherited as a birthright.

On the pretext of unchaining the enslaved people of other lands, we first chain our own people with preposterous and unprecedented measures, knowing full well that usurpations of power, once submitted to, will never hereafter be voluntarily restored to the people.

I think all men recognize that in time of war the citizen must surrender some rights for the common good which he is entitled to enjoy in time of peace. *But, sir, the right to control their own Government, according to constitutional forms, is not one of the rights that the citizens of this country are called upon to surrender in time of war.*

Rather, in time of war, the citizen must be more alert to the preservation of his right to control his Government. He must be most watchful of the encroachment of the military upon the civil power. He must beware of those precedents in support of arbitrary action by administrative officials which, excused on the plea of necessity in wartime, become the fixed rule when the necessity has passed and normal conditions have been restored.

More than all, the citizen and his representative in Congress in time of war must maintain his right of free speech. More than in times of peace, it is necessary that the channels for free public discussion of governmental policies shall be open and unclogged.

I believe, Mr. President, that I am now touching upon the most important question in this country today—and that is the right of the citizens of this country and their representatives in Congress to discuss in an orderly way, frankly and publicly and without fear, from the platform and through the press, every important phase of this war; its causes, the manner in which it should be conduced, and the terms upon which peace should be made. . . .

I am contending for this right, because the exercise of it is necessary to the welfare, to the existence, of this Government, to the successful conduct of this war, and to a peace which shall be enduring and for the best interest of this country. . . .

Mr. President, our Government, above all others, is founded on the right of the people freely to discuss all matters pertaining to their Government, in war not less than in peace. . . . How can that popular will express itself between elections except by meetings, by speeches, by publications, by petitions, and by addresses to the representatives of the people?

Any man who seeks to set a limit upon those rights, whether in war or peace, aims a blow at the most vital part of our Government. And then as the time for election approaches, and the official is called to account for his stewardship—not a day, not a week, not a month, before the election, but a year or more before it, if the people choose—they must have the right to the freest possible discussion of every question upon which their representative has acted, of the merits of every measure he has supported or opposed, of every vote he has cast and every speech that he has made. And before this great fundamental right every other must, if necessary, give way, for in no other manner can representative government be preserved.

VIEWPOINT 2

"The executive departments of the State and Nation are under a very solemn obligation to do whatever is necessary to prevent action . . . which will . . . bring aid and comfort to our enemies."

War Dissenters' Freedoms of Speech and Assembly Must Be Limited

Outlook

In the United States during World War I, the political activities of organizations seen as opposing the war effort were often suppressed. For example, the People's Council for Democracy and Peace, a prominent antiwar organization, experienced such repression when it attempted to hold its national convention in 1918. The group—whose membership included labor activists, socialists, and some German-American and Irish-American workers—favored repeal of draft laws, called for the government to issue a public statement of war aims, and adopted the slogan "Peace By Negotiation—Now."

The organization had scheduled a national convention to be held on September 1, 1918, in Minneapolis, Minnesota. The governor of that state, Joseph A.A. Burnquist, issued a proclamation on August 28 forbidding all meetings of the People's Council in any city in Minnesota on the grounds that such a meeting would give aid and comfort to America's enemies. Partly because of this proclamation, the council was unable to secure a meeting facility. Attempted relocations to North Dakota and Wisconsin also ran aground against local opposition. The council eventually convened in Chicago, Illinois, on September 1 for three hours before

Reprinted from "The Right of Public Assembly," Editorial, *Outlook*, September 12, 1917.

the meeting was broken up by local police and state militia.

The following viewpoint is taken from an editorial in the magazine *Outlook*. Referring to the recent controversy over the People's Council's troubles in assembling, the editors argue that speech and public meetings that give "aid and comfort to the enemy" are not protected under the Constitution. Therefore, they insist, federal and state government authorities have the right to prevent such meetings from taking place. People and organizations have no constitutional right to engage in activities that could do the American public harm by hindering the war effort, the editors of *Outlook* conclude.

There are no rights which do not imply corresponding duties and obligations. Of no rights is this truer than of the right of free speech and public assembly.

Apparently the great majority of those who are agitating against the Draft Law [the 1917 Selective Service Act] and who are pleading for an early peace—a peace which of necessity would be a German peace—have failed to understand this fundamental principle which underlies the right of free speech and free public assembly. A concrete instance of this misunderstanding has recently occupied a larger space than it deserved in the public prints. We refer to the agitation over the pacifist convention which has been denied the right of assembly in more than one State of the Union.

A Fundamental Right

No one denies, on the one hand, that the right of free assembly in a republic is one of the fundamental rights of the citizen. Democracy is imperiled without it. The people must be free to meet and to discuss public questions. And the mere fact that there is such a state of public feeling that an assembly may be broken into by a mob does not justify the prohibition of such an assembly. The right of free assembly must, however, be maintained by the authorities even in the face of threatened riots. This right to assemble is based on the purpose of the assembly. It is not limited by the danger or lack of danger of public disorder.

For example, the citizens of East St. Louis have a lawful right to meet and protest against the recent lynching of Negroes in that city. Any fear of riots caused by the rougher elements of East St. Louis would not justify the authorities from prohibiting such an assembly. If the Mayor did not have the power to protect such an assembly, he might temporarily postpone it, but only in order to enable him to call on the Governor, and, if necessary, on the President, for forces sufficient to keep order and to protect the right of free assembly. It must always be remembered that this right to free assembly even under the circumstances which we have described does not justify any body of citizens in claiming a right to use the public streets or the public parks for the purpose of such an assembly. They have no more right to take public property for such a purpose than they have to take private property without the consent of its owner.

For services rendered.

During World War I, war dissenters were often viewed as traitors. This Los Angeles Daily Times *cartoon from April 6, 1917, depicts Wisconsin senator Robert La Follette—who opposed U.S. entry into World War I—as receiving a medal from Germany.*

There is, on the other hand, nothing in the right of free assembly which entitles any body of citizens to hold a meeting for an unlawful purpose on either public or private property, no matter how freely permission to hold such a meeting may be granted by the owners or owner. Burglars or train robbers have no right to meet for the purpose of planning a robbery. Before the Civil War the border ruffians of Missouri had no right to meet for the purpose of planning a raid upon Kansas, and to-day the liquor-sellers and bootleggers of Kansas have no right to meet in order to plan a scheme of organized resistance to the Prohibition Law of that State.

Such offenses against the public peace can be readily recognized by even the most pro-German of our pacifists. But they fail to recognize what the overwhelming majority of our citizens do recognize—that treason in time of war is an attack on public security enormously greater than any of the peace-time offenses which we have above described.

War and Treason

In time of war any overt act which gives aid and comfort to the enemy is treason. The intent of an act is determined by its evident effect. It is entirely possible that the effect of the mere call for such an assembly as certain pacifists have recently attempted to hold was to give aid and comfort to the enemies of the United States. the effect of such a call is rightly judged, not only from the announced purpose of the assembly, but also from the private utterances of the leaders of the movement. Certainly, in any case, the people of the country have a right to assume that the decisions of the governors and mayors who prohibit such an assembly within their several jurisdictions were based on just and reasonable grounds. If these executive officers were convinced that the intent or effect of such a meeting would have been to give aid and comfort to our enemies, no one, no matter how passionate his championship of the right of free assembly, need complain of its prohibition.

Preventive law is as legitimate as preventive medicine. The law continually steps in to prevent a wrong from being perpetrated. It does not wait until it is perpetrated before it attempts to prohibit or punish. If a policeman sees a thug holding a blackjack over the head of an unarmed citizen, he does not wait until the blackjack falls before he attempts to arrest the offender.

In war time the duty of prompt preventive action is especially laid upon the executive. We do not have to wait until injury is done, until the blackjack falls, or conscription is halted or the collection of taxes made difficult, or until that public confidence necessary to the vigorous prosecution of a war is undermined, before our executives can act. The executive departments of the State and Nation are under a very solemn obligation to do whatever is necessary to prevent action by irresponsible or malicious parties which will interfere with the prosecution of the war, and so bring aid and comfort to our enemies.

The outcry that is now heard against conscription or war taxes or military despotism or interference with free assembly and free speech was much more virulent and widespread in the North during the Civil War than it has been against the loyal executives of our cities, our States, and our National Government to-day. Nevertheless, our present-day pacifists can learn much to their advantage if they study the comment of history upon the Copperheads [Confederate sympathizers from the North] of the Civil War. To-day the leaders of the South who fought in the open are honored throughout the United States on a common footing with the soldiers who fought to preserve the Union. But there will never be any monuments erected, either North or South, to the Vallandighams and Copperheads who stabbed in the back the Government they did not have the courage to fight against in the open.

"The compelling motive for refusing to comply with the draft act is my uncompromising opposition to the principle of conscription of life by the State for any purpose whatever."

A Defense of Draft Law Defiance

Roger N. Baldwin (1884–1981)

Thousands of men drafted during World War I chose to become conscientious objectors (COs) because of their political and/or religious beliefs opposing war. Roger N. Baldwin was one of several hundred COs who were imprisoned for refusing to serve in the U.S. military.

In 1917, Baldwin helped found and direct the Civil Liberties Bureau, an office of the American Union Against Militarism. The bureau, which later became an independent organization, provided legal counsel to conscientious objectors and war dissenters who had been victimized by mob violence or who faced criminal prosecution for hindering the war effort. In October 1918 Baldwin received a summons to report for an army physical examination; he instead turned himself in to the civil authorities as a willful violator of the military draft.

On October 30, 1918, Baldwin was sentenced by federal judge Julius M. Mayer to the maximum prison term of one year. In many ways, however, Baldwin was fortunate. Most of the 20,900 COs who were drafted during World War I were inducted into the army, where many were subject to brutal mistreatment in army camps. Several hundred "absolutists" (who refused to perform noncombatant service or cooperate with military authorities in any way) were tried by military courts and sentenced up to twenty years in military prison.

Reprinted from Roger N. Baldwin, *The Individual and the State: The Problem as Presented by the Sentencing of Roger N. Baldwin* (New York, n.p., 1918).

The following viewpoint is taken from the statement Baldwin made before the court just prior to his sentencing. Explaining why he has taken a position of disobedience, Baldwin argues that he has no choice but to obey his conscience and refuse to serve in the U.S. military or to cooperate with the U.S. government in matters concerning the war. Following the completion of his sentence, Baldwin resumed his work in the area of civil liberties. He was one of the founders of the American Civil Liberties Union in 1920 and served as its director from 1920 until 1950.

I am before you as a deliberate violator of the draft act. On October 9, when ordered to take a physical examination, I notified my local board that I declined to do so, and instead presented myself to the United States Attorney for prosecution. . . .

The compelling motive for refusing to comply with the draft act is my uncompromising opposition to the principle of conscription of life by the State for any purpose whatever, in time of war or peace. I not only refuse to obey the present conscription law, but I would in future refuse to obey any similar statute which attempts to direct my choice of service and ideals. I regard the principle of conscription of life as a flat contradiction of all our cherished ideals of individual freedom, democratic liberty and Christian teaching.

I am the more opposed to the present act, because it is for the purpose of conducting war. I am opposed to this and all other wars. I do not believe in the use of physical force as a method of achieving any end, however good.

The District Attorney calls your attention, your Honor, to the inconsistency in my statement to him that I would, under extreme emergencies, as a matter of protecting the life of any person, use physical force. I don't think that is an argument that can be used in support of the wholesale organization of men to achieve political purposes in nationalistic or domestic wars. I see no relationship at all between the two.

My opposition is not only to direct military service but to any service whatever designed to help prosecute the war. I could accept no service, therefore, under the present act, regardless of its character. . . .

I realize that to some this refusal may seem a piece of wilful defiance. It might well be argued that any man holding my views might have avoided the issue by obeying the law, either on the chance of being rejected on physical grounds, or on the chance of the war stopping before a call to service. I answer that I am not seeking to evade the draft; that I scorn evasion, compromise and gambling with moral issues. It may further be argued that the War Department's liberal provision for agricultural service on furlough for conscientious objectors would be open to me if I obey the law and go to camp, and that there can be no moral objection to farming, even in time of war. I answer first, that I am opposed to any service under conscription, regardless of whether that service is in itself morally objectionable; and second, that even if that were not the case, and I were opposed only to war, I can make no moral distinction between the various services which assist in prosecuting the war—whether rendered in the trenches, in the purchase of bonds or thrift stamps at home, or in raising farm products under the lash of the draft act. All serve the same end—war. Of course all of us render involuntary assistance to the war in the processes of our daily living. I refer only to those direct services undertaken by choice.

I am fully aware that my position is extreme, that it is shared by comparatively few, and that in the present temper it is regarded either as unwarranted egotism or as a species of feeble-mindedness. I cannot, therefore, let this occasion pass without attempting to explain the foundations on which so extreme a view rests.

An American Upbringing

I have had an essentially American upbringing and background. Born in a suburban town of Boston, Massachusetts, of the stock of the first settlers, I was reared in the public schools and at Harvard College. Early my mind was caught by the age-old struggle for freedom; America meant to me a vital new experiment in free political institutions; personal freedom to choose one's way of life and service seemed the essence of the liberties brought by those who fled the medieval and modern tyrannies of the old world. But I rebelled at our whole autocratic industrial system—with its wreckage of poverty, disease and crime, and childhood robbed of its right to free growth. So I took up social work upon leaving college, going to St. Louis as director of a settlement and instructor in sociology at Washington University. For ten years I have been professionally engaged in social work and political reform, local and national. That program of studied, directed social progress, step by step, by public agitation and legislation, seemed to me the practical way of effective service to gradually freeing the mass of folks from industrial and political bondage. At the same time I was attracted to the solutions of our social problems put forth by the radicals. I studied the programs of socialism, the I.W.W. [Industrial Workers of the World], European syndicalism and anarchism. I attended their meetings, knew their leaders. Some of them became my close personal friends.

Sympathizing with their general ideals of a free society, with much of their program, I yet could see no effective way of practical daily service. Some six years ago, however, I was so discouraged with social work and reform, so challenged by the sacrifices and idealism of some of my I.W.W. friends, that I was on the point of getting out altogether, throwing respectability overboard and joining the I.W.W. as a manual worker.

I thought better of it. My traditions were against it. It was more an emotional reaction than a practical form of service. But ever since, I have felt myself heart and soul with the world-wide radical movements for industrial and political freedom,—wherever and however expressed—and more and more impatient with reform.

Personally, I share the extreme radical philosophy of the future society. I look forward to a social order without any external restraints upon the individual, save through public opinion and the opinion of friends and neighbors. I am not a member of any radical organization, nor do I wear any tag by which my views may be classified. I believe that all parts of the radical movement serve the common end—freedom for the individual from arbitrary external controls.

When the war came to America, it was an immediate challenge to me to help protect those ideals of liberty which seemed to me not only the basis of the radical economic view, but of the radical political view of the founders of this Republic, and of the whole medieval struggle for religious freedom. Before the war was declared I severed all my connections in St. Louis, and offered my services to the American Union Against Militarism to help fight conscription. Later, that work developed into the National Civil Liberties Bureau, organized to help maintain the rights of free speech and free press, and the Anglo-Saxon tradition of liberty of conscience, through liberal provisions for conscientious objectors. This work has been backed by both pro-war liberals and so-called pacifists. It is not anti-war in any sense. It seemed to me the one avenue of service open to me, consistent with my views, with the country's best interest, and with the preservation of the radical minority for the struggle after the war. Even if I were not a believer in radical theories and movements, I would justify the work I have done on the ground of American ideals and traditions alone—as do many of those who have been associated with me. They have stood for those enduring principles which the revolutionary demands of war have temporarily set aside. We have stood against hysteria, mob-violence, unwarranted prosecution, the sinister use of patriotism to cover attacks on radical and labor movements, and for the unabridged right of a fair trial under war statutes. We have tried to keep open those channels of expression which stand for the kind of world order for which the President is battling today against the tories and militarists.

Now comes the Government to take me from that service and to demand of me a service I cannot in conscience undertake. I refuse it simply for my own peace of mind and spirit, for the satisfaction of that inner demand more compelling then any consideration of punishment or the sacrifice of friendships and reputation. I seek no martyrdom, no publicity. I merely meet as squarely as I can the moral issue before me, regardless of consequences.

I realize that your Honor may virtually commit me at once to the military authorities, and that I may have merely taken a

---

The Social Value of Heresy

Norman Thomas was one of the leading defenders of conscientious objectors during World War I. A Presbyterian minister who in future years would run for president as the nominee of the Socialist Party, Thomas was a close friend of Roger N. Baldwin and worked for him in the Civil Liberties Bureau. The following passage is taken from Thomas's 1917 pamphlet War's Heretics: A Plea for the Conscientious Objector.

We are not now pleading that our critics recognize that conscientious objectors are right in their opposition to war. We are not claiming a monopoly of idealism for ourselves or denying that men may seek our name from unworthy motives. Our interest is deeper than securing justice for ourselves. We are pleading for recognition of the social value of heresy. Every movement worth while began with a minority. Democracy degenerates into mobocracy unless the rights of the minority are respected. The church of the Middle Ages made the sincerest, most magnificent effort in history to coerce the individual's conscience for the sake not only of the eternal welfare of his soul, but of the church universal. At last she recognized her failure, but not until she had done incalculable damage. Her own sons rejoice in that failure. Now the state, less universal in its outlook, less definite in its dogma, sets itself up as a secular deity and demands not the outward conformity which usually satisfied the church, but active participation in doing that which is to its heretic sons the supreme denial of their sense of righteousness. It deliberately thinks it can save democracy by this final act of autocracy. Gone is our belief in the power of ideas, in the might of right. America, founded by exiles for conscience's sake, their refuge in all generations, gives her sons the option of service in the trenches or imprisonment and thereby wounds her very soul as no outward victory of Prussian power can do. The heretic may be very irritating, he may be decidedly wrong, but the attempt to choke heresy or dissent from the dominant opinion by coercing the conscience is an incalculable danger to society. If war makes it necessary, it is the last count in the indictment against war.

quicker and more inconvenient method of arriving at a military camp. I am prepared for that—for the inevitable pressure to take an easy way out by non-combatant service—with guard-house confinement—perhaps brutalities, which hundreds of other objectors have already suffered and are suffering today in camps. I am prepared for court martial and sentence to military prison, to follow the 200–300 objectors already sentenced to terms of 10–30 years for their loyalty to their ideals. I know that the way is easy for those who accept what to me is compromise, hard for those who refuse, as I must, any service whatever. And I know further, in military prison I shall refuse to conform to the rules for military salutes and the like, and will suffer solitary confinement on bread and water, shackled to the bars of a cell eight hours a day—as are men of like convictions at this moment.

I am not complaining for myself or others. I am merely advising the court that I understand full well the penalty of my heresy, and am prepared to pay it. The conflict with conscription is irreconcilable. Even the liberalism of the President and Secretary of War in dealing with objectors leads those of us who are "absolutists" to a punishment longer and severer than that of desperate criminals.

But I believe most of us are prepared even to die for our faith, just as our brothers in France are dying for theirs. To them we are comrades in spirit—we understand one another's motives, though our methods are wide apart. We both share deeply the common experience of living up to the truth as we see it, whatever the price.

Though at the moment I am of a tiny minority, I feel myself just one protest in a great revolt surging up from among the people—the struggle of the masses against the rule of the world by the few—profoundly intensified by the war. It is a struggle against the political state itself, against exploitation, militarism, imperialism, authority in all forms. It is a struggle to break in full force only after the war. Russia already stands in the vanguard, beset by her enemies in the camps of both belligerents—the Central Empires break asunder from within—the labor movement gathers revolutionary force in Britain—and in our own country the Nonpartisan League, radical labor and the Socialist Party hold the germs of a new social order. Their protest is my protest. Mine is a personal protest at a particular law, but it is backed by all the aspirations and ideals of the struggle for a world freed of our manifold slaveries and tyrannies.

I ask the Court for no favor. I could do no other than what I have done, whatever the Court's decree. I have no bitterness or hate in my heart for any man. Whatever the penalty I shall endure it, firm in the faith that whatever befalls me, the principles in which I believe will bring forth out of this misery and chaos, a world of brotherhood, harmony and freedom for each to live the truth as he sees it.

I hope your Honor will not think that I have taken this occasion to make a speech for the sake of making a speech. I have read you what I have written in order that the future record for myself and for my friends may be perfectly clear. . . . I know that it is pretty nigh hopeless in times of war and hysteria to get across to any substantial body of people the view of an out and out heretic like myself. I know that as far as my principles are concerned, they seem to be utterly impractical—mere moonshine. They are not the views that work in the world today. I fully realize that. But I fully believe that they are the views which are going to guide in the future.

Having arrived at the state of mind in which those views mean the dearest things in life to me, I cannot consistently, with self-respect, do other than I have, namely, to deliberately violate an act which seems to me to be a denial of everything which ideally and in practice I hold sacred.

VIEWPOINT 4

"A Republic can last only so long as its laws are obeyed."

Military Draft Laws Must Be Obeyed

Julius M. Mayer (1865–1925)

Of the 23.8 million Americans who registered for the military draft during World War I, 64,700 sought conscientious objector (CO) status. The 1917 Selective Service Act provided for such applications; the decision of who would be granted CO status rested with local community draft boards staffed by civilian volunteers. These boards generally granted CO status to Quakers, Mennonites, and members of other historical "peace" churches whose religious teachings forbade all violence. Those granted CO status were allowed to choose noncombatant service within the military. This arrangement failed to resolve all conflicts, however. A minority of COs refused noncombatant service or any cooperation with the military, leading to numerous confrontations with civilian and military authorities. In addition, many objectors were not members of peace churches, but instead refused military service based on economic, political, or ethical reasons. Such stances were not provided for in the draft law or recognized as valid by most draft boards.

Opinion about COs, both within the American military and the general public, was harsh; COs were often seen as shirkers, cowards, or traitors. One minister defined a CO as "a man who uses his religion to cloak a yellow streak." Nonreligious objectors were especially viewed as insincere. Leonard Wood, commanding general of several army training camps, wrote in a letter to the father of a draft resister that many "alleged conscientious objectors" were not "sincere religious objectors" but instead were "avowed

Reprinted from Julius M. Mayer remarks on sentencing Roger N. Baldwin in *The Individual and the State: The Problem as Presented by the Sentencing of Roger N. Baldwin* (New York, n.p., 1918).

enemies of this Government" who were "opposing the Government in the efforts which it is making to crush autocracy." Such persons, many Americans believed, should not be allowed to evade their responsibilities to the nation when called to military service or to defy the legal authority of the U.S. government.

Federal judge Julius M. Mayer, a former New York state attorney general, presided over several cases involving World War I dissenters (including the 1917 trial of anarchists Emma Goldman and Alexander Berkman, who were convicted and sentenced to prison for conspiracy to organize draft resistance). On October 30, 1918, Mayer served as the sentencing judge of Roger N. Baldwin, a civil liberties activist who had voluntarily turned himself in as a draft violator. The following viewpoint is taken from Mayer's remarks made in sentencing Baldwin to the maximum sentence of one year—comments made in part to respond to Baldwin's own statement of views (see prior viewpoint). Mayer argues that obedience to the law is essential for the United States to maintain "a Government of free people." He charges that the stance of disobedience taken by Baldwin and other draft resisters not only harms America's war effort but could conceivably lead to the destruction of America's system of government.

I have not any question at all in my mind that the position which you have announced as being held by you is honestly and conscientiously held.

In one regard, out of a considerable number of cases that are of similar character, you do stand out in that you have retained your self-respect, because you state to the Court your position without quibble, and you don't seek to avoid the consequences of that position, as some others, who have been much louder in words, have done, by taking the chance of a trial and the possibility of escaping through either some technicality of the law or through some inability of a Jury to decide appropriately on the facts.

And therefore I want you to distinctly understand, as I think you will, with your ability and intelligence, that I deal with the disposition of your case entirely from the standpoint of the law. And although our individual views are not considered as a matter of import, it may or may not be some satisfaction to know, that while your views are exactly opposite to those that I entertain, I cannot help but contrast in my mind your self-respecting and manly position in stating views which to my mind are intolerable, but which are so stated as to at least put your case in a somewhat different position from that of others to which I referred.

Now, it may be impossible for me to convey to your mind successfully the point of view which I think is entertained by the great masses of the people, and which must be entertained by the Courts and by those, such as the Department of Justice, who are charged with the administration of the law.

Laws Must Be Obeyed

In all that you have said, I think that you have lost sight of one very fundamental and essential thing for the preservation of that American liberty of which by tradition you feel that you are a genuine upholder. A Republic can last only so long as its laws are obeyed. The freest discussion is permitted, and should be invited in the processes that lead up to the enactment of a statute. There should be the freest opportunity of discussion as to the methods of the administration of the statutes. But the Republic must cease to exist if disobedience to any law enacted by the orderly process laid down by the constitution is in the slightest degree permitted. That is, from my point of view, fundamental. That is the sense, not only from an ideal standpoint, but from a practical standpoint. We should not be able, as I think most Americans believe, to maintain what we regard as a Government of free people, if some individual, whether from good or bad motives, were able successfully to violate a statute, duly and constitutionally and properly passed, because his own view of the same might differ from that entertained by the law makers who have enacted the law, and from that of the Executive who has given it his approval.

Now that is my point of view, based upon a system whose perpetuity rests upon obedience of the law.

It may often be that a man or woman has greater foresight than the masses of the people. And it may be that in the history of things, he, who seems to be wrong today, may be right tomorrow. But with those possible idealistic and academic speculations a Court has nothing to do.

I don't take into consideration any of the details of the organization [the National Civil Liberties Bureau] with which you were connected. I cannot and will not endeavor to arrive at any conclusions as to whether its activities were good, bad, or indifferent. If it should come before the Court sometime, why then the Court, however composed, will deal with the subject matter as the evidence may justify. I am concerned only with your perfectly definite, frank statement that you decline to take a step which the law provides. I am directing my mind solely to the indictment to which you plead guilty. You are entirely right. There can be no compromise. There can be neither compromise by you as the defendant, as you say, because you don't wish to compromise. Nor

168

can there be compromise by the Court, which, for the moment, represents organized society as we understand it in this Republic. He who disobeys the law, knowing that he does so, with the intelligence that you possess, must, as you are prepared to do—take the consequences.

Slackers and Pro-Germans

In a September 1918 speech in Minneapolis, Minnesota, former president Theodore Roosevelt expressed the views of many Americans toward conscientious objectors.

We have heard much of the conscientious objectors to military service, the outcry having been loudest among those objectors who are not conscientious at all but who are paid or unpaid agents of the German Government.

It is certain that only a small fraction of the men who call themselves conscientious objectors in this matter are actuated in any way by conscience. The bulk are slackers, pure and simple, or else traitorous pro-Germans. Some are actuated by lazy desire to avoid any duty that interferes with their ease and enjoyment, some by the evil desire to damage the United States and help Germany, some by sheer, simple, physical timidity.

When at times there have been brought in here, ignorant men—men of low intelligence—men who have lacked opportunity of education and cannot see things clearly—the Court, by whatever judge may be sitting, has seen its way clear to make the punishment light, where theoretically, under the statutes it might be made severe. You have made my task this morning an entirely easy one. I have no difficulty in concluding how your case will be treated, because at the moment you represent one extreme of thought, and in my capacity at the moment, I represent another. I cannot emphasize too strongly that in my view, not only could this war not have been successfully and in a self-respecting way carried on by the United States Government if such an attitude as yours had prevailed, but I think such an attitude would have led inevitably to disorder and finally to the destruction of a Government, which with all of the imperfections that may attach to human government, has proved itself, as I view it, to be a real people's Government, as evidence by the millions upon millions of men who voluntarily obey the laws—and some of them requiring great sacrifice—which, as enacted by the legislature, embody the judgment of the people at large.

Now in such circumstances, you representing the utterly contrary view, you representing—although possibly not meaningly—a position which in my judgment if carried out would mean the subversion of all the principles dear to the American people, and the ultimate destruction of the Republic, there is nothing left for me to do except to impose the full penalty of the statute. It would be obviously most unwise to permit you to go into the army now, and there become a disturbing element and cause the military authorities only an increase to the many great and difficult problems with which they are now dealing. The case is one, from the standpoint of the penalty to be imposed, no different from that which has been imposed in many similar cases. The maximum penalty, as I understand it, is one year in the penitentiary. You have already spent twenty days in imprisonment. You ask for no compromise. You will get no compromise. You are sentenced to the penitentiary for eleven months and ten days.

"Every man and woman in this country must realize that the first duty they can perform for their country is to take some of these bonds."

War Funds Can Be Raised Through Bonds

William Gibbs McAdoo (1863–1941)

An important question the United States faced after it entered World War I was how to raise the enormous sums of money necessary for its prosecution (the total direct cost of the war would eventually amount to $35.5 billion, a greater sum than the entire expenditures of the U.S. government in its first century of existence). Americans were divided on how best to raise this money. The approach eventually favored by William Gibbs McAdoo, secretary of the treasury from 1913 to 1918, was to obtain the bulk of the funds through a series of government bond drives. McAdoo named the bonds "Liberty Loans" and orchestrated a massive public relations campaign that included posters, speeches by motion picture stars, and other features designed to raise general public support for the war effort as well as financial backing.

McAdoo announced the first of the Liberty Loans on May 14, 1917: a $2 billion offering of bonds with an interest rate of 3½ percent, exempt from federal taxes, and convertible to a higher rate if the government raised interest rates for future Liberty Loans. The following viewpoint is taken from a speech that McAdoo made one week later before bankers and business executives in Des Moines, Iowa. McAdoo describes the features of the Liberty Loan and urges patriotic Americans to subscribe. He maintains that such bond measures are the best way to finance both the war effort and the credits and loans America has extended to the Allies.

Reprinted from William Gibbs McAdoo, address entered into S. Doc. 40, 65th Cong., 1st sess., May 21, 1917.

Wars can not be fought without money. The very first step in this war, the most effective step that we could take, was to provide the money for its conduct. The Congress quickly passed an act authorizing a credit of $5,000,000,000, and empowered the Secretary of the Treasury, with the approval of the President, to extend to the allied Governments making war with us against the enemies of our country, credits not exceeding $3,000,000,000. Since that law was passed—it was only passed on the 24th of April, less than a month ago—the financial machinery of your Government has been speeded up to top notch to give relief to the allies in Europe, in order that they might be able to make their units in the trenches, their machinery which is there on the ground, tell to the utmost, and tell, if possible, so effectively that it might not be necessary to send American soldiers to the battle fields. As a result, we have already extended in credits to these Governments—Great Britain, France, Italy, Russia, and Belgium—something like $745,000,000, and we shall have to extend before this year is out, if the war lasts that long, not $3,000,000,000 of credits, but probably five billions or six billions. But it makes no difference how much credit we extend, we are extending it for a service which is essential . . . for your own protection, if no other grave issues were involved in this struggle.

Extending Credit

This initial financing was not an easy thing to do. The Congress authorized the Secretary of the Treasury to issue, in addition to bonds, $3,000,000,000 of one-year debt certificates. Their purpose is to bridge over any chasms, so to speak, so that if the Treasury is short at any time, because of extraordinary demands, we can sell these temporary certificates, supply the need, and then sell bonds to take up these certificates. We have been selling temporary debt certificates in anticipation of the sale of these Liberty bonds. The first issue of bonds,—$2,000,000,000,—has not been determined by any arbitrary decision or judgment; it has been determined by the actual necessities of the situation. It is the least possible sum that we can afford to provide for the immediate conduct of the war. We are trying to spread the payment for the bonds over as large a period as possible, so that there shall be no interference with business. This money is not going to be taken out of the country. All of this financing is largely a matter of shifting credits; it is not going to involve any loss of gold; it is not going to involve any loss of values. These moneys are going to be put back into circulation, put back promptly into the channels of business and circulated and recirculated to take care of the abnormal prosperity of the country, a prosperity that will be greater in the present year than ever before in our history. As we sell these bonds we take back from the foreign governments, under the terms of the act, their obligations, having practically the same maturity as ours, bearing the same rate of interest as ours, so that as their obligations mature the proceeds will be employed to pay off the obligations issued by this Government to provide them with credit. So you can see, fellow citizens, that in extending credit to our allies we are not giving anything to them. So far as that is concerned, for the purposes of this war, I would be willing to give them anything to gain success, but they don't ask that. They are glad and grateful that the American Government is willing to give them the benefit of its matchless credit, a credit greater and stronger than any nation on the face of the globe. We give them credit at the same price our Government has to pay you, its people, for the use of the money, because we do not want to make any profit on our allies. We do not want to profit by the blood that they must shed upon the battle field in the same cause in which we are engaged.

Colorful posters were a mainstay of the campaigns to persuade Americans to take out "Liberty Loans" or "Liberty Bonds."

What Must Be Done

What can you do to make this loan a success? You have got to work, gentlemen, to make this loan a success. America never before was offered a $2,000,000,000 issue of bonds. This Government never has had to borrow so much money at one time. The money is in the country and can be had if you men will simply say that the Government can have it. The annual increase of our wealth is estimated to be fifty billions of dollars. You are asked not to give anything to your Government, but merely to invest 4 per cent of the annual increase of wealth in this country, to take back from your Government the strongest security on the face of God's earth, and to receive in return for it 3½ per cent per annum, exempted from all taxation, with the further provision that if the Government issues any other bonds during the period of this war at a higher rate of interest than 3½ per cent every man who has bought a 3½ per cent bond may turn it in and get a new bond at the higher rate of interest. Could anything be fairer than that? Could anything be more secure than an obligation of your Government, an obligation backed not alone by the honor of the American people—which of itself is sufficient—but backed also by the resources of the richest nation in the world, a nation whose aggregate wealth to-day is two hundred and fifty billions of dollars; so that you take no risk, my friends, in buying these bonds.

This bond offering is not going to be successful of its own momentum. Every man and woman in this country must realize that the first duty they can perform for their country is to take some of these bonds. Those who are not able to take some of these bonds ought to begin saving monthly to take some of them; and if they can not save monthly, or at all, they ought to make some man or woman who is able to take some of these bonds subscribe. If you do that, my friends, this first issue of $2,000,000,000 will be largely oversubscribed. It depends, however, upon you. Your Government can not do what you can do for your Government. A government is not worth a continental unless it has the support of the people of the country. And one thing that makes me glad—I ought not to be glad that there is a war—but I can not help feeling a certain amount of reverent elation that God has called us to this great duty, not alone to vindicate the ideals that inspire us but also because it has, for the time being, eliminated detestable partisanism from our national life and made us one solid people. As one people, my friends, with such an ideal, the Republic is invincible and irresistible, and there can be no doubt whatever of the outcome. I want you to give a thunderous reply on the 15th of June—Liberty bond subscription day—to the enemies of your country.

VIEWPOINT 6

"We should collect more taxes in proportion to the amount of bonds that are being sold to finance the war."

War Funds Should Be Raised Through Increased Taxes

George Huddleston (1869–1960)

During World War I, Congress grappled with the question of what ratio of war costs should be raised by taxation and what part by borrowing through government bonds. Many in Congress believed that raising the federal income tax and taxes on business profits would not only help pay for the war but would also help equalize the nation's distribution of wealth.

George Huddleston was a veteran of the Spanish American War and a Democratic representative from Alabama from 1915 to 1937. In the following viewpoint, Huddleston argues that too much money has been raised by borrowing, thereby weakening the war effort by causing inflation and stimulating nonproductive use of America's resources. Responding to critics who believe increased taxes would harm businesses, he examines the profits made by one of America's largest companies, the United States Steel Corporation. That company and others can well afford to pay additional taxes and therefore should be taxed more on their profits, Huddleston concludes.

Both government borrowing and taxation reached unprecedented heights during World War I. The national debt increased from about a billion dollars in 1915 to more than twenty billion in

Reprinted from George Huddleston, address to the U.S. House of Representatives, April 6, 1918, *Congressional Record*, vol. 56, part 5, 65th Cong., 2nd sess., pp. 4738–39.

1920. The war also resulted in a permanent shift in the nation's tax policies. Prior to the war, three- quarters of federal tax revenues came from customs and excise taxes. After the war about the same proportion would come from taxes on incomes, estates, and business profits.

A few days ago I took occasion to comment in the House upon the unwisdom of our ratio of bond issues to taxation. I expressed the opinion that we should collect more taxes in proportion to the amount of bonds that are being sold to finance the war. The view was expressed at that time by certain Members that business could not stand higher taxation; that higher taxes would cripple business.

Examining One Company

I desire now to further refer to that subject and to answer the claim that business will be crippled by increased taxes. I wish to take up the case of the United States Steel Corporation. I refer to that concern for a number of reasons. The first is that it employs 25,000 men, or thereabouts, in my own district, and I believe that comment of this kind ought, like charity, to begin at home. I refer to that concern also because it is the largest employer of labor in the United States.

I refer to it because, on account of its wealth and influence, of the power that it wields, it has been able to get along and carry on its operations without recognizing the right of men who toil to organize, to form themselves into labor unions. The United States Steel Corporation has never recognized any such right upon the part of the men who work for it. Itself constituting the greatest industrial organization in this country, having, as has been charged in the courts, a monopoly of ore supplies, enjoying enormous influence and wealth, thoroughly organized itself, its vast activities carried on under the direction of one or two supreme heads, it has denied to the 275,000 men who work for it the same right, the right to organize and to bargain collectively with their employer.

I also refer to this corporation because it has steadfastly refused to give recognition to the basic eight-hour day. It has refused to allow the principle advocated by the President of the United States, that society has reached the point where it recognizes the justice of the eight-hour day. Men are now compelled to work for the Steel Corporation 8 hours, or 10, or 12 hours, or whatever number of hours the employer demands, without any regard to overtime or of the justice of the eight-hour principle. Therefore it seems fair, in view of all these things that distinguish this great industrial concern, that we should take it as a type and look to it and see what it is doing in this time of war and national distress and what profits it is realizing.

I hold in my hand the report for 1917, recently issued to its stockholders by the United States Steel Corporation. It is not a clear report. I do not think that an accountant could take this report and find out what the net profits of the Steel Corporation were for last year. I will not presume to say that the report is intended to mislead; I will not make that charge. I do say that the profits that the Steel Corporation was able to make during last year are so covered up in it that, although it purports to be a real exposition of that subject, it is impossible for any man, accountant, layman, or whatever he may be, to tell from the report just what it earned.

The Need for Fair Taxation

On May 27, 1918, shortly before Congress was to adjourn, President Woodrow Wilson asked the members to approve additional revenues for the war and called for greater taxation to raise the money.

The facts are these: Additional revenues must manifestly be provided for. It would be a most unsound policy to raise too large a proportion of them by loan, and it is evident that the four billions now provided for by taxation will not of themselves sustain the greatly enlarged budget to which we must immediately look forward. . . .

Enormous loans freely spent in the stimulation of industry of almost every sort produce inflations and extravagances which presently make the whole economic structure questionable and insecure and the very basis of credit is cut away. Only fair, equitably distributed taxation, of the widest incidence and drawing chiefly from the sources which would be likely to demoralize credit by their very abundance, can prevent inflation and keep our industrial system free of speculation and waste. We shall naturally turn, therefore, I suppose, to war profits and incomes and luxuries for the additional taxes.

There are, however, statements in this report that throw some light upon its operations. For illustration, the report states that the net earnings of the Steel Corporation for last year were $304,000,000. That is to say, the net earnings, after deducting *"allowances for estimated proportion of extraordinary cost of facilities installed by reason of war requirements and conditions, also taxes—in-*cluding an estimate of $233,465,435 for account of Federal income, war income, and war excess-profits taxes payable in

1918—but exclusive of charge for interest on outstanding bonds, mortgages, and purchase obligations of the subsidiary companies," amounted to $304,161,471.53.

The report states that after making those deductions the net earnings of the corporation were $304,161,471.53. How much would have been shown if those legitimate items had been added—and they ought to have been added if the statement was intended as a candid presentation of the earnings of the company—how much they would have been shown to be with such items included can not be learned from this report.

I do observe, however, the statement that $233,465.435 has been set apart to pay Federal income, war income, and war excess-profits taxes payable in 1918. Using that as a basis, and making the best calculation that an expert can make from these figures, which is, take them as 32 per cent of the taxable income of the company, the net earnings of the Steel Corporation for last year was in the neighborhood of $729,000,000. So much for that.

Now, let us see what the earnings of the concern applicable to dividends were according to its own statement. This corporation has $508,302,500 common stock, commonly believed to be practically pure water, without hardly the color of value having gone into the assets of the company. It has $360,281,100 of 7 per cent preferred stock and has a bonded debt, it and its subsidiaries, of $586,828,875.89. Out of the $304,161,471.53 net earnings, as shown by its report to remain after making all deductions for taxes, replacements, and so forth, charged off, the Steel Corporation paid $25,219,677 as the dividend of 7 per cent on its preferred stock, and the interest on all its bonded indebtedness amounting to $30,125,594.67, making a total of $55,345,271.67, which, taken from the earnings of $304,161,471.53, shows that for 1917 alone the net profits of this corporation applicable to the common stock were $248,816,199.86, which was 49 per cent earnings upon the common stock of that corporation for the space of one year.

Corporations Can Pay More Taxes

How can it be argued that a corporation earning such dividends as that can not stand further taxation? How can it be argued that corporations which earn practically 50 per cent upon their common stock, after paying all charges of every kind, should not in this time submit to further taxation? In 1914 the Steel Corporation made only $23,496,796; in 1915, $75,833,833; in 1916, $271,531.730, compared with its prewar average profits of $63,585,777 for the years 1911, 1912, and 1913.

What would have been the taxes of this corporation under the British law, according to the British rate of 80 per cent on excess profits and 25 per cent on average prewar earnings? The Steel

Corporation for the prewar years of 1911, 1912, and 1913 earned an average of $63,585,777 annually. On this average the British rate is 25 per cent, or $15,896,44, with a rate of 80 per cent upon the excess above that, which would have yielded the further sum of $371,531,378.40. The figures are based upon the statement in the report of net earnings of $304,161,471.53 plus the sum set apart for Federal taxes, $233,465,435, which makes a total income upon which taxes are to be paid, as admitted by the report, of $537,625,906.53. So that if the Steel Corporation had been doing business in Great Britain instead of America, in place of paying taxes of only $233,465,435 to the Government, it would pay $387,427,822 taxes to the Government. *So that by being in the United States instead of in Great Britain this corporation saves the tidy sum of $153,962,387 in taxes in one year.*

Had this corporation paid taxes according to the British rate of 80 per cent upon their excess profits it would still be able to place to the credit of the common stock 18.9 per cent for 1917 alone. Is not that enough in these war times? Is not that enough profit for even a war contractor to make in this time when men are laying down their lives for the flag?

The Steel Corporation is merely a type; it is merely one of many concerns which are making enormous profits. Such profit-making concerns may be numbered in thousands. I have no sympathy with corporation baiting, and I hope never to be guilty of it. But also I have no sympathy with profiteering when the country is torn with distress, when a million firesides are desolate, and when anguish is entering into a million American homes.

The matter of vast profits being earned that I have referred to relates to the ability of concerns situated as the United States Steel Corporation is to pay a greater rate of taxation than they are now paying. It relates to the justice of requiring higher rates of taxes from such concerns. It relates to the necessity, if we are going to present a clean face to our soldier boys when they come back from France, of having done our duty here while they are doing their duty over there, that we shall increase the taxes on those who are making big profits out of the war and make them furnish the money, so far as they are able while our boys are furnishing the manhood on the battle line.

Bonds and Inflation

But there is another aspect to this matter, a purely economic aspect, which does not heed the question of justice, which assumes that profiteers have the right to make all the money that can and that they should not be stayed in their operations. That is, whether it is good from an economic standpoint that we should allow such low rates of taxation at this time, and to issue bonds to get money to carry on the war. We are faced with an inflation of prices such as this country never saw. It began with the outbreak of the war in Europe. We then began to issue more money in this country. We have inflated the per capita circulation from $34.35 in 1914 until it is $49.70 per capita at this time. Practically all of that inflation took place before we entered the war. The result of that inflation was that prices went up and up and up until when we entered the war there had been an increase of over 50 per cent above prewar prices.

Of course, not all of that increase in prices was due to the inflation of circulation. Some of it was due to the laws of supply and demand. The least part of it was due to such laws. The most of it, in my judgment, was due to the fact that we inflated the circulation in this country and that there was a great return of American securities held in Europe prior to the outbreak of the war, those securities being sent back and resold in this country, which furnished a basis of credit and thereby business was stimulated and credits inflated and prices grossly increased. In addition to that, of course, was the fact that foreign countries were permitted to float their own securities in the United States to the extent of—I do not know how much—perhaps as much as $2,000,000,000, and that also furnished a basis of credit and aggravated the inflation.

But the fact remains that we have had an increase in prices of the necessaries of life since we went into the war of 21 per cent, according to the statement issued the other day by the Department of Labor. Now, we have not inflated the circulation very much since we entered the war. But we have issued bonds to the amount of billions of dollars. The bonds that have been issued in this country have been used largely as a basis of credit. There has been a tremendous stimulation of business. There has been a great increase in circulation due to that fact, and the result is that we have had this further increase of 21 per cent in prices since we entered the war. That great increase I attribute principally to the fact that we have been financing this war with bonds instead of financing it with taxes. The result, stated in another way, is that a man who had a dollar last April now has only 79 cents. The men with money all did one of two things. Either they were content with what they had, as far as a man with money is ever content with what he has, and they invested it in tax-free Government bonds and hid their money away so that we could not take it to help pay for the war, or they put it out and started it to work doing something. A man can not afford to hold idle money when it is going down as it has gone down in purchasing power during the past year. A man can not afford to hold idle money to-day, because it is going down still further, if we continue these bond issues. Therefore, he has got to put it into business or industry. And what is the result? There has been a tremendous stimulation of industry. Business is stimulated to a point that this country never saw before.

Hurting the Nation

The inflation of circulation and stimulation of business has made money plentiful, it has fallen into the hands of almost every class of citizens, and the people of the country are going on a joy ride of extravagance and financial profligacy. That applies to all persons more than professional men and those working for salaries; they have had the least out of this change. Practically all other classes are spending money with a free hand as they never did before; they are consuming more than they ever did before; they are eating more food and better food; they are throwing more food away; they are throwing away money on automobiles, find clothes, and luxuries as they never did before. All this means a waste of our strength and resources. Business is so stimulated that there is a greater consumption of raw materials of all kinds. There is a congestion in transportation; there is a general riot, as you might call it, of waste, lost motion, and extravagance going on all down the line. This does not injure alone the people who are spending the money, it does not hurt alone those who are wasting it, or the business men who are making the money freely and spending it in the same way; it hurts the Nation and it hurts the country as a whole and hinders us in carrying on the war.

Now, I have got to the point. It seems to me that every man who loves this country would want to devote its energies to essential things. We are giving too much of America's strength to things that have no relation to this war. Not one-tenth of our possible strength is going into pressing the war to victory. Men are busying themselves with making money. No man has the right to make money at this time beyond his absolute needs. We must curb business activity by laying a heavy tax on its profits; we must take away the inducement to profiteer; we must turn back into channels of war use all the waste of raw materials and muscle now consumed in profit-making business enterprises; we must release for war purposes the men, the capital, and the materials which have been diverted to activities which have no bearing on the war. This can be done effectively only by heavy taxation on profits.

CHAPTER 5

The Treaty of Versailles and the League of Nations

Chapter Preface

America declared war in April 1917, but most U.S. soldiers did not arrive in Europe until the following year. American forces first participated in combat in significant numbers in May and June 1918, when they helped the Allies contain Germany's spring offensive. Beginning in September 1918, 1.2 million soldiers under the command of General John J. Pershing participated in the Saint-Mihiel and Meuse-Argonne offensives as part of a general Allied campaign on the western front. American troops were successful in driving back the Germans, and many historians credit U.S. intervention for Germany's decision to seek an armistice in November 1918. Others argue, however, that it was the prospect of more and more American reinforcements, rather than U.S. victories on the battlefield, that caused the leaders of Germany to give up all hope of victory.

President Woodrow Wilson wanted more than just an Allied victory: He hoped that American military intervention would increase U.S. influence on the peace talks after the war. Maintaining that the United States had entered the conflict as an "associated" rather than an "allied" power, he sought to differentiate American goals from those of the Allies. Wilson summarized his vision of what the peace settlement should be in his famous "Fourteen Points" speech in January 1918. These war aims included an end to the making of secret treaties, a reduction of armaments, and the creation of an "association of nations" to prevent future wars.

Many Europeans on both sides of the war embraced Wilson's Fourteen Points, which were distributed in leaflet form throughout the western front as the fighting continued during most of 1918. When German leaders concluded in October that victory was impossible in the wake of Allied gains on the western front (and the surrender or impending surrender of all of Germany's military allies), they proposed to Wilson an armistice based on the Fourteen Points. After a month of negotiations between Germany, the United States, and the Allies (during which time Kaiser Wilhelm II abdicated and a German republic was proclaimed), Germany signed an armistice on November 11, 1918, ending the fighting that day at 11 A.M.

To help make his postwar vision a reality, President Wilson decided to travel to Europe himself as head of the American peace delegation at the Paris Peace Conference. This action made him the first U.S. president to leave the United States while in office. Arriving in France in December 1918, he was greeted by ecstatic crowds hailing him as a hero. Wilson's goal at Paris was to negotiate a peace treaty that would implement his Fourteen Points. He was especially anxious to replace the system of international diplomacy that had existed prior to World War I with a "League of Nations" that would preserve international law, protect the territorial integrity of nations, and prevent future wars through a system of collective security and negotiation.

In Paris, however, the Fourteen Points faced obstacles, primarily because America's allies did not share Wilson's idealism. Prior to U.S. entry into the war, the Allies had already signed secret treaties dividing territory and other spoils of war among themselves. The leaders of the major Allied nations, including Prime Minister David Lloyd George of Great Britain and Premier Georges Clemenceau of France, were skeptical of most of Wilson's proposals. After four years of war, they were intent on punishing Germany. Over the course of negotiations, Wilson agreed to the Allies' punitive demands. The resulting Treaty of Versailles officially pronounced Germany responsible for the war and made it liable for billions of dollars in reparations. Wilson compromised many of his original Fourteen Points in order to win diplomatic support for the League of Nations. He personally wrote much of the League Covenant (constitution) and insisted on incorporating it within the treaty itself, which was signed by Germany, the Allies, and the United States on June 28, 1919.

However, like all U.S. treaties, the Treaty of Versailles had to be ratified by a two-thirds vote in the Senate. Wilson returned to the United States in July 1919 with the Treaty of Versailles only to face opposition in the Republican-majority Senate. Some opponents of the treaty criticized it for its harsh demands on Germany, arguing that it betrayed too much of Wilson's original Fourteen Points. Others focused their objections on the League of Nations Covenant, especially Article X. This clause pledged mutual support of the territorial integrity and political independence of its members. By ensuring a united response of all member states against any nation using war to threaten another country, Wilson believed, the League could prevent future wars. Isolationists in the Senate feared instead that Article X would compel America to fight more wars—and to go to war without congressional approval. Senator Hiram Johnson of California spoke out against this provision, declaring "I am opposed to American boys policing Europe and quelling riots in every nation's back yard." Other critics, such as Henry Cabot Lodge, wanted to ensure that the United States would take military action only on its own terms and in defense of its own interests.

Attempting to appeal directly to the American people, Wilson embarked on a nationwide campaign to raise support for the League of Nations. The strenuous speaking tour was cut short, however, when the president collapsed from exhaustion after a speech in Pueblo, Colorado. Shortly after his return to Washington, he suffered a stroke that kept him bedridden and unable to work for months. Due to congressional opposition and Wilson's refusal to accept amendments or to compromise regarding the Covenant (a stubbornness some historians attribute to his ailing health), the Treaty of Versailles failed to win ratification in the Senate. The sweeping 1920 presidential election victory of Warren G. Harding, a Republican who called for a return to "normalcy," was viewed by many as a repudiation of Wilson's foreign policy and an expression of the American people's wishes to put World War I firmly behind them.

VIEWPOINT 1

"The peace that we win must guarantee full reparation for the awful cost of life and treasure which . . . Germany . . . has inflicted on the entire world."

Germany and Its Allies Must Be Punished

Theodore Roosevelt (1858–1919)

Theodore Roosevelt, president of the United States from 1901 to 1909 and the presidential candidate of the Progressive Party in 1912, remained an outspoken and influential voice in American public affairs during World War I. A frequent critic of Woodrow Wilson both before and after American entry into the war, Roosevelt unsuccessfully sought permission to raise and command an American volunteer division in Europe. (His four sons did fight in World War I; the youngest son was killed in combat.)

The following viewpoint is taken from a speech Roosevelt gave in New York City on September 6, 1918 (a day commemorating the Marquis de Lafayette, a French nobleman who assisted the United States in the American Revolution). Anticipating the continuation of the war into 1919, Roosevelt argues that only a complete victory and harsh punishment of the Central Powers—especially Germany—will make American sacrifices in war worthwhile. Roosevelt also expresses some doubts as to the efficacy of international organizations and agreements, such as the League of Nations proposed by Wilson, in preventing future wars. Roosevelt's views were shared by many in the Allied camp: The Treaty of Versailles that was negotiated after World War I would contain harsh punitive measures against Germany.

Reprinted from Theodore Roosevelt, *The Great Adventure* (New York: Scribner, 1919).

Lafayette Day commemorates the services rendered to America in the Revolution by France. I wish to insist with all possible emphasis that in the present war France and England and Italy and the other Allies have rendered us similar services. The French at the battle of the Marne four years ago, and at Verdun, and the British at Ypres—in short, the French, the English, the Italians, the Belgians, the Serbians have been fighting for us when they were fighting for themselves. Our army on the other side is now repaying in part our debt, and next year we have every reason to hope, and we must insist, that the fighting army in France from the United States shall surpass in numbers the fighting army in France, of either France or England. It is now time—and it long has been time—for America to bear her full share of the common burden, the burden borne by all the Allies in this great war for liberty and justice.

The Peace of Overwhelming Victory

We must win the war as speedily as possible. But we must set ourselves to fight it through no matter how long it takes, with the resolute determination to accept no peace until, no matter at what cost, we win the peace of overwhelming victory. The peace that we win must guarantee full reparation for the awful cost of life and treasure which the Prussianized Germany of the Hohenzollerns [the German emperors] has inflicted on the entire world; and this reparation must take the form of action that will render it impossible for Germany to repeat her colossal wrong-doing. Germany has been able to wage this fight for world dominion because she has subdued to her purpose her vassal allies, Austria, Turkey, and Bulgaria. Serbia and Roumania must have restored to them what Bulgaria has taken from them. The Austrian and Turkish Empires must both be broken up, all the subject peoples liberated, and the Turk driven from Europe. We do not intend that German or Magyar shall be oppressed by others, but neither do we intend that they shall oppress and domineer over others. France must receive back Alsace and Lorraine. Belgium must be restored and indemnified. Italian Austria must be restored to Italy, and Roumanian Hungary to Roumania. The heroic Czech-Slovaks must be made into an independent commonwealth. The southern Slavs must be united in a great Jugo-Slav commonwealth. Poland as a genuinely independent commonwealth must receive back Austrian and Prussian Poland, as well as Russian Poland, and have her coast line on the Baltic. Lithuania, the Baltic Provinces of Russia, Ukrania, and Finland must be guaranteed their independence, and no part of the ancient empire of Russia left under the German yoke, or subject in any way to German influence. Northern Schleswig should go back to the Danes. Britain and Japan should keep the colonies they have conquered. Armenia must be freed, Palestine made a Jewish state, the Greeks guaranteed their rights, and the Syrians liberated—all of them, Mohammedans, Jews, Druses, and Christians, being guaranteed an equal liberty of religious belief, and required to work out their independence on the basis of equal political and civil rights for all creeds.

Nationalism and Internationalism

It is sometimes announced that part of the peace agreement must be a League of Nations, which will avert all war for the future, and put a stop to the need of this nation preparing its own strength for its own defense. Many of the adherents of this idea grandiloquently assert that they intend to supplant nationalism by internationalism.

In deciding upon proposals of this nature it behooves our people to remember that competitive rhetoric is a poor substitute for the habit of resolutely looking facts in the face. Nothing in the world can alter facts. Patriotism stands in national matters as love of family does in private life. Nationalism corresponds to the love a man bears for his wife and children. Internationalism corresponds to the feeling he has for his neighbors generally. The sound nationalist is the only type of really helpful internationalist, precisely as in private relations it is the man who is most devoted to his own wife and children who is apt, in the long run, to be the most satisfactory neighbor. To substitute internationalism for nationalism means to do away with patriotism, and is as vicious and as profoundly demoralizing as to put promiscuous devotion to all other persons in the place of steadfast devotion to a man's own family. Either effort means the atrophy of robust morality. The man who loves other countries as much as his own stands on a level with the man who loves other women as much as he loves his own wife. One is as worthless a creature as the other. The professional pacifist and the professional internationalist are equally undesirable citizens. The American pacifist has in actual fact shown himself to be the tool and ally of the German militarist. The professional internationalist is a man who, under a pretense of diffuse attachment for everybody hides the fact that in reality he is incapable of doing his duty by anybody.

We Americans should abhor all wrong-doing to other nations. We ought always to act fairly and generously by other nations. But we must remember that our first duty is to be loyal and patriotic citizens of our own nation, of America. These two facts should always be in our minds in dealing with any proposal for a

League of Nations. By all means let us be loyal to great ideals. But let us remember that, unless we show common sense in action, loyalty in speech will amount to considerably less than nothing.

The Crimes of Germany

Much American writing about World War I focused on reported or rumored German atrocities, suggesting that Germany deserved punishment. The following passage from a 1918 article in the Northwestern Christian Advocate *by William A. Quayle, a Methodist bishop, is typical of these accounts.*

Let us set down sternly that we are at war with the Germans, not the Junkers [German aristocrats], not autocracy, not Prussianism, not the Kaiser. . . . The German people is what we war with. The German people is committing the unspeakable horrors which set the whole world aghast. The German people is not and has not been conducting war. It is and has been conducting murder. Hold fast to that. The Supreme Court of New York declared the sinking of the *Lusitania* an act of piracy. Piracy is not war. All decencies, honors, humanities, international agreements, and laws have been smashed by them day and night from the first rape of Belgium to now. The new atrocity which appeared this week was spraying prisoners with burning oil. This is Germany's most recent jest. It makes them laugh so!

They have violated every treaty with the United States; they have lied from start to finish and to everybody. . . .

Germany has stolen things little and big: playthings from children, finery from women, pictures of incalculable worth, bank-deposits, railroads, factories. Germany has sunk hospital-ships, has bombed hospitals and Red Cross camps. Germany has disclosed neither decency nor honor from the day it started war, nor has a single voice in Germany to date been lifted up against the orgies of ruthlessness which turn the soul sick and which constitute the chief barbarity of history. Germany remains unblushing and unconscious of its indecency. Germany's egotism still struts like a Kaiser. And to climax its horrid crimes, Germany has inflicted compulsory polygamy on the virgins of its own land.

Test the proposed future League of Nations so far as concerns proposals to disarm, and to trust to anything except our own strength for our own defense, by what the nations are actually doing at the present time. Any such league would have to depend for its success upon the adhesion of the nine nations which are actually or potentially the most powerful military nations, and these nine nations include Germany, Austria, Turkey, and Russia. The first three have recently and repeatedly violated, and are now actively and continuously violating, not only every treaty, but every rule of civilized warfare and of international good faith. During the last year Russia, under the dominion of the Bolshevists, has betrayed her allies, has become the tool of the German autocracy, and has shown such utter disregard of her national honor and plighted word, and her international duties, that she is now in external affairs the passive tool and ally of her brutal conqueror, Germany. What earthly use is it to pretend that the safety of the world would be secured by a League in which these four nations would be among the nine leading partners? Long years must pass before we can again trust any promises these four nations make. Any treaty of any kind or sort which we make with them should be made with the full understanding that they will cynically repudiate it whenever they think it to their interest to do so. Therefore, unless our folly is such that it will not depart from us until we are brayed in a mortar, let us remember that any such treaty will be worthless unless our own prepared strength renders it unsafe to break it

Punish the Wrong-Doers

After the war the wrong-doers will be so punished and exhausted that they may for a number of years wish to keep the peace. But the surest way to make them keep the peace in the future is to punish them heavily now. And don't forget that China is now useless as a prop to a League of Peace, simply because she lacks effective military strength for her own defense.

Let us support any reasonable plan, whether in the form of a League of Nations or in any other shape, which bids fair to lessen the probable number of future wars, and to limit their scope. But let us laugh out of court any assertion that any such plan will guarantee peace and safety to the foolish, weak or timid creatures who have not the will and the power to prepare for their own defense. Support any such plan which is honest and reasonable. But support it as an addition to, and never as a substitute for, the policy of preparing our own strength for our own defense. To follow any other course would turn this country into the China of the Occident. We cannot guarantee for ourselves or our children peace without effort, or safety without service and sacrifice. We must prepare both our souls and our bodies, in virile fashion, alike to secure justice for ourselves and to do justice to others. Only thus can we secure our own national self-respect. Only thus can we secure the respect of other nations and the power to aid them when they seek to do well.

In sum, then, I shall be delighted to support the movement for a League to Enforce Peace, or for a League of Nations, if it is developed as a supplement to, and not a substitute for, the preparation of our own strength. I believe that this preparation should be by the introduction in this country of the principle of universal training and universal service, as practised in Switzerland, and modified, of course, both along the lines indicated in Australia and in accordance with our own needs. There will be no taint of Prussian militarism in such a system. It will merely mean ability to fight for self-defense in a great democracy in which law, order, and liberty are to prevail.

VIEWPOINT 2

"The Treaty . . . commits the national democracies to a permanent policy of inhumane violence."

The Treaty of Versailles Is Too Punitive

The New Republic

The Treaty of Versailles was the product of negotiations held in Paris, France, between January 18, 1919, when the Paris Peace Conference opened, and June 28, 1919, when the treaty was signed by a German delegation who had had little say in its creation. Most of the major decisions were made by the Council of Four, which consisted of the four political leaders of the Allies: U.S. president Woodrow Wilson, British prime minister David Lloyd George, French premier Georges Clemenceau, and Italian prime minister Vittorio Orlando.

The treaty that emerged from the proceedings in Paris was in many respects harshly punitive of Germany, which was forced to admit sole blame for the war, disarm itself, and commit to heavy reparation payments to the Allies. It also lost significant amounts of territory: France regained the Alsace and Lorraine provinces lost to Germany in 1871 and took control of Germany's Saar province for the next fifteen years; Poland (restored to independent status) and the newly created nation of Czechoslovakia also gained former German territory.

Some observers both within and outside the United States criticized the treaty's harshness toward Germany. The following viewpoint is taken from an editorial published in the May 24, 1919, issue of the *New Republic*, a liberal and politically influential journal. The magazine's official editorial stance had been one of strong approval of Wilson's decision to take the United States into this "war to end all wars." The *New Republic* also endorsed

Reprinted from Editorial, *New Republic*, May 24, 1919.

the president's declared intentions of securing a peace agreement that would reshape global politics and prevent future conflict. However, in the following viewpoint the editors express bitter disappointment over the Treaty of Versailles. They argue that the treaty imposes burdensome commitments and reparations that Germany cannot realistically be expected to fulfill, raises the specter of future class conflict, and scuttles any hopes of a new world order that transcends nationalistic competition and strife.

The U.S. Senate ultimately refused to ratify the Treaty of Versailles, mostly because of controversy over the League of Nations rather than because of the arguments expressed here. The United States and Germany finally signed a separate peace agreement in 1921. However, the Treaty of Versailles did go into effect between Germany and most of the Allies. Many historians believe the treaty's harshness was one of the factors that led to World War II.

In their comments on the Treaty of Versailles, the newspapers published in the Allied countries confine themselves chiefly to the expression of two sharply contrasted verdicts. Those which have vigorously supported the war praise the Treaty as a document, which, however harsh its terms may appear to be, is defensible as a stern but just attempt to make the punishment of Germany fit her crimes. Those which did not support the war or conditioned their support on the fulfillment of definite political objects are equally uncompromising in their rejection of the Treaty. They consider it a flagrant and perfidious repudiation of all the more generous, humane, and constructive objects in the name of which the people in the Allied countries were induced to shed their blood and sacrifice their lives.

A Third State of Mind

These hostile verdicts attract to themselves the limelight of public attention, but particularly in this country we should not overlook the third state of mind about the Treaty which is obtaining expression in some of the Western journals. There are many of our fellow countrymen, both in the East and in the West, whose sense of justice and fair-dealing is outraged by the Treaty, but who cannot quite decide to place themselves in open and uncompromising opposition to it. Their state of mind is analogous to that of those Americans in August 1914 whose consciences were troubled by the wanton violence of the German invasion of Belgium, but who did not know how, as American citizens, they could assume effective responsibility for defeating the monster of militant imperialism.

To Americans who share this third state of mind, we should like to address an appeal. They are in danger now of committing a mistake similar to that which their fellow countrymen committed in the fall of 1914. During the early months of the war the majority of uneasy Americans compromised with their consciences. They usually became definitely pro-Ally in opinion, but they were mentally unprepared for war, and they considered it unnecessary to consider any method, short of an actual declaration of war, which would bring American political influence and economic power to the support of democratic Europe. In an analogous spirit, Americans who are deeply troubled by the proposed treaty of peace are feeling for a way out which does not imply outspoken and uncompromising opposition. Just as four and one-half years ago they shrank from breaking down the traditional aloofness of this country from European political and military controversies, so now they shrink from parting company with their recent companions in arms. The bonds forged by their fight against a common enemy are hard to break. If they reject the Treaty they are afraid of looking to themselves and to their European friends like quitters. They are longing for peace and are tempted to accept it at any price.

Yet if they connive at this Treaty they will, as liberal and humane American democrats who seek by social experiment and education to render their country more worthy of its still unredeemed national promise, be delivering themselves into the hands of their enemies, the reactionaries and the revolutionists. The future of liberal Americanism depends upon a moral union between democracy and nationalism. Such a union is compromised so long as nationalism remains competitive in policy, exclusive in spirit, and complacently capitalist in organization. Liberals all over the world have hoped that a war, which was so clearly the fruit of competition and imperialist and class-bound nationalism, would end in a peace which would moralize nationalism by releasing it from class bondage and exclusive ambitions.

An Inhuman Monster

The Treaty of Versailles does not even try to satisfy these aspirations. Instead of expressing a great recuperative effort of the conscience of a civilization, which for its own sins has sweated so much blood, it does much to intensify and nothing to heal the old and ugly dissensions between political nationalism and social democracy. Insofar as its terms are actually carried out, it is bound to provoke the ultimate explosion of irreconcilable warfare. It weaves international animosities and the class conflict into the very fabric of the proposed new system of public law. The European politicians, who with American complicity have hatched this inhuman monster, have acted either cynically, hypocritically, or vindictively, and their handwork will breed cynicism, hypocrisy, or vindictiveness in the minds of future generations. The moral source of the political life of modern nations remains polluted.

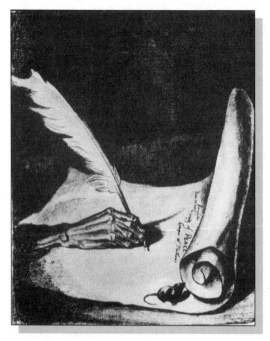

Cartoonist Boardman Robinson responded to the signing of the Treaty of Versailles in June 1919 with this darkly prophetic illustration titled "Signed."

The authors of the Treaty of Versailles are the victims of the blind interests and the imperious determinism of an inhumane class economy. They admit in private conversation the diseased nature of their own offspring. "Even conservative opinion in Europe," says William Allen White, "is frankly cynical about Germany's fulfillment of the terms imposed. They are too severe for Germany to live under for a generation. . . . They practically exterminate her as a nation." Why, then, did they do it? Why do they propose to terminate a war, fought in part to vindicate the sacredness of public treaties, by compelling the vanquished enemy to sign a bond which they know he cannot fulfill? The answer is not pleasant. They do this thing because they themselves are the unconscious servants of the cupidity and the vindictiveness which infect the psychology of an inhumane and complacent capitalist society.

They crave at any cost the emotional triumph of imposing on the German nation the ultimate humiliation of solemnly consenting to its own abdication as a self-governing and self-respecting community. To satisfy this craving they are so far as possible depriving the German people by public law of the status of economic citizens with rights which other nations are bound to respect. Thus they are deliberately raising the question of working class solidarity. They are defying the community of interest and the feeling of brotherhood which unites the socially alert workers of all the European peoples. They are subsidizing the growth of class-conscious and class-bound proletarian internationalism dominated by the conviction of the incorrigible inhumanity of a capitalist national economy. They are demonstrating by example what a perfidious protectorate nationalism exercises over the common human interests of all peoples.

The Socialist Response

The Socialists are fully alive to this deeper and less obvious meaning of the Treaty. They will flourish it as a complete vindication of the Marxian dogma that, as long as capitalism prevails, war necessarily operates as the instrument of class aggrandizement and popular exploitation. The Treaty proposes the exploitation of the German people only, but an international organization whose chief object it is to profit by the exploitation of a subject people can survive only through the exploitation and deception of its own workers. The Treaty is, consequently, greeted as a declaration of a class war by organized society against the proletariat of all nations. It is condemned as a final exposure of the hypocrisy and inhumanity of a national economy.

Hitherto, in spite of all their propaganda and of the grievances of the wage-earning class, the Socialists have never persuaded the workers to believe in the need of a class war, or to undermine the popular confidence in nationalism. Now, as they believe, their class enemies have provided them with an unanswerable demonstration, and they are looking forward jubilantly to the inevitable revolution. The New York *Nation* announces confidently that all recent political and social convulsions are only "the preliminaries of the great revolution to whose support the friends of freedom must now rally everywhere."

A Decisive Test

In our opinion the Treaty of Versailles subjects all liberalism, and particularly that kind of liberalism which breathes the Christian spirit, to a decisive test. Its very life depends upon the ability of the modern national state to avoid the irreconcilable class conflict to which, as the Socialists claim, capitalism condemns the future of society. In the event of such a conflict, liberalism is ground, as it is being ground in Russia, between the upper and lower millstones of reaction and revolution. The Treaty, insofar as it commits the national democracies to a permanent policy of inhumane violence, does weave this conflict into the fabric of international law. It is the most shameless and, we hope, the last of those treaties which, while they pretend to bring peace to a mortified world, merely write the specifications for future revolution and war. It presents liberalism with a perfect opportunity of proving whether or not it is actually founded in positive moral and religious conviction.

If a war which was supposed to put an end to war culminates without strenuous protest by humane men and women in a treaty of peace which renders peace impossible, the liberalism which preached this meaning for the war will have committed suicide. That such a protest on the part of national liberals may not have much immediate success in defeating the ratification of the Treaty is not essential. The Treaty of Versailles, no matter under what kind of compulsion it is ratified by the nations, is impossible of execution and will defeat itself.

But it is essential that the ratification should not take place with the connivance of the sincerely liberal and Christian forces in public opinion. For in that event national liberalism in the Allied countries will be following the example and inviting the fate of national liberalism in imperial Germany. It will become the dishonored accomplice of its own downfall. It will abandon society to an irresistible conflict between the immoral and intransigent forces of Junkerism [Prussian aristocracy] and revolutionary socialism.

The calamity of the war descended on the Western nations because of the existence of one crying weakness in Western civilization. The organized Christian nations could never agree upon an effective method of subordinating the exercise of political and economic power to moral and humane purposes. Many liberals have hoped that at the end of the war the enlightened conscience of the Western people would arise and exert itself to cure this weakness. The Treaty of Versailles is damned because it does nothing to moralize the future exercise of political and economic power. On the contrary, it conceives the victors who exercise the power as possessing only rights and the vanquished who have lost the power as possessing only duties. The powerful are permitted to abuse it as much as they please, and, in their relations to the defeated Hungary, Austria, Russia, and Germany, they are encouraged and licensed to abuse it.

The past sins of the Hungarian and German ruling classes afford no justification for such a convenient and drastic system of future discrimination. Those who will not subordinate the exercise of power to rules of impartial justice sacrifice their moral right to inflict punishment. The Treaty does not embody either the spirit or method even of punitive justice. What it does embody and strain to the breaking point is the pagan doctrine and spirit of retaliation. What it treats with utter ignorance is the Christian doctrine of atonement and redemption. At a crisis in the history of civilization, the rulers of the victorious Christian states conclusively demonstrate their own contemptuous disbelief in the practical value of Christian moral economy.

The Treaty and the League

Just as the acceptance of the Treaty of Versailles without protest will undermine the moral foundation of nationalism and menace civilization with an uncontrollable class conflict, so its defeat or discredit will clearly and emphatically testify to a formative connection between religion and morals and economics and politics. It would begin the cure of the spiritual anarchy in Western civilization which the recent war and the proposed peace both exemplify. It would constitute the first step in the moral preparation of the Western democracies for a League of Nations.

For the possibility of any vital League of Nations does not depend, as so many liberals seem to suppose, on the ratification of the Treaty. It depends on the rejection of the Treaty. The League is not powerful enough to redeem the Treaty. But the Treaty is vicious enough to incriminate the League. It would convert the League into the instrument of competitive imperialist nationalism whose more disinterested members would labor in vain to mold it into a cooperative society. Liberal democrats cannot honestly consent to peace on the proposed terms. If it was wrong when confronted by the imperialist aggression of Germany to tolerate peace by conniving at such an attack, it is equally wrong when confronted by a treaty which organizes competitive imperialism into an international system to pay so high a price for the ending of the war. This above all others is the time and the occasion to repudiate the idea of peace at any price, to reject immediate peace at the price of permanent moral and economic warfare.

"Unless you get the united . . . power of the great Governments of the world behind this settlement, it will fall down like a house of cards."

America Must Join the League of Nations

Woodrow Wilson (1856–1924)

On June 28, 1919, the Paris Peace Conference concluded when delegates representing Germany and most of the Allied nations (including the United States) signed the Treaty of Versailles. In July 1919, after nearly six months spent almost entirely abroad as the leader of the American peace delegation, President Woodrow Wilson returned home and submitted the Treaty of Versailles to the Senate for ratification. Embedded within the treaty was the League of Nations Covenant. The covenant provided for the creation of an Assembly with delegations from all member nations, a Council controlled by the leading Allied nations, and a Permanent Court of International Justice. Wilson, who had compromised his original peace aims in negotiating other parts of the Treaty of Versailles, viewed the inclusion of the League of Nations Covenant in the treaty as his most important achievement. "At least," he wrote his adviser Edward House, "we are saving the Covenant, and that instrument will work wonders, bring the blessing of peace."

Many members of Congress, however, opposed the inclusion of the League in the peace treaty. These critics expressed misgivings about the likelihood that the wording of the covenant would enable other nations to entangle the United States in future foreign wars. In September 1919, with the treaty bottled up in the Senate, Wilson embarked on a nationwide speaking tour in which he hoped to raise public support for the treaty and the League. The

Reprinted from Woodrow Wilson, address on the League of Nations, Pueblo, Colorado, September 25, 1919.

following viewpoint is taken from a speech Wilson made in Pueblo, Colorado, on September 25, in which he defends the League against critics and argues that its creation will secure future peace. Shortly after this speech, Wilson collapsed from exhaustion and was forced to end his speaking tour. He later suffered several major strokes that left him an invalid during the remainder of his term.

There have been unpleasant impressions as well as pleasant impressions, my fellow citizens, as I have crossed the continent. I have perceived more and more that men have been busy creating an absolutely false impression of what the treaty of peace and the covenant of the League of Nations contain and mean. . . . Therefore, in order to clear away the mists, in order to remove the impressions, in order to check the falsehoods that have clustered around this great subject, I want to tell you a few very simple things about the treaty and the covenant. . . .

It is a people's treaty, that accomplishes by a great sweep of practical justice the liberation of men who never could have liberated themselves, and the power of the most powerful nations has been devoted not to their aggrandizement but to the liberation of people whom they could have put under their control if they had chosen to do so. Not one foot of territory is demanded by the conquerors, not one single item of submission to their authority is demanded by them. The men who sat around that table in Paris knew that the time had come when the people were no longer going to consent to live under masters, but were going to live the lives that they chose themselves, to live under such governments as they chose themselves to erect. That is the fundamental principle of this great settlement. . . .

The League of Nations

At the front of this great treaty is put the covenant of the League of Nations. . . . Unless you get the united, concerted purpose and power of the great Governments of the world behind this settlement, it will fall down like a house of cards. There is only one power to put behind the liberation of mankind, and that is the power of mankind. It is the power of the united moral forces of the world, and in the covenant of the League of Nations the moral forces of the world are mobilized. . . . They enter into a solemn promise to one another that they will never use their power against one another for aggression; that they never will impair the

200

territorial integrity of a neighbor; that they never will interfere with the political independence of a neighbor; that they will abide by the principle that great populations are entitled to determine their own destiny and that they will not interfere with that destiny; and that no matter what differences arise amongst them they will never resort to war without first having . . . either submitted the matter of controversy to arbitration, in which case they agree to abide by the result without question, or submitted it to the consideration of the Council of the League of Nations . . . agreeing that there shall be six months allowed for the mature consideration of . . . the Council, and agreeing that at the expiration of the six months, even if they are not then ready to accept the advice of the Council with regard to the settlement of the dispute, they will still not go to war for another three months. In other words, they consent, no matter what happens, to submit every matter of difference between them to the judgment of mankind, and just so certainly as they do that, . . . war will be pushed out of the foreground of terror in which it has kept the world for generation after generation, and men will know that there will be a calm time of deliberate counsel. The most dangerous thing for a bad cause is to expose it to the opinion of the world. The most certain way that you can prove that a man is mistaken is by letting all his neighbors know what he thinks, by letting all his neighbors discuss what he thinks, and if he is in the wrong you will notice that he will stay at home, he will not walk on the street. He will be afraid of the eyes of his neighbors. He will be afraid of their judgment of his character. He will know that his cause is lost unless he can sustain it by the arguments of right and of justice. The same law that applies to individuals applies to nations. . . .

Article 10

When you come to the heart of the covenant, my fellow citizens, you will find . . . there is something in article 10 that you ought to realize and ought to accept or reject. Article 10 is the heart of the whole matter. . . . Article 10 provides that every member of the League covenants to respect and preserve the territorial integrity and existing political independence of every other member of the League as against external aggression. Not against internal disturbance. There was not a man at that table who did not admit the sacredness of the right of self-determination, the sacredness of the right of any body of people to say that they would not continue to live under the Government they were then living under, and under article 11 of the covenant they are given a place to say whether they will live under it or not. For following article 10 is article 11, which makes it the right of any member of the League at any time to call attention to anything, anywhere, that is likely to disturb the peace of the world or the good understanding between nations upon which the peace of the world depends. . . . Now, read articles 10 and 11. You will see that international law is revolutionized by pulling morals into it. Article 10 says that no member of the League, and that includes all these nations that have demanded these things unjustly of China, shall impair the territorial integrity or the political independence of any other member of the League. [During the nineteenth century, Japan and the western European powers had impinged on China's sovereignty by carving out separate spheres of influence.] China is going to be a member of the League. Article 11 says that any member of the League can call attention to anything that is likely to disturb the peace of the world or the good understanding between nations, and China is for the first time in the history of mankind afforded a standing before the jury of the world. I, for my part, have a profound sympathy for China, and I am proud to have taken part in an arrangement which promises the protection of the world to the rights of China. The whole atmosphere of the world is changed by a thing like that, my fellow citizens. The whole international practice of the world is revolutionized.

But you will say, "what is the second sentence of article 10? That is what gives very disturbing thoughts." The second sentence is that the Council of the League shall advise what steps, if any, are necessary to carry out the guaranty of the first sentence, namely, that the members will respect and preserve the territorial integrity and political independence of the other members. I do not know any other meaning for the word "advise" except "advise." The Council advises, and it can not advise without the vote of the United States. Why gentlemen should fear that the Congress of the United States would be advised to do something that it did not want to do I frankly can not imagine, because they can not even be advised to do anything unless their own representative has participated in the advice. It may be that that will impair somewhat the vigor of the League, but, nevertheless, the fact is so, that we are not obliged to take any advice except our own, which to any man who wants to go his own course is a very satisfactory state of affairs. Every man regards his own advice as best, and I dare say every man mixes his own advice with some thought of his own interest. Whether we use it wisely or unwisely, we can use the vote of the United States to make impossible drawing the United States into any enterprise that she does not care to be drawn into.

Yet article 10 strikes at the taproot of war. Article 10 is a statement that the very things that have always been sought in imperialistic wars are henceforth forgone by every ambitious nation in the world. I would have felt very lonely, my fellow countrymen, and I would have felt very much disturbed if, sitting at the peace table in Paris, I had supposed that I was expounding my own ideas. Whether you believe it or not, I know the relative size of my own ideas; I know how they stand related in bulk and proportion to the moral judgments of my fellow countrymen, and I proposed nothing whatever at the peace table at Paris that I had not sufficiently certain knowledge embodied the moral judgment of the citizens of the United States. I had gone over there with, so to say, explicit instructions. Don't you remember that we laid down fourteen points which should contain the principles of the settlement? They were not my points. In every one of them I was conscientiously trying to read the thought of the people of the United States, and after I uttered those points I had every assurance given me that could be given me that they did speak the moral judgment of the United States and not my single judgment. . . .

Articles 10 and 11

In his Pueblo speech, Wilson refers to Articles 10 and 11 of the League of Nations Covenant. Article 10 was perhaps the most controversial section of the covenant. Critics argued that it would create a blanket commitment for the United States to intervene in military conflicts at the discretion of the League of Nations rather than of Congress.

Article 10. The Members of the League undertake to respect and preserve as against external aggression the territorial integrity and existing political independence of all Members of the League. In case of any such aggression or in case of any threat or danger of such aggression the Council shall advise upon the means by which this obligation shall be fulfilled.

Article 11. Any war or threat of war, whether immediately affecting any of the Members of the League or not, is hereby declared a matter of concern to the whole League, and the League shall take any action that may be deemed wise and effectual to safeguard the peace of nations. In case any such emergency should arise the Secretary General shall on the request of any Member of the League forthwith summon a meeting of the Council.

It is also declared to be the friendly right of each Member of the League to bring to the attention of the Assembly or of the Council any circumstance whatever affecting international relations which threatens to disturb international peace or the good understanding between nations upon which peace depends.

I am dwelling upon these points, my fellow citizens, in spite of the fact that I dare say to most of you they are perfectly well known, because in order to meet the present situation we have got to know what we are dealing with. We are not dealing with the kind of document which this is represented by some gentlemen to be; and inasmuch as we are dealing with a document simon-pure in respect of the very principles we have professed and lived up to, we have got to do one or other of two things— we have got to adopt it or reject it. There is no middle course. You can not go in on a special-privilege basis of your own. I take it that you are too proud to ask to be exempted from responsibilities which the other members of the League will carry. We go in upon equal terms or we do not go in at all; and if we do not go in, my fellow citizens, think of the tragedy of that result—the only sufficient guaranty to the peace of the world withheld! Ourselves drawn apart with that dangerous pride which means that we shall be ready to take care of ourselves, and that means that we shall maintain great standing armies and an irresistible navy; that means we shall have the organization of a military nation; that means we shall have a general staff, with the kind of power that the general staff of Germany had, to mobilize this great manhood of the Nation when it pleases, all the energy of our young men drawn into the thought and preparation for war. What of our pledges to the men that lie dead in France? We said that they went over there, not to prove the prowess of America or her readiness for another war but to see to it that there never was such a war again. It always seems to make it difficult for me to say anything, my fellow citizens, when I think of my clients in this case. My clients are the children; my clients are the next generation. They do not know what promises and bonds I undertook when I ordered the armies of the United States to the soil of France, but I know, and I intend to redeem my pledges to the children; they shall not be sent upon a similar errand.

Those Who Have Perished

Again and again, my fellow citizens, mothers who lost their sons in France have come to me and, taking my hand, have shed tears upon it not only, but they had added, "God bless you, Mr. President!" Why, my fellow citizens, should they pray God to bless me? I advised the Congress of the United States to create the situation that led to the death of their sons. I ordered their sons overseas. I consented to their sons being put in the most difficult parts of the battle line, where death was certain, as in the impenetrable difficulties of the forest of Argonne. Why should they weep upon my hand and call down the blessings of God upon me? Because they believe that their boys died for something that vastly transcends any of the immediate and palpable objects of the war. They believe, and they rightly believe, that their sons saved the liberty of the world. They believe that wrapped up with the liberty of the world is the continuous protection of that liberty by the concerted powers of all civilized people. They believe that this sacrifice was made in order that other sons should not be called upon for a similar gift—the gift of life, the gift of all that died—and if we did not see this thing through, if we fulfilled the dearest present wish of Germany and now dissociated ourselves from those alongside whom we fought in the war, would not something of the halo go away from the gun over the mantelpiece, or the sword? Would not the old uniform lose something of its significance? These men were crusaders. They were not going forth to prove the might of the United States. They were going forth to prove the might of justice and right, and all the world accepted them as crusaders, and their transcendent achievement has made all the world believe in America as it believes in no other nation organized in the modern world. There seems to me to stand between us and the rejection or qualification of this treaty the serried ranks of those boys in khaki, not only these boys who came home, but those dear ghosts that still deploy upon the fields of France.

My friends, on last Decoration Day I went to a beautiful hillside near Paris, where was located the cemetery of Suresnes, a cemetery given over to the burial of the American dead. Behind me on the slopes was rank upon rank of living American soldiers, and lying before me upon the levels of the plain was rank upon rank of departed American soldiers. Right by the side of the stand where I spoke there was a little group of French women who had adopted those graves, had made themselves mothers of those dear ghosts by putting flowers every day upon those graves, taking them as their own sons, their own beloved, because they had died in the same cause—France was free and the world was free because America had come! I wish some men in public life who are now opposing the settlement for which these men died could visit such a spot as that. I wish that the thought that comes out of those graves could penetrate their consciousness. I wish that they could feel the moral obligation that rests upon us not to go back on those boys, but to see the thing through, to see it through to the end and make good their redemption of the world. For nothing less depends upon this decision, nothing less than the liberation and salvation of the world.

VIEWPOINT 4

"I object in the strongest possible way to having the United States agree . . . to be controlled by a league which may at any time . . . be drawn in to deal with internal conflicts in other countries."

America Must Not Join the League of Nations

Henry Cabot Lodge (1850–1924)

Before the United States could join the League of Nations created by the Treaty of Versailles, that treaty had to be ratified by the U.S. Senate. However, passage of the treaty faced formidable opposition in Congress by those who believed that joining the League would harm the United States. A central figure of this opposition was the Republican majority leader, Henry Cabot Lodge.

A Massachusetts senator and chair of the Foreign Relations Committee, Lodge was one of Woodrow Wilson's principal political adversaries. During the summer of 1919, Lodge held lengthy hearings on the Treaty of Versailles and the League of Nations. The following viewpoint is taken from his first major speech concerning the League, made on the floor of the Senate on August 12, 1919. Expressing his misgivings about the League of Nations, Lodge argues that American freedom of action in foreign policy should not be compromised by membership in the organization as presently arranged.

Unlike the so-called irreconcilables who opposed any American participation in an international body, Lodge eventually offered a compromise. In November 1919 he submitted to the Senate floor a ratification resolution accompanied by fourteen "Lodge reservations" placing limits on America's international obligations under the League and preserving Congress's authority to declare

Reprinted from Henry Cabot Lodge, address to the U.S. Senate, August 12, 1919, *Congressional Record*, 66th Cong., 1st sess., pp. 3778–84.

war or commit troops. Wilson refused to accept these reservations, and the Treaty of Versailles ultimately failed to win ratification in the Senate.

The Treaty of Versailles—without American participation—took effect on January 20, 1920, at which time the League of Nations began operations in Geneva, Switzerland. Its subsequent effectiveness, however, was severely hampered by the absence of U.S. membership.

I object in the strongest possible way to having the United States agree, directly or indirectly, to be controlled by a league which may at any time, and perfectly lawfully and in accordance with the terms of the covenant, be drawn in to deal with internal conflicts in other countries, no matter what those conflicts may be. We should never permit the United States to be involved in any internal conflict in another country, except by the will of her people expressed through the Congress which represents them.

Article 10

With regard to wars of external aggression on a member of the league, the case is perfectly clear. There can be no genuine dispute whatever about the meaning of the first clause of article 10. In the first place, it differs from every other obligation in being individual and placed upon each nation without the intervention of the league. Each nation for itself promises to respect and preserve as against external aggression the boundaries and the political independence of every member of the league. . . .

It is, I repeat, an individual obligation. It requires no action on the part of the league, except that in the second sentence the authorities of the league are to have the power to advise as to the means to be employed in order to fulfill the purpose of the first sentence. But that is a detail of execution, and I consider that we are morally and in honor bound to accept and act upon that advice. The broad fact remains that if any member of the league suffering from external aggression should appeal directly to the United States for support the United States would be bound to give that support in its own capacity and without reference to the action of other powers, because the United States itself is bound, and I hope the day will never come when the United States will not carry out its promises. If that day should come, and the United States or any other great country should refuse, no matter how specious the reasons, to fulfill both in letter and spirit every obligation in this covenant, the United States would be dishonored and the league would crumble into dust, leaving behind it a legacy of wars. If China should rise up and attack Japan in an effort to undo the great wrong of the cession of the control of Shantung to that power, we should be bound under the terms of article 10 to sustain Japan against China, and a guaranty of that sort is never involved except when the question has passed beyond the stage of negotiation and has become a question for the application of force. I do not like the prospect. It shall not come into existence by any vote of mine. . . .

An Alliance

Any analysis of the provisions of this league covenant, however, brings out in startling relief one great fact. Whatever may be said, it is not a league of peace; it is an alliance, dominated at the present moment by five great powers, really by three, and it has all the marks of an alliance. The development of international law is neglected. The court which is to decide disputes brought before it fills but a small place. The conditions for which this league really provides with the utmost care are political conditions, not judicial questions, to be reached by the executive council and the assembly, purely political bodies without any trace of a judicial character about them. Such being its machinery, the control being in the hands of political appointees whose votes will be controlled by interest and expedience it exhibits that most marked characteristic of an alliance—that its decisions are to be carried out by force. Those articles upon which the whole structure rests are articles which provide for the use of force; that is, for war. This league to enforce peace does a great deal for enforcement and very little for peace. It makes more essential provisions looking to war than to peace for the settlement of disputes. . . .

Taken altogether, these provisions for war present what to my mind is the gravest objection to this league in its present form. We are told that of course nothing will be done in the way of warlike acts without the assent of Congress. If that is true let us say so in the covenant. But as it stands there is no doubt whatever in my mind that American troops and American ships may be ordered to any part of the world by nations other than the United States, and that is a proposition to which I for one can never assent. It must be made perfectly clear that no American soldiers, not even a corporal's guard, that no American sailors, not even the crew of a submarine, can ever be engaged in war or ordered anywhere except by the constitutional authorities of the United States. To Congress is granted by the Constitution the right to declare war, and nothing that would take the troops out of the country at the bidding or demand of other nations should ever be permitted except through congressional action. The lives of Americans must never be sacrificed except by the will of the American people expressed through their chosen Representatives in Congress. This is a point upon which no doubt can be permitted. American soldiers and American sailors have never failed the country when the country called upon them. They went in their hundreds of thousands into the war just closed. They went to die for the great cause of freedom and of civilization. . . . We were late in entering the war. We made no preparation, as we ought to have done, for the ordeal which was clearly coming upon us; but we went and we turned the wavering scale. It was done by the American soldier, the American sailor, and the spirit and energy of the American people. They overrode all obstacles and all shortcomings on the part of the administration or of Congress and gave to their country a great place in the great victory. It was the first time we had been called upon to rescue the civilized world. Did we fail? On the contrary, we succeeded, succeeded largely and nobly, and we did it without any command from any league of nations. When the emergency came, we met it and we were able to meet it because we had built up on this continent the greatest and most powerful Nation in the world, built it up under our own policies, in our own way, and one great element of our strength was the fact that we had held aloof and had not thrust ourselves into European quarrels; that we had no selfish interest to serve. We made

"Interrupting the Ceremony," a cartoon by John T. McCutcheon of the Chicago Tribune, depicts Senate opposition to U.S. membership in the League of Nations.

great sacrifices. We have done splendid work. I believe that we do not require to be told by foreign nations when we shall do work which freedom and civilization require. I think we can move to victory much better under our own command than under the command of others. Let us unite with the world to promote the peaceable settlement of all international disputes. Let us try to develop international law. Let us associate ourselves with the other nations for these purposes. But let us retain in our own hands and in our own control the lives of the youth of the land. Let no American be sent into battle except by the constituted authorities of his own country and by the will of the people of the United States.

Responding to Charges of Isolationism

Those of us, Mr. President [of the Senate], who are either wholly opposed to the league, or who are trying to preserve the independence and the safety of the United States by changing the terms of the league, and who are endeavoring to make the league, if we are to be a member of it, less certain to promote war instead of peace have been reproached with selfishness in our outlook and with a desire to keep our country in a state of isolation. So far as the question of isolation goes, it is impossible to isolate the United States. I well remember the time, 20 years ago, when eminent Senators and other distinguished gentlemen who were opposing the Philippines and shrieking about imperialism sneered at the statement made by some of us, that the United States had become a world power. I think no one now would question that the Spanish war marked the entrance of the United States into world affairs to a degree which had never obtained before. It was both an inevitable and an irrevocable step, and our entrance into the war with Germany certainly showed once and for all that the United States was not unmindful of its world responsibilities. We may set aside all this empty talk about isolation. Nobody expects to isolate the United States or to make it a hermit Nation, which is a sheer absurdity. But there is a wide difference between taking a suitable part and bearing a due responsibility in world affairs and plunging the United States into every controversy and conflict on the face of the globe. By meddling in all the differences which may arise among any portion or fragment of humankind we simply fritter away our influence and injure ourselves to no good purpose. We shall be of far more value to the world and its peace by occupying, so far as possible, the situation which we have occupied for the last 20 years and by adhering to the policy of [George] Washington and [Alexander] Hamilton, of [Thomas] Jefferson and [James] Monroe, under which we have risen to our present greatness and prosperity. The fact that we have been separated by our geographical situation and by our consistent policy from the broils of Europe has made us more than any one thing capable of performing the great work which we performed in the war against Germany and our disinterestedness is of far more value to the world than our eternal meddling in every possible dispute could ever be.

Reservations on Article 10

Of the fourteen reservations submitted by Henry Cabot Lodge as a necessary condition of Senate approval of the League of Nations, perhaps the most important was the second. This reservation sought to circumscribe America's commitment to international military action under Article 10 of the League of Nations Covenant.

The United States assumes no obligation to preserve the territorial integrity or political independence of any other country or to interfere in controversies between nations—whether members of the league or not—under the provisions of Article 10, or to employ the military or naval forces of the United States under any article of the treaty for any purpose, unless in any particular case the Congress, which, under the Constitution, has the sole power to declare war or authorize the employment of the military or naval forces of the United States shall by act or joint resolution so provide.

Now, as to our selfishness, I have no desire to boast that we are better than our neighbors, but the fact remains that this Nation in making peace with Germany had not a single selfish or individual interest to serve. All we asked was that Germany should be rendered incapable of again breaking forth, with all the horrors, incident to German warfare, upon an unoffending world, and that demand was shared by every free nation and indeed by humanity itself. For ourselves we asked absolutely nothing. We have not asked any government or governments to guarantee our boundaries or our political independence. We have no fear in regard to either. We have sought no territory, no privileges, no advantages, for ourselves. That is the fact. It is apparent on the face of the treaty. I do not mean to reflect upon a single one of the powers with which we have been associated in the war against Germany, but there is not one of them which has not sought individual advantages for their own national benefit. I do not criticize their desires at all. The services and sacrifices of England and France and Belgium and Italy are beyond estimate and beyond praise. I am glad they should have what they desire for their own welfare and safety. But they all receive under the peace territorial and commercial benefits. We are asked to give, and we in no way seek to take. Surely it is not too much to insist that when we are offered nothing but the opportunity to give and to aid others we should have the right to say what sacrifices we shall make and what the magnitude of our gifts shall be. In the prosecution of the war we gave unstintedly American lives and American treasure. When the war closed we had 3,000,000 men under arms. We were turning the country into a vast workshop for war. We advanced ten billions to our allies. We refused no assistance that we could possibly render. All the great energy and power of the Republic were put at the service of the good cause. We have not been ungenerous. We have been devoted to the cause of freedom, humanity, and civilization everywhere. Now we are asked, in the making of peace, to sacrifice our sovereignty in important respects, to involve ourselves almost without limit in the affairs of other nations and to yield up policies and rights which we have maintained throughout our history. We are asked to incur liabilities to an unlimited extent and furnish assets at the same time which no man can measure. I think it is not only our right but our duty to determine how far we shall go. Not only must we look carefully to see where we are being led into endless disputes and entanglements, but we must not forget that we have in this country millions of people of foreign birth and parentage.

Other Concerns

Our one great object is to make all these people Americans so that we may call on them to place America first and serve America as they have done in the war just closed. We cannot Americanize them if we are continually thrusting them back into the quarrels and difficulties of the countries from which they came to us. We shall fill this land with political disputes about the troubles and quarrels of other countries. We shall have a large portion of our people voting not on American questions and not on what concerns the United States but dividing on issues which concern foreign countries alone. That is an unwholesome and perilous condition to force upon this country. We must avoid it. We ought to reduce to the lowest possible point the foreign questions in which we involve ourselves. Never forget that this league is primarily—I might say overwhelmingly—a political organization, and I object strongly to having the politics of the United States turn upon disputes where deep feeling is aroused but in which we have no direct interest. It will all tend to delay the Americanization of our great population, and it is more important not only to the United States but to the peace of the world to make all these people good Americans than it is to determine that some piece of territory should belong to one European country rather than to another. For this reason I wish to limit strictly our interference in the affairs of Europe and of Africa. We have interests of our own in Asia and in the Pacific which we must guard upon our own account, but the less we undertake to play the part of umpire and thrust ourselves into European conflicts the better for the United States and for the world.

It has been reiterated here on this floor, and reiterated to the point of weariness, that in every treaty there is some sacrifice of sovereignty. That is not a universal truth by any means, but it is true of some treaties and it is a platitude which does not require reiteration. The question and the only question before us here is how much of our sovereignty we are justified in sacrificing. In what I have already said about other nations putting us into war I have covered one point of sovereignty which ought never to be yielded—the power to send American soldiers and sailors everywhere, which ought never to be taken from the American people or impaired in the slightest degree. Let us beware how we palter with our independence. We have not reached the great position from which we were able to come down into the field of battle and help to save the world from tyranny by being guided by others. Our vast power has all been built up and gathered together by ourselves alone. We forced our way upward from the days of the Revolution, through a world often hostile and always indifferent. We owe no debt to anyone except to France in that Revolution, and those policies and those rights on which our power has been founded should never be lessened or weakened. It will be no service to the world to do so and it will be of intolerable injury to the United States. We will do our share. We are ready and anxious to help in all ways to preserve the world's peace. But we can do it best by not crippling ourselves. . . .

We are told that we shall "break the heart of the world" if we do not take this league just as it stands. I fear that the hearts of the vast majority of mankind would beat on strongly and steadily and without any quickening if the league were to perish altogether. If it should be effectively and beneficently changed the people who would lie awake in sorrow for a single night could be easily gathered in one not very large room but those who would draw a long breath of relief would reach to millions. . . .

This Deformed Experiment

Ideals have been thrust upon us as an argument for the league until the healthy mind which rejects cant revolts from them. Are ideals confined to this deformed experiment upon a noble purpose, tainted, as it is, with bargains and tied to a peace treaty which might have been disposed of long ago to the great benefit of the world if it had not been compelled to carry this rider on its back? "Post equitem sedet atra cura [behind the rider sits dark

213

anxiety]," Horace tells us, but no blacker care ever sat behind any rider than we shall find in this covenant of doubtful and disputed interpretation as it now perches upon the treaty of peace.

No doubt many excellent and patriotic people see a coming fulfillment of noble ideals in the words "league for peace." We all respect and share these aspirations and desires, but some of us see no hope, but rather defeat, for them in this murky covenant. For we, too, have our ideals, even if we differ from those who have tried to establish a monopoly of idealism. Our first ideal is our country, and we see her in the future, as in the past, giving service to all her people and to the world. Our ideal of the future is that she should continue to render that service of her own free will. She has great problems of her own to solve, very grim and perilous problems, and a right solution, if we can attain to it, would largely benefit mankind. We would have our country strong to resist a peril from the West, as she has flung back the German menace from the East. We would not have our politics distracted and embittered by the dissensions of other lands. We would not have our country's vigor exhausted or her moral force abated, by everlasting meddling and muddling in every quarrel, great and small, which afflicts the world. Our ideal is to make her ever stronger and better and finer, because in that way alone, as we believe, can she be of the greatest service to the world's peace and to the welfare of mankind.

CHAPTER 6

Woodrow Wilson's Decision to Go to War in Retrospect

Chapter Preface

During World War I, the majority of Americans supported the war effort and President Woodrow Wilson's ideas of a new world order. The hopes and enthusiusm of the American people, created in part by the propaganda efforts of the Committee on Public Information, quickly gave way to disappointment when the peace negotiated after the war failed to live up to Wilson's idealistic vision and Congress rejected U.S. inclusion in the League of Nations.

The postwar disappointment caused many historians and other commentators to reinvestigate America's decision to enter the war. Instead of accepting that German submarine warfare forced U.S. involvement or concluding that U.S. participation was inevitable because of America's position as a world power, dissatisfied scholars looked to economic interests as a potential motive. Under this theory, leading munitions manufacturers and bankers who had loaned money to the Allies sought American entry into the war to preserve and expand their profits. This capitalist scheming—as well as British propaganda and Wilson's personal bias in favor of the Allies—drew the United States into a war that it could have avoided. Such arguments were voiced by New York *Herald-Tribune* journalist Walter Millis in his bestselling 1935 book *Road to War*. The claims were soon echoed by historian Charles C. Tansill in *America Goes to War*, published in 1938. Due partially to such writings, many Americans in the 1930s considered their country's involvement in World War I to be a tragic blunder. A January 1937 Gallup poll showed that 70 percent of Americans believed that the United States should not have entered the conflict.

This critical view of World War I became less prevalent after World War II, which placed the previous conflict in a new perspective (some historians argue that World War I and World War II were essentially a single war punctuated by an uneasy truce). Scholars have continued to disagree in rating Woodrow Wilson's leadership and policy decisions before, during, and after World War I, but most post–World War II analysts concurred that Germany's submarine warfare was the primary cause for Wilson's decision to enter the war. During the 1950s, historians Arthur Link in *Wilson the Diplomatist* and Ernest E. May in *The World War and American Isolation* both concluded that the actions of the German government left Wilson with little choice but to militarily intervene in the war. Their opinions, however, are still not universally accepted. The following pair of viewpoints present sharply differing assessments of Wilson's momentous decision to forgo American neutrality and commit U.S. soldiers to the war in Europe.

VIEWPOINT 1

"National need and interests were such that it was nearly impossible to avoid the problems which led the nation into war."

Woodrow Wilson's Decision to Take the United States into War Was Justified

Ross Gregory (b. 1933)

Ross Gregory, a history professor at Central Michigan University at Kalamazoo, is the author of several books on U.S. history, including *America 1941: A Nation at the Crossroads* and *Modern America, 1914–1945*. The following viewpoint is taken from the concluding chapter of his book *The Origins of American Intervention in the First World War*. Gregory argues that President Woodrow Wilson's decision to call for American entry into the war was inevitable given German actions, especially its resumption of unrestricted submarine warfare in 1917. According to Gregory, Wilson believed that as a major world power, the United States had to defend its rights and interests and that war, although undesirable, was a better alternative than surrendering those prerogatives. Although Wilson attempted to keep the United States neutral, by 1917 he had little choice but to enter the war in order to preserve America's security, economic strength, and national honor, Gregory concludes.

From *The Origins of American Intervention in the First World War* by Ross Gregory. Copyright ©1971 by W.W. Norton & Company, Inc. Reprinted by permission of W.W. Norton & Company, Inc.

In light of the controversy which later surrounded America's entry into the First World War, and the momentous effect that war had on the future of the world, it seems appropriate . . . to offer some . . . observations about Wilsonian diplomacy and the factors responsible for intervention. Wilson asked Congress to declare war in 1917 because he felt Germany had driven him to it. He could find no way, short of an unthinkable abandonment of rights and interests, to avoid intervention. He briefly had tried armed neutrality, and as he said in the war message, that tactic had not done the job. Germany was making war on the United States, and Wilson had no reasonable alternative to a declaration of hostilities. Hence submarine warfare must bear the immediate responsibility for provoking the decision for war. It nonetheless is not enough to say that the United States went to war simply because of the submarines, or that the events of January–March 1917 alone determined the fate of the United States, for a number of factors helped bring the nation to that point where it seemed impossible to do anything else. During the period of neutrality the American government made certain decisions, avoided others, found itself pulled one way or another by national sentiment and need and by the behavior of the belligerent nations.

Any account of American intervention would go amiss without some reference to the pro-Ally nature of American neutrality. American money and supplies allowed the Allies to sustain the war effort. While Wilson did not act openly partial to the Allies, he did promote American economic enterprise and declined to interfere—indeed showed no signs of dismay—when the enterprise developed in ways that were beneficial to Britain and France. Although Wilson did experience a considerable hardening of attitude toward the Allies in 1916 (his major advisers did not), he could not bring himself to limit the provisioning of Britain and France; and it was this traffic that brought on submarine warfare. Without American assistance to the Allies, Germany would have had no reason to adopt policy injurious to the interests of the United States.

Favoring the Allies

There were several reasons why American policy functioned in a manner which favored the Allies. The first was a matter of circumstances: Britain controlled the sea, and the Allies were in desperate need of American products—conditions which assured that most American trade would go to Britain and France. The second factor was an assumption by much of the American population, most members of the administration, and the president that the political and material well-being of the United States was associated with preservation of Britain and France as strong, independent states. Germany unintentionally confirmed the assumption with the [1914] invasion of Belgium, use of submarines, and war tactics in general. While pro-Ally feeling was tempered by a popular desire to stay out of the conflict and by the president's wish to remain fair and formally neutral, it was sufficiently strong to discourage any policy that would weaken the Allied war effort. [Wilson's adviser and envoy Edward] House, [Secretary of State Robert] Lansing, and [Walter Hines] Page were so partial to the Allies that they acted disloyally to the president. Wilson frequently complained about Britain's intolerable course; he sent notes of protest and threatened to do more. He grumbled about Page's bias for the British and questioned the usefulness of his ambassador in Britain. Yet he did nothing to halt Britain's restrictions on trade with continental Europe, and Page stayed on in London until the end of the war. Wilson declined to press the British because he feared that such action would increase Germany's chances of winning and lead to drastic economic repercussions in the United States. Favoritism for the Allies did not cause the United States to go to war with Germany. It did help create those conditions of 1917 in which war seemed the only choice.

The United States (or much of the population) preferred that Britain and France not collapse, and the nation was equally anxious that Germany not succeed, at least not to the extent of dominating Europe. A prewar suspicion of German militarism and autocratic government, and accounts, during the war, of "uncivilized" German warfare influenced Wilson and a majority of the American people to believe that the United States faced an evil world force, that in going to war with Germany the nation would be striking a blow for liberty and democracy. This general American attitude toward the war of 1914–18 probably influenced Wilson's decision to resist submarine warfare, and thus affected his neutrality policies. More important, it made the decision to intervene seem all the more noble and did much to determine the way the United States, once it became belligerent, prosecuted the war. It was not, however, the major reason for accepting intervention. For all the popular indignation over the invasion of Belgium and other allegedly atrocious German warfare, there still did not develop in the United States a large movement for intervention. Even in 1917 Wilson showed the utmost reluctance to bring the nation into the war. Americans evidently were willing to endure German brutality, although they did not like it, as long as it did not affect their interests; and one must wonder what the American response—and the response of the president—would have been had no Americans been aboard the *Lusitania*. Wilson's vilification on April 2 of the German political system was more a means of sanctifying the cause than a reason for undertaking it. He was a curious crusader. Before April 1917 he would not admit that there was a need for America to take up the sword of righteousness. Against his will he was driven to the barricades, but once he was in the streets he became the most thorough and enthusiastic of street fighters.

America's World Position

The most important influence on the fate of the United States 1914–17 was the nation's world position. National need and interests were such that it was nearly impossible to avoid the problems which led the nation into war. Even if the administration had maintained a rigidly neutral position and forced Britain to respect all maritime rights of the United States, it is doubtful that the result would have been different. [British foreign secretary Sir Edward] Grey testified that Britain would have yielded rather than have serious trouble with the United States, which means that, faced with American pressure, Britain would have allowed a larger amount of American trade through to Germany. This was the most the Germans could have expected from the United States, and it would not have affected the contraband trade with the Allies. Germany used submarines not because of the need to obtain American supplies, but from a desire to prevent the Allies from getting them.

The course that would have guaranteed peace for the United States was unacceptable to the American people and the Wilson administration. Only by severing all its European ties could the nation obtain such a guarantee. In 1914 that act would have placed serious strain on an economy that already showed signs of instability; by 1916 it would have been economically disastrous. At any time it would have been of doubtful political feasibility, even if one were to premise American popular disinterest in who won the war. The British understood this fact and reacted accordingly. If such thoughts suggest that the United States was influenced by the needs of an expanding capitalist economy, so let it be. It is by no means certain that another economic structure would have made much difference.

One might argue that measures short of a total embargo, a different arrangement of neutral practices—for instance, stoppage of the munitions traffic, and/or a ban on American travel on belligerent ships—would have allowed a profitable, humane, yet nonprovocative trade with Europe. Though a reply to that contention can offer no stronger claim to truth than the contention itself, one can offer these points: Wilson argued that yielding one concession on the seas ultimately would lead to pressure to abandon all rights. The pragmatic behavior of belligerents, especially the Germans, makes that assessment seem fair. Lest the German chancellor appear a hero to opponents of American intervention, it is well to remember that [Theobald von] Bethmann[-Hollweg]'s views on submarine warfare were not fashioned by love of the United States, or by the agony of knowing his submarines were sending innocent victims to their death. He was guided by simple national interest and the desire to use submarines as fully as circumstances allowed. It also is worth noting that Germany, when it reopened submarine warfare in 1917, was interested not merely in sinking munitions ships, but wanted to prevent all products going to Britain and was especially anxious to halt shipments of food. Had the United States wished to consider [then-secretary of state William Jennings] Bryan's proposals, keeping people and property out of the danger zone, it would have been easier early in the war, perhaps in February 1915, than after the sinkings began, and above all after the *Lusitania* went down. Yielding in the midst of the *Lusitania* crisis involved nothing short of national humiliation. If Bryan's proposals would have eliminated the sort of incident that provoked intervention, they also would have required a huge sacrifice—too great, as it turned out, for Wilson to accept. The United States would have faced economic loss, loss of national prestige, and probably the eventual prospect of a Europe dominated by [German rulers Paul von] Hindenburg, [Erich von] Ludendorff, and Wilhelm II.

Principle vs. Practical Considerations

No less than the nation as a whole, Wilson found himself accountable for the world standing of the United States. He felt a need and an obligation to promote economic interests abroad. When dealing with Germany he usually spoke in terms of principle; in relations with the Allies he showed awareness of practical considerations. In the hectic days of August 1914, he took steps to get American merchant ships back to sea. In the summer of 1915, advisers alerted him to the financial strain Britain had come to experience, the weakening of the pound sterling and the need to borrow funds in the United States. The secretary of the treasury [William G. MacAdoo] recommended approval of foreign loans. "To maintain our prosperity we must finance it," he said. Lansing, who believed similarly, wrote the president: "If the European countries cannot find the means to pay for the excess of goods sold them over those purchased from them, they will have to stop buying and our present export trade will shrink proportionately. The result will be restriction of output, industrial depression, idle capital, idle labor, numerous failures, financial demoralization, and general unrest and suffering among the laboring masses."

Shortly afterward the administration acquiesced as the House of Morgan floated loans of $500 million for the British and French governments. War traffic with the Allies prompted the German attempt to stop it with submarines. Submarine warfare led to destruction of property and loss of American lives. What had started as efforts to promote prosperity and neutral rights developed into questions of national honor and prestige. Wilson faced not merely the possibility of abandoning economic rights but the humiliating prospect of allowing the Germans to force him to it. The more hazardous it became to exercise American rights, the more difficult it was to yield them.

A Matter of National Honor

Wilson's definition of right and honor was itself conditioned by the fact that he was president of the United States and not some less powerful nation. His estimate of what rights belonged to the United States, what was for belligerents fair and humane warfare, rested not simply on a statement of principle, but on the power of the United States to compel observance of these principles. He could not send demands to the German government without some reason for believing the Germans would obey. Interpretation of national honor varies with national economic and military strength. The more powerful the nation, the more the world expects of it and the more the nation expects of itself. Such small seafaring states as Denmark and the Netherlands suffered extensive losses from submarine warfare, and yet these governments did not feel themselves honor bound to declare war. Wilson credited his right to act as a mediator to his position as leader of the most powerful neutral state. Indeed, he sometimes felt obligated to express moral principle. He could not, and would not, have acted these ways had he been, let us say, president of the Dominican Republic. It is thus possible to say that despite Wilson's commanding personality, his heavy-handedness in foreign policy and flair for self-righteousness, American diplomacy in final analysis was less a case of the man guiding affairs of the nation than the nation, and belligerent nations, guiding the affairs of the man.

It is tempting to conclude that inasmuch as the United States was destined to enter the conflict, it might as well have accepted that fact and reacted accordingly. Presumably this response would have involved an earlier declaration of war, certainly a large and rapid rearmament program. In recent years some "realist" scholars, notably George F. Kennan, have considered that this course would have been practical. However wise that policy might have been, it did not fit conditions of the period of neutrality. Wilson opposed entering the war earlier, and had he thought differently, popular and congressional support were highly questionable. People did not know in 1914 that commercial relations would lead them into the World War; most of them believed during the entire period that they could have trade and peace at the same time. The body of the United States was going one way during the period of neutrality, its heart and mind another. For a declaration of war there needed to be a merging of courses.

The Decisive Event

In his book America in the Twentieth Century, *historian George Moss maintains that President Woodrow Wilson strove to keep the United States out of World War I until Germany's submarine warfare made that impossible.*

Although it is accurate to say that popular pro-Ally sentiments, economic and financial ties to the Allies, and Wilson's pro-Ally preferences made genuine neutrality impossible, it is important to stress that Wilson did not seek to bring the United States into the war. He wanted desperately to avoid war, and he crafted a foreign policy that avoided war for nearly three years at the same time it protected vital American interests and national honor. Repeatedly, Wilson sent his personal representative, Colonel Edward House, to Europe to try to mediate an end to the conflict. In early 1917, Wilson cried: "It would be a crime against civilization if we went in." No modern president has felt a greater horror of war and none tried harder to avoid engulfing his people in war.

But Americans got caught in an Allies–Central Powers conflict. . . .

The decisive event which brought the United States into World War I was the German decision to resume unrestricted submarine warfare in early 1917. This decision nullified Wilson's neutrality policy based upon "strict accountability" and forced Wilson to choose between war and appeasement. Wilson's critics have cited his rigid conception of international law, which did not fit the reality of submarine tactics. They have also faulted his unyielding defense of the right of Americans to travel on belligerent ships, even those hauling contraband. But most Americans supported his neutrality policy, and when he told the people on April 2, 1917 that "neutrality was no longer feasible nor desirable," most supported his request for war.

Then, too, it was not absolutely certain that the United States had to enter the conflict, for the nation after all did avoid intervention for over two and one-half years, two-thirds of the war's fighting time. That same strength which eventually brought the nation into the war for a while helped it avoid intervention. From this perspective the campaign for mediation might have represented some of Wilson's soundest thinking. German officials never were certain about American strength, and the longer they had to endure a costly, indecisive conflict, the more they were willing to consider the type of gamble taken in 1917. American intervention was all but certain unless the United States made a drastic change in policy—which, as we have seen, it was unwilling to do—or unless someone beforehand brought the war to an end. It incidentally also seems fair to say that an indecisive settlement, a "peace without victory," would have better served the interests of the United States, not to mention the interests of the world, than the vindictive treaty drawn up in 1919. These thoughts, of course, are hindsight, but it is ironic that Wilson made the same observations weeks before the United States entered the war.

Why did the peace effort fail? In some small measure it was due to Wilson's inability to maintain the loyalty of his advisers. House, Page, and Lansing helped convince the Allies that Wilson did not intend to bring to bear on them the tremendous power at his disposal. The movement failed in 1917 largely because American power was not clearly observable to the German government. A better indication of American might, a military force visibly large enough to ensure German defeat, probably would have prevented resumption of submarine warfare and forced the Germans to negotiate. Thus, perhaps the major weakness of Wilson's war policies was an unwillingness to promote a more vigorous preparedness campaign. Even these thoughts are speculative, based on the assumption that Wilson could have done as he wished. Rearmament was no easy burden to impose upon the American people, and even if the United States had possessed a formidable force, there is no way to tell what it would have done with it. Huge armies can be a deterrent to war; they also can hasten its coming.

Wilsonian Diplomacy

One of the most provocative features of Wilsonian diplomacy was the president's apparent obsession with moral principle and international law. To critics this tendency suggested blindness to realistic goals, ignorance of the way nations deal with one another, if not a profession of personal superiority. In some ways the critics were right. Wilson was dedicated to principle. He thought the old system of interstate relations was unsatisfactory and looked to a time when nations would find rules to govern relations among themselves no less effective than laws within individual states. He wished to have a large part in making those rules. His propensity to quibble about shipments of cargo and techniques of approaching ships at sea seemed a ridiculous and remote abstraction at a time when the fate of nations hung in balance. It was naive to expect nations to respect legal principles when they had so much at stake. If they obeyed Wilson's command, their obedience was due less to principle than to his nation's ability to retaliate. At the same time international law was to Wilson more than an ideal; it was a manifestation of neutral intent and a device for defining American neutrality. Unless the United States decided to declare war or to stay out of the mess entirely, it would have to deal with complicated questions of neutral rights. International law was not merely convenient, it was the only device available. There fortunately was no conflict between Wilsonian principle and American rights and needs—the principle could be used to uphold the need. That the United States found an attraction for international law is not surprising: the restraints the law placed on belligerents would benefit any nation wishing to engage in neutral wartime commerce. International law looked to an orderly international society, and the United States, a satisfied nation, would profit from order. The chaos of 1914–17 strengthened feeling in the United States that American interests coincided with world interests, or, put another way, that what was good for the United States was good for the world.

Wilson's Goals

Even so, it is not adequate to say that Wilson was a realist who clothed practical considerations with moral rhetoric. He was both practical and idealistic, at least during the period of American neutrality. If he believed that upholding principle would advance American interests, he also hoped that promoting American interests would serve the cause of international morality. By demonstrating that the United States would not condone brutality, disorder, and lawlessness, he hoped to set a standard for other nations to follow. Wilson wanted to help reform the world, but he would have settled for protecting the interests of the United States and keeping the nation at peace.

Evidence from various quarters supports these final conclusions: there is no indication that Wilson went to war to protect American loans to the Allies and large business interests, although these interests, and economic factors in general, helped bring the United States to a point where war seemed unavoidable. There is no evidence that Wilson asked for war to prevent the defeat of Britain and France. It could well have been, as several scholars have written, that preservation of Britain and France was vital to the interests of the United States. American neutrality, incidentally or by design, functioned to sustain that thesis. Even so, Wilson did not intervene to prevent these nations' collapse; the Allies, while not winning, were not on the verge of losing in the spring of 1917. Nor did Wilson go to war to preserve American security. This is not to say that he was not concerned with security; he simply did not see it in jeopardy. The president did ask his countrymen for war as a means of protecting American honor, rights, and general interest—for both moral and practical reasons. He saw no contradiction between the two. But Wilson's idea of right and interest grew out of what the nation was at the time, and the First World War made clear what had been true for some years: the United States was in all respects a part of the world, destined to profit from its riches and suffer from its woes.

VIEWPOINT 2

"The presence of American troops in battle surely was not the only or most effective way to use American influence to bring the war to an end."

Woodrow Wilson's Decision to Take the United States into War Was Not Justified

Henry Fairlie (1924–1990)

Henry Fairlie was a prominent British journalist and author; his books include *The Kennedy Promise* and *The Life of Politics*. Fairlie spent the last twenty-five years of his life in the United States, where he was an editor for the *New Republic*. The following viewpoint is taken from an article published in a special edition of the *New Republic* commemorating its seventy-fifth anniversary. Fairlie notes that the journal, founded in the year World War I began in Europe, was an early and consistent advocate of American intervention in the war. This advocacy was misguided, he argues, as was President Woodrow Wilson's ultimate decision to call for a declaration of war in April 1917. Fairlie maintains that although some form of American diplomatic intervention in World War I was inevitable, the United States did not need to send American troops in order to bring about an end to the war. Wilson's actions, he concludes, actually contributed to the failure to secure a lasting peace and helped set the groundwork for the next world war.

From Henry Fairlie, "War Against Reason," *New Republic*, November 6, 1989. Reprinted by permission of the *New Republic*; ©1989, The New Republic, Inc.

War broke out in Europe on August 4, 1914. Three months later the first issue of *The New Republic* proclaimed "The End of American Isolation," and its second issue ruled out "comfortable neutrality." Remorselessly, for the next two years and five months, the editors of *TNR* developed the case for direct American intervention, until the entire issue of March 10, 1917, was devoted to extracts from its previous editorials, illustrating "The Evolution of a National Policy in Relation to the Great War." Three weeks later Woodrow Wilson's chief clerk in the White House saw him "sitting before his little typewriting machine," a Hammond portable, "slowly but accurately and neatly" composing the message that took his country into war. Of all the voices that prepared American public opinion (and to some extent, Wilson's own mind) to accept the inevitability of that decision, the most consistent, intellectually forceful, and zealous was that of this then infant magazine.

The Wilsonian case for going to war has been the conventional wisdom for 75 years. So dense is the consensus, only occasionally challenged by revisionist historians, that it seems almost a heresy to suggest that Wilson's decision was unnecessary and unwise, that there was no justification for it; and that the manner in which he took it has (with a brief interruption in the 1920s) been responsible for a mindset that still bedevils American policy and the nation's life.

Alternatives to War

By 1917 the European powers had fought themselves to a standstill. Amid the ruin of their continent and the carnage in the trenches, neither side was capable of winning or ending the war. America had to intervene. The question is whether entering the war as a combatant was the only or even the most effective way of bringing America's weight to bear. It was not.

The United States had become the leading manufacturing nation in the world. The value of its exports doubled between 1876 and 1900, giving it a net surplus in its balance of payments, and then, amazingly, doubled again before 1914. An influential British book of 1901 carried the title *The Americanization of the World.* Every great power listened to the puissant new nation across the Atlantic. The most obvious evidence was that, as Britain felt its supremacy slipping westward, a spontaneous cry arose there around 1900, calling for a "special relationship" with America (the birth of the term) and an "Anglo-Saxon" condominium to rule the world—and save the British Empire! It was the time when [British writer Rudyard] Kipling exhorted Americans:

"Take up the White Man's burden."

With this immense prowess and influence, America could have exerted its diplomacy with more consistency and skill. It is true that Wilson made peace efforts in 1916, and that Germany was foolishly in no mood to accept a negotiated peace. But these efforts were not persistent or well informed, and were frustrated by personal considerations, such as Wilson's choice of his ubiquitous adviser, Colonel [Edward] House, to be his negotiator. If America had remained neutral, the war (which, after all, ended in armistice, not unconditional surrender) probably could have been brought to a close just as quickly, and America would have retained its moral authority, which it forfeited by becoming merely another combatant. The hostility that Wilson aroused among European nations at the Versailles peace conference, and his loss of authority at home in failing to win support for the League of Nations, were the result of his abandonment of American neutrality, so that the New World became (and has remained ever since) only the latest contributor to the Old World's sorry record of folly.

There was no pretext for going to war until 1917, when the kaiser supported his more belligerent admirals (and general staff) in resuming a policy of unrestricted submarine warfare. Thus he gave Wilson, and the editors of *TNR*, a plausible casus belli. On February 10, 1917, *TNR* said that America was "being drawn into war" to keep open the Atlantic sea-lane. "We shall uphold the dominion of the ocean highway as men upheld the Union in 1861." The secondary question is whether this was a sufficient reason to become a belligerent. Again, it was not. The ease with which almost two million American troops were transported to France, mostly in a few months in 1918, suggests that the menace of the U-boat warfare, barbarous as it was, was greatly exaggerated.

It is not even clear what those pushing America into war thought it could accomplish militarily. When Wilson read his war message to Congress, the strength of the American regular Army stood at only 127,588 men. There were 200 German divisions massed on the western front, and in the next two months the British army alone lost 177,000 men in a single offensive. (Britain eventually lost three-quarters of a million men, and France, with half the population, double that number.) Although most of the two million American troops never saw action, I am not denying their contribution or valor in battle. But the presence of American troops in battle surely was not the only or most effective way to use American influence to bring the war to an end.

American Views on the Military

Americans in 1917 were a generally pacific people who had never expected to participate in a great foreign war. Before 1914 it was extremely rare for even one percent of the male population between 20 and 39 to see military service, and for the annual military expenditure to reach as much as one percent of the GNP. [Republican senator] Mark Hanna said in 1897 that the War Department was the only Cabinet office for which a busy man could spare the time from his own affairs. Appointed to the supreme command of the [American] Expeditionary Force, [John J.] Pershing gazed on the little continental army. "We still maintained our troops in small posts," he wrote later, "as in the days of Indian warfare." That is it in a nutshell. America had barely finished mopping up a few intransigent Indians when Wilson took it into a war between the great monarchies of Europe.

The traditional hostility of the American people to a standing army was still so pronounced that in 1911 Congress enacted a law imposing a $500 fine on any public place of entertainment that discriminated against men in uniform. When the proposal for a draft was submitted to Congress in 1917, the Speaker of the House [Champ Clark] went to the floor to oppose it, comparing the conscript to a convict. As Wilson took the nation to war, he was using martial language. "Force, Force to the utmost, Force without stint or limit," he proclaimed on Flag Day 1917. But where was the martial nation?

Transforming the Country

It had to be created. This was the work of an extraordinary harmony between the drives of big business and the variety of "progressivism" represented by the editors of *TNR*. It is here that we come close to the idea that carried America into a foreign war, and changed Wilson from the insistent advocate of American neutrality into a war leader of inflammatory rhetoric, ruthless execution, and global pretensions.

At the conclusion of his *History of the American People* (1902), Wilson noted that they had turned from a deliberate preoccupation with their domestic development to "make conquest of the markets of the world." Seven years later S.D. Scudder of the International Banking Corporation trumpeted to the National Association of Manufacturers: "You have completed the home task. . . . The world is ours!" The phenomenal energy of American industry was of course accompanied by its rapid consolidation into huge corporations, and the impulse was more than aggrandizement for profit. The industrial process, from start to finish, was to be made more rational; and becoming so—this was the astonishing leap—it would make society more rational.

"Rationalization" was the dynamic idea of the time. The needs of industry were obvious. With its consolidation, and the explosive expansion of consumption and production, a much higher degree of standardization was required. The new chemical and electrical industries depended on scientific research and highly developed technologies. In 1901 General Electric announced that it had created its own laboratory "devoted exclusively to original research," and with Westinghouse and Bell also leading the way, scientists were being employed (as David Noble says in his path-breaking study *America by Design*, 1979) "by hundreds where Edison employed them by tens."

The belief that science had given men the opportunity to create a new and beneficent order was never more widespread. It was the time also of Taylorism: Frederick Taylor published his *Principles of Scientific Management* in 1911, and its influence extended far beyond industry. There was a great deal of talk of "rational planning" and "social engineering." All these voices and more can be found in the early *TNR*, not only in its editorials, but in such an important contributor as John Dewey, whose belief in the scientific method imparted an extraordinary optimism to the seemingly endless programs for reorganizing society that poured forth. . . .

In the famous rift in progressivism—between those looking back to an idealized age of small units and communities, and those looking forward to directing the large units and corporations—the editors of *TNR* had moved far from the progressivism of [jurist Louis] Brandeis, with its Jeffersonian emphasis on pluralism and decentralized power. What is more, although Wilson still consulted Brandeis, by 1914 he was looking for a new idea in anticipation of his campaign for re-election two years later. As Max Lerner has written, "Democratic reformism of the Wilson variety had already pretty much run its course before we entered the war; *in fact, that may have been one of the things pushing us in.*" (Italics added.) Between 1914 and 1917 the compact between big business, progressivism, and Wilson was forged. A compelling idea was in the air, and it was in Wilson's mind as he sat before his Hammond portable.

War and Big Business

Industrialists in those days spoke more candidly. It is almost engaging that Howard E. Coffin, vice president of the Hudson Motor Company, should tell Congress that "the war in Europe is the greatest business proposition in all time." The purpose of the "war preparedness campaign" after 1914, largely inspired by big business while *TNR* supplied the intellectual arguments, was to prepare the mind of the nation for war, as if Ypres were to be fought at Hoboken. Since the Germans, according to Allied propaganda, raped Belgian nuns, New Jersey farm girls must be saved from a fate worse than death. In his best seller of that time, Hudson Maxim spoke of *Defenseless America*. Defenseless before whom? The penguins might as well have marched from the South Pole as the army of any nation was likely to invade the United States. But with its monster parades around the country, the preparedness campaign even accustomed the American people to the weapons of modern war on their Main Streets.

The collusion of Wilson's administration was the true beginning of the "military-industrial complex." As early as the middle of 1915, representatives of the leading industrial and engineering associations were summoned by Josephus Daniels, Secretary of the Navy, to act as unpaid consultants. This led to the formation of the Naval Consulting Board, which in turn created an Industrial Preparedness Committee. Its director was Walter S. Gifford, chief statistician of AT&T. (Statistics were to the "corporate liberals" and progressives an important instrument for mastering modern society.) These arrangements were formalized in 1916, when Congress established a Council on National Defense. This body then appointed seven "experts" (i.e., industrialists) to act as a National Defense Advisory Commission, with Gifford again its director. When the commission first met in a hotel room, it recommended that in the event of war the government should depend "largely upon private plants for war matériel." The recommendation cannot have been painful: the recommenders commanded the private plants. In the hundred or so committees they established, the responsibility for transport and communications was entrusted to the president of the Baltimore & Ohio Railroad; for supplies, including clothes, to Sears, Roebuck; and so to the committee on canned goods, placed in the hands of the California Packing Corporation, Libby, and H.J. Heinz.

An entire society was to be organized in detail from the center. And none of this elaborate meshing of industry with government was intended only for the emergency. When Wilson announced the names of the seven commissioners, he said that "it opens up a new and direct channel of communication between business and scientific men and all the departments of government." In 1919 the chairman of a select committee of the House investigating the activities of the commission before and during the war reported:

> . . . a commission of seven men chosen by the President seems to have devised the entire system of purchasing war supplies, planned a press censorship, designed a system of food control . . . , determined on a daylight-saving scheme, and in a word designed practically every measure which Congress subsequently enacted, and did all this behind closed doors, weeks and even months before the Congress of the United States declared war against Germany.

He had reason to be flabbergasted.

None were more zealous in advocating the use of greater centralized authority than the progressives. Wilson chose Newton Baker, one of the "Holy Trinity" of progressive Mayors who won in Ohio before the war, to be his Secretary of War. In 1916 Baker wrote to Wilson that many concerns that he would have left to state governments 20 years before he now considered appropriate for national legislation, "and so I do not know that I have reached any clear conclusion as to where the Federal government ought to stop." Even Brandeis by 1918 advised Wilson to create the War Industries Board under Bernard Baruch, the final apotheosis of the peacetime preparedness committees. The war did not move Wilson into this path; it merely hastened his progress down it. . . .

So when Wilson rode to Congress to deliver his War Message on April 2, 1917, Baker provided a troop of cavalry, who did not regard it as a favor to be called out on an evening when the day-long rain was still gusting down Pennsylvania Avenue. Only four weeks before he had ridden the same route for his second inauguration in an open carriage with Mrs. Wilson. Now it was lined thickly with soldiers of two regiments of the New York National

Wilson's Failure to Maintain U.S. Neutrality

Many historians—including John G. Coogan, a history professor at Michigan State University—have argued that despite his public pro-nouncements to the contrary, President Woodrow Wilson failed to maintain American neutrality in World War I prior to America's dec-laration of war on Germany. The following passages are excerpted from Coogan's 1981 book The End of Neutrality: The United States, Britain, and Maritime Rights, 1899–1915.

[On April 2, 1917,] Woodrow Wilson asked the Congress of the United States to declare war on Germany. He emphasized in his re-quest that, although other concerns had influenced his decision, the primary motivation had been defense of American maritime rights against the German submarine: "We enter this war only where we are clearly forced into it because there are no other means of defend-ing our rights." At best this statement indicates Wilson's capacity for self-delusion; at worst it demonstrates his capacity for hypocrisy. The system for international law Wilson claimed to be defending in 1917 had been undermined two years earlier by his own failure to maintain American neutrality. The United States went to war not in defense of neutral rights, but to enforce the principle that a nation purporting to be neutral could violate the rules of neutrality while avoiding the consequences of belligerency. . . .

Woodrow Wilson publicly pledged in August 1914 to maintain American neutrality. He did not keep this pledge. . . . American pol-icy toward Britain during the [1899–1902] Boer War had been benev-olent neutrality. American policy during World War I was precisely

Guard. There was nothing ceremonial about the squads of secret service men forming a tight square around his carriage; and most astonishing of all, machine guns were "set at every street corner." But it was to precisely all this that the "war preparedness campaign" had sought to accustom the American people with parades. Thus did Wilson lead the pacific nation into war, with soaring rhetoric and uncontained, missionary idealism: to use "the righteous and triumphant force which shall make right the law of the world, and cast every self dominion down in the dust."

In spite of some outbursts of whipped-up patriotic hysteria, the incessant war propaganda, and the unnecessary prosecution of many dissidents (including Eugene Debs, who had to wait to be released until 1921, not by Wilson, but as one of the first acts of [President Warren G.] Harding when he replaced Wilson!), the American people were never enthusiastic about the war and barely touched by it. Brandeis warned the British foreign secretary that the war was not popular with the people, and that they would not undertake any responsibility beyond it: e.g., joint re-

what [State Department official] James Brown Scott had warned it would be if the United States failed to defend its rights against flagrant British violation: "non-neutrality toward Germany" and "a manifest failure to safeguard the interests of United States citizens engaged in perfectly legitimate business." American maritime neutrality during the first eight months of World War I was incompatible with the traditional American principles contained in John Bassett Moore's magisterial 1907 *Digest of International Law,* incompatible with John Hay's statements during the Boer and Russo-Japanese Wars, incompatible with the Naval War Code of 1900 and the teachings of the Naval War College, [and] incompatible with the positions taken by the United States at the Hague and London Conferences. . . .

Several historians have concluded from this evidence that Wilson deliberately compromised American neutrality in order to aid the Allies and eventually bring the United States into the war at their side. For the first eight months of war, at least, this interpretation overestimates Wilson's deviousness and underestimates his capacity for self-delusion. The president did shape American neutrality so it aided the Allies, but there is no evidence that he recognized his actions were in any way unneutral. On the contrary, surrounded by advisers eager to present Allied actions in the best possible light and convinced of his own moral superiority, Wilson continued to believe that he could define true neutrality better than could lawyers and textbooks. [Secretary of State Robert] Lansing and [Secretary of War Lindley] Garrison saw the flaw in this reasoning—that other nations were more likely to accept the rule of law than to accept the rule of Wilson—but they were never able to make the president see it.

sponsibility for a mandate in Palestine. In fact, the revulsion of the American people (and intellectuals) against the war when it was over was in part a rejection of the sweep of the American intervention in the world that Wilson imagined.

Nothing in the argument advanced here is intended to support the isolationism of men such as Robert La Follette and William Borah, who said that America went to war with the dollar sign on the flag. There was no conspiracy. There was merely the unchecked sway of a propelling idea. More important, I am not arguing a case for isolationism in general. I am talking only of America's intervention *in that war*, and of the messianic manner in which Wilson chose to enter it. (Knowing that Wilson was about to announce his Fourteen Points, Lloyd George, like other European statesmen, was so scared by what he regarded as its profound naïveté that he tried to forestall it in the House of Commons with some less far-reaching statements of the Allies' war aims.)

It seems, if one restudies the facts, that if America had stood outside the conflict, its overwhelming economic presence in the world by 1914 could have been used better, both to end the war and to make a lasting peace, instead of one that fell calamitously to pieces within 20 years. The story of the 1920s, now that some historians have demythologized it, is confirmation of this claim. America in the 1920s was not isolationist: in no way. Virtually disarmed but economically dominant, America was a constant presence in Europe, even if its influence was not always wisely used. The European nations could barely move without America, as in the matter of German reparations, and the Dawes Plan and then the Young Plan, both the work of Americans. Economic power is usually worth more than military power.

Warping America's Sense of Itself

When American intellectuals (in this case, speaking for the people) lamented after 1919 that America had lost its innocence in 1917, they were not being sentimental. Wilson had tragically warped America's own sense of itself, and for the past 50 years this has been most evident in the too often indiscriminate and ignorant American intervention around the globe; a profligate expenditure on arms in peacetime; and the growth of what is in many respects a garrison state of centralized power and cynical manipulation of its citizens. One of the instruments for which Wilson's administration reached during the war was the more professional advertising that had been developed by big business as part of its rationalization.

Abroad, since Wilson's war, America has become merely another power. At home, it has lost much of its confident pluralism, of which there was one eloquent, visionary spokesman within

TNR in those years. Randolph Bourne was already at odds with the progressivism of [*New Republic* editors Herbert] Croly and [Walter] Lippmann before 1917. With the entry of America into the war, his break with *TNR* (and not least with his mentor, Dewey) was complete and embittered. Apart from his famous formulation "War is the health of the state"—that the prosperity of the nation was being made dependent on an industrial war machine with government support—he developed, with the arrival of the mass immigrants, a remarkably coherent notion of a new multiethnic trans-Allegheny pluralism that would release, not constrict, America's founding sense to itself. It was precisely against the "rationalization" of American society, through a centralized power and intellectual elite, that Bourne revolted. Bourne was right.

Appendix

Wilson's Fourteen Points

On January 8, 1918, in an address before a joint session of Congress, President Woodrow Wilson presented what he held to be the fundamental war aims of the United States—the Fourteen Points. Included within these points were general principles for a future peace settlement, including open negotiations (no secret treaties), reduction of armaments, and freedom of the seas. Several points concerned specific territorial adjustments, adhering to the general principle of self-determination for European national groups. A final point dealt with the creation of what became the League of Nations. Distributed throughout Europe, the Fourteen Points were accepted by Germany and became the basis of the November 1918 armistice that ended the fighting in World War I. However, many of the goals of the Fourteen Points were opposed by the leaders of France, Great Britain, and Italy at the 1919 Paris Peace Conference and were ultimately compromised in the negotiations that produced the Treaty of Versailles.

The following excerpt from Wilson's speech includes the full text of the Fourteen Points.

We entered this war because violations of right had occurred which touched us to the quick and made the life of our own people impossible unless they were corrected and the world secured once for all against their recurrence. What we demand in this war, therefore, is nothing peculiar to ourselves. It is that the world be made fit and safe to live in; and particularly that it be made safe for every peace-loving nation which, like our own, wishes to live its own life, determine its own institutions, be assured of justice and fair dealing by the other peoples of the world as against force and selfish aggression. All the peoples of the world are in effect partners in this interest, and for our own part we see very clearly that unless justice be done to others it will not be done to us. The program of the world's peace, therefore, is our program; and that program, the only possible program, as we see it, is this:

I. Open covenants of peace, openly arrived at, after which there shall be no private international understandings of any kind but diplomacy shall proceed always frankly and in the public view.

II. Absolute freedom of navigation upon the seas, outside territorial waters, alike in peace and in war, except as the seas may be closed in whole or in part by international action for the enforcement of international covenants.

III. The removal, so far as possible, of all economic barriers and the establishment of an equality of trade conditions among all the nations consenting to the peace and associating themselves for its maintenance.

IV. Adequate guarantees given and taken that national armaments will be reduced to the lowest point consistent with domestic safety.

V. A free, open-minded, and absolutely impartial adjustment of all colonial claims, based upon a strict observance of the principle that in determining all such questions of sovereignty the interests of the populations concerned must have equal weight with the equitable claims of the government whose title is to be determined.

VI. The evacuation of all Russian territory and such a settlement of all questions affecting Russia as will secure the best and freest coöperation of the other nations of the world in obtaining for her an unhampered and unembarrassed opportunity for the independent determination of her own political development and national policy and assure her of a sincere welcome into the society of free nations under institutions of her own choosing; and, more than a welcome, assistance also of every kind that she may need and may herself desire. The treatment accorded Russia by her sister nations in the months to come will be the acid test of their good will, of their comprehension of her needs as distinguished from their own interests, and of their intelligent and unselfish sympathy.

VII. Belgium, the whole world will agree, must be evacuated and restored, without any attempt to limit the sovereignty which she enjoys in common with all other free nations. No other single act will serve as this will serve to restore confidence among the nations in the laws which they have themselves set and determined for the government of their relations with one another. Without this healing act the whole structure and validity of international law is forever impaired.

VIII. All French territory should be freed and the invaded portions restored, and the wrong done to France by Prussia in 1871 in the matter of Alsace-Lorraine, which has unsettled the peace of the world for nearly fifty years, should be righted, in order that peace may once more be made secure in the interest of all.

IX. A readjustment of the frontiers of Italy should be effected along clearly recognizable lines of nationality.

X. The peoples of Austria-Hungary, whose place among the nations we wish to see safeguarded and assured, should be accorded the freest opportunity of autonomous development.

XI. Rumania, Serbia, and Montenegro should be evacuated; occupied territories restored; Serbia accorded free and secure access to the sea; and the relations of the several Balkan states to one another determined by friendly counsel along historically established lines of allegiance and nationality; and international guarantees of the political and economic independence and territorial integrity of the several Balkan states should be entered into.

XII. The Turkish portions of the present Ottoman empire should be assured a secure sovereignty, but the other nationalities which are now under Turkish rule should be assured an undoubted security of life and an absolutely unmolested opportunity of autonomous development, and the Dardanelles should be permanently opened as a free passage to the ships and commerce of all nations under international guarantees.

XIII. An independent Polish state should be erected which should include the territories inhabited by indisputably Polish populations, which should be assured a free and secure access to the sea, and whose political and economic independence and territorial integrity should be guaranteed by international covenant.

XIV. A general association of nations must be formed under specific covenants for the purpose of affording mutual guarantees of political independence and territorial integrity to great and small states alike. . . .

For such arrangements and covenants we are willing to fight and to continue to fight until they are achieved; but only because we wish the right to prevail and desire a just and stable peace such as can be secured only by removing the chief provocations to war, which this program does remove. . . .

An evident principle runs through the whole program I have outlined. It is the principle of justice to all peoples and nationalities, and their right to live on equal terms of liberty and safety with one another, whether they be strong or weak. Unless this principle be made its foundation no part of the structure of international justice can stand. The people of the United States could act upon no other principle; and to the vindication of this principle they are ready to devote their lives, their honor, and everything that they possess. The moral climax of this the culminating and final war for human liberty has come, and they are ready to put their own strength, their own highest purpose, their own integrity and devotion to the test.

For Discussion

Chapter One

1. What lessons of history have Americans neglected, according to Leonard Wood? In his opinion, how have international conditions changed with regard to foreign military threats to America? Considering Wood's viewpoint, how do you think he might respond to George Nasmyth's arguments regarding the possibility of foreign invasion?

2. Charles E. Jefferson outlines a broad definition of "preparedness" that includes nonmilitary matters. In your opinion, does this tactic effectively counter the arguments of Wood and other advocates of military preparedness? Why or why not?

3. How does Charles W. Eliot dismiss pacifist and philosophical objections to military conscription and preparedness? Are his arguments against "non-resistance" convincing? Explain your answer, using examples from the viewpoint.

4. George Nasmyth argues that a system of compulsory military service might eventually result in the disappearance of freedom of the press and other rights enjoyed by Americans. Do you believe he successfully links conscription to the loss of democracy? Why or why not?

Chapter Two

1. What predictions does William Howard Taft make about the war's outcome? Do any of them pertain to Lewis Einstein's main concern i.e., whether the war will upset Europe's balance of power in favor of Germany? Does Einstein raise possible negative ramifications of American neutrality that Taft overlooks? Explain.

2. After reading the viewpoints by the *Fatherland* and Henry Watterson, which nation or party do you believe is most responsible for the loss of American lives on the *Lusitania?* Defend your answer.

3. Woodrow Wilson argues in his war message that neutrality is impossible because of German attacks on U.S. ships and other aggressive acts. William La Follette contends that neutrality was never really practiced by the United States. Compare their supporting arguments. Which do you find more convincing? Explain.

Chapter Three

1. The Socialist Party states that the war in Europe "was the logical outcome of the competitive capitalist system." In your opinion, does the party's entire case against the war rest upon this single premise? Explain your answer, citing specific arguments in the viewpoint.

2. Both Samuel Gompers and the editors of the *New Republic* support Wilson's decision to take the United States into war. However, while Gompers says he would rather have had Wilson enter the United States into the war sooner, the editors of the *New Republic* give special praise to Wilson's timing. Can you find other subtle differences between the two? In your opinion, do Gompers and the *New Republic* writers support different objectives for the war? List the objectives that Gompers and the *New Republic* editors discuss, both those they may share and those they may hold separately.

3. Randolph Bourne dismisses the argument that the United States is intervening in World War I "to save the world from subjugation" by asserting that all the warring nations in the conflict have made similar self-justifications for going to war. In your opinion, is this a compelling rebuttal? Is it logically sound? Defend your answer.

4. Both Harriot Stanton Blatch and Crystal Eastman direct much of their arguments toward a female audience. List some of the supporting reasons Blatch cites in maintaining why women as a class should support the war effort. Do the same for the arguments of Eastman. Which author, in your opinion, makes a more convincing case about what women should do regarding the war? Explain.

Chapter Four

1. Robert La Follette acknowledges that "in time of war the citizen must surrender some rights for the common good." In your opinion, does this concession strengthen or weaken his arguments? Explain.

2. What analogy do the authors of the *Outlook* editorial make between pacifists and train robbers? Do you believe the analogy is close enough to justify laws aimed at restricting the activities of pacifist groups? Why or why not?

3. What kind of future social order does Roger N. Baldwin look forward to? How does it differ from the social order Julius M. Mayer defends in his viewpoint? Which vision of society do you find more appealing? Which vision do you find more realistic? Explain, using examples from the viewpoints.

Chapter Five

1. Compare the visions that Woodrow Wilson and Theodore Roosevelt have regarding what the League of Nations should do and the powers it should possess. In what aspects are the visions compatible? In what aspects are they furthest apart?

2. Compare the *New Republic* editorial in this chapter with the one in Chapter Three (in which the editors endorsed Wilson's war address and the goals of the war). Are they consistent in their ideas of why the war was necessary and what it should accomplish? Does this consistency, or lack thereof, strengthen or weaken their conclusions? Explain.

3. Some historians have argued that Woodrow Wilson and Henry Cabot Lodge shared many ideas concerning diplomacy and American foreign policy and that their failure to reach a compromise over the League of Nations stemmed from political and personal rivalries rather than from fundamental differences in principle. Other scholars contend that compromise between the two was impossible because their disagreements ran too deep. Judging from the viewpoints presented here, which explanation do you find most convincing? Use examples from the viewpoints to support your answer.

Chapter Six

1. According to Henry Fairlie, what alternatives to military intervention did President Wilson have at his disposal? Are these alternative courses of action discussed or dispensed within Ross Gregory's viewpoint, in which he concludes that Wilson had little choice but to declare war? Which author, in your opinion, presents a more convincing case of the options Wilson had? Explain.
2. What aspects of Woodrow Wilson's personality emerge from the viewpoints of Ross Gregory and Henry Fairlie? For each viewpoint, list five statements about President Wilson you believe are based on fact and five statements that are, in your judgment, based on opinion. Compare the lists. Can you find cases of different opinions being drawn from the same set of facts?

General

1. Based on the viewpoints in this volume, do you think that the United States had viable alternatives to declaring war on Germany in April 1917? What other courses could the nation possibly have taken? Explain.
2. Many of the disagreements in the United States during World War I were more about American domestic issues than foreign policy. Which viewpoints in this volume fall into this category? What generalizations can you make connecting authors' domestic views with their views about the war?
3. In its critique of the war, the Socialist Party said it would create "a sinister spirit of passion, unreason, race hatred, and false patriotism." Are there examples in the viewpoints in this volume that, in your opinion, support this claim? Are there viewpoints that refute it? Explain.

Chronology

June 28, 1914	The assassination in Sarajevo of Archduke Franz Ferdinand, heir to the Hapsburg monarchy of Austria-Hungary, by a Serbian nationalist sets in motion the series of events that initiate World War I.
July 28, 1914	Austria-Hungary declares war on Serbia.
July 30, 1914	Russia mobilizes its military forces.
August 1, 1914	Germany declares war on Russia.
August 3, 1914	Germany declares war on France; its troops enter neutral Belgium, prompting an ultimatum from Great Britain.
August 4, 1914	Great Britain declares war on Germany.
	President Woodrow Wilson formally proclaims American neutrality in the war, which by now involves all of Europe's major powers: Great Britain, France, Russia, Germany, and Austria-Hungary.
August 15, 1914	The U.S. government announces that loans to belligerents violate American neutrality.
August 18, 1914	Wilson asks the American people to be "impartial in thought as well as in action."
August 20, 1914	The British government issues a broad definition of war contraband and declares its intention to intercept American ships bound for Germany.
August 25–31, 1914	In a major setback for the Allies, Russia is defeated by Germany in the Battle of Tannenberg.
August 26, 1914	German troops burn the Belgian city of Louvain, including its university and library, actions publicized in America as part of the "rape of Belgium."
September 5, 1914	Great Britain, France, and Russia agree not to seek a separate peace in the Pact of London.
September 6–10, 1914	German hopes for rapid victory in France are destroyed at the Battle of the Marne; the western front becomes a trench war stalemate that will last for three years.
November 3, 1914	The British government declares the North Sea a war zone and begins to mine its waters.
December 1914	The National Security League, a private organization, is established to promote American military preparedness.

December 21, 1914	The first German air raid is launched against Great Britain.
December 29, 1914	Wilson protests British detention of American ships in search of contraband.
January 30, 1915	Wilson sends a personal emissary, Colonel Edward House, on a fruitless peace mission to Europe.
February 4, 1915	Germany declares a war zone around the British Isles to begin on February 18.
February 10, 1915	The State Department formally protests the German declaration of a war zone and declares that the Berlin government will be held to "strict accountability" if American ships are sunk.
March 1, 1915	A German torpedo sinks the British passenger liner *Falaba*; one American citizen is killed in the attack.
March 11, 1915	The British government announces its blockade of German ports; Wilson issues a formal protest of the blockade on March 30.
April 11, 1915	The German ambassador to the United States calls on Americans to stop exporting arms to the Allies.
April 22, 1915	Poison gas is used in war for the first time by Germany in the Second Battle of Ypres.
April 26, 1915	France, Russia, Italy, and Great Britain conclude the secret treaty of London.
May 7, 1915	The British passenger liner *Lusitania* is sunk without warning by a German submarine, killing 1,198 people, including 128 Americans. Wilson responds by declaring in a May 10 speech that the United States is "too proud to fight."
May 12, 1915	The British government issues the Bryce Report, detailing alleged German atrocities against Belgium.
May 13, 1915	The Wilson administration issues its first diplomatic response to the sinking of the *Lusitania*, upholding the "indisputable" right of American citizens to travel the high seas and demanding reparations from Germany.
May 23, 1915	Italy declares war against Austria-Hungary, almost a month after signing a secret treaty with the Allies.
June 6, 1915	Unwilling to provoke the United States, the German government issues a secret order to submarine commanders to spare passenger liners from torpedo attacks.
June 9, 1915	Wilson issues a stronger protest of submarine warfare to the German government. Secretary of State William Jennings Bryan resigns and is replaced by his deputy, Robert Lansing.

August 4, 1915	The United States receives Britain's response to blockade protests; Great Britain defends its blockade as legal but offers to submit disputed cases of seizure to arbitration.
August 10, 1915	An American civilian military training camp experiment opens at Plattsburg, New York; other "Plattsburg camps" soon follow.
August 15, 1915	The New York *World* begins publication of documents captured by the U.S. Secret Service detailing German espionage and sabotage activities in the United States.
August 19, 1915	In violation of secret instructions, a German submarine sinks the British passenger ship *Arabic*; two American citizens die.
September 1915	Wilson reverses previous policy and permits private American firms to lend money to the Allies.
September 1, 1915	Germany agrees in the *Arabic* pledge to sink no more passenger liners without warning; the pledge, made public on October 15, is viewed as a diplomatic victory for America.
December 4, 1915	Henry Ford's peace ship, *Oskar II*, begins its voyage to Europe.
December 7, 1915	Wilson addresses Congress and urges legislation that would provide for major expansion of the army and navy.
January 27, 1916	Wilson embarks on a speaking tour urging Americans to support military preparedness.
February 1916	Congress debates the Gore-McLemore Resolutions, which call for either a warning or a ban against Americans traveling on belligerent ships in wartime; the resolution is tabled on March 3.
February 21, 1916	The monumental Battle of Verdun begins; it will last for ten months and claim a million French and German casualties.
February 22, 1916	A second Colonel House peace mission to Europe results in the issuance of the House-Grey Memorandum, which offers American mediation of the war. Included is the veiled threat of U.S. entrance into the war if the German government refuses the American offer of mediation.
March 7, 1916	Newton Baker is appointed secretary of war by President Wilson; he replaces Lindley M. Garrison, who resigned in February in a dispute over national versus state control of National Guard units.
March 15, 1916	General John J. Pershing leads six thousand American troops into Mexico following raids on American soil by Mexican rebel leader Pancho Villa.

March 24, 1916	In violation of the *Arabic* pledge, a German submarine torpedoes an unarmed French passenger ship, the *Sussex*, as it crosses the English Channel; several Americans are injured, none fatally.
April 18, 1916	Secretary of State Lansing warns the German government that further acts of submarine warfare will lead to the severing of diplomatic relations between the two countries.
	Seven Americans from a fighter plane squadron, the Escadrille Lafayette, volunteer to fight for France.
April 24, 1916	The Easter Rebellion rocks Ireland; many Americans criticize Great Britain for its actions in putting down the Irish nationalist revolt and executing its leaders.
May 4, 1916	The German government responds to Secretary Lansing by announcing that there will be no further surprise submarine attacks against either merchant ships or passenger liners. However, Germany reserves the right to use submarines in self-defense.
June 3, 1916	The National Defense Act becomes law, authorizing a five-year expansion of the American army to 223,000, establishing officer training programs in universities, and including provisions on industrial preparedness.
July 1, 1916	The Battle of the Somme begins; the British suffer more than sixty thousand casualties on the first day.
July 18, 1916	The British government issues a blacklist of some eighty American firms or individuals who may not engage in trade with Great Britain because of their German connections.
July 30, 1916	An explosion at a munitions plant on Black Tom Island in New Jersey is one of several incidents attributed to German sabotage.
August 1916	Congress passes and Wilson signs the Naval Act of 1916, which represents the largest peacetime military appropriation to date in American history.
August 29, 1916	The Council of National Defense is established; it consists of six cabinet members under the direction of Secretary of War Baker and is charged with coordinating industry and resources.
August 31, 1916	Germany announces a suspension of submarine attacks.
September 15, 1916	Great Britain uses tanks for the first time in battle.
October 15, 1916	Germany resumes submarine attacks under search-and-destroy rules.

November 7, 1916	Wilson, campaigning on a "He kept us out of war" slogan, is reelected to a second term.
December 12, 1916	The German government issues a statement indicating a willingness to discuss peace terms.
December 18, 1916	Wilson sends a note to the warring countries offering American services as a mediator and asking them to state their conditions for peace negotiations. The British angrily, but wrongly, assume that this note has been coordinated with the German statement of December 12.
January 16, 1917	German foreign minister Arthur Zimmermann sends a coded telegram to the German minister in Mexico instructing him to propose a German-Mexican alliance that could possibly lead to Mexico's recovery of territory lost to the United States during the Mexican War.
January 22, 1917	After his mediation efforts have been rebuffed, Wilson delivers his "peace without victory" speech to Congress, in which he calls on all warring parties to settle for less than victory.
January 31, 1917	Germany resumes unrestricted submarine warfare, meaning that American and all other neutral ships traveling within war zones are subject to attack without warning.
February 3, 1917	The United States breaks off diplomatic relations with Germany.
February 26, 1917	Wilson asks Congress to pass legislation arming American merchant ships for defense against submarines.
March 1, 1917	The contents of the Zimmermann telegram (which had been intercepted by the British and passed on to the U.S. government) are revealed to the American press by the State Department.
March 12, 1917	After failing to get Senate approval, Wilson announces the arming of merchant ships by executive order.
March 15, 1917	Czar Nicholas II of Russia abdicates; a provisional government takes power, promising to simultaneously keep Russia in the war and build Russian democracy. Its authority is undercut by the Petrograd Soviet, a revolutionary council, which on March 17 calls on Russian soldiers to support its authority and to retain their weapons for internal revolution.
March 29, 1917	Wilson calls for a national army to be "raised and maintained exclusively by selective draft."

March 31, 1917	The General Munitions Board is established by the Council on National Defense to coordinate war industries and military procurement; its abilities are hampered by lack of enforcement authority.
April 1917	Lenin and other radical Bolshevik political exiles in Switzerland return, with German help, to Russia, where they take control of the Soviet Petrograd and plot a revolt against the Russian provisional government.
	German destruction of Allied shipping peaks during the month of April at 881,000 tons.
	French soldiers begin to mutiny following failure in the Aisne and Champagne offensives.
April 1, 1917	Wilson is informed that the American army is able to muster 5,791 officers and 121,797 enlisted men; during the war the number of men in the army will grow to 4 million.
April 2, 1917	Wilson asks for an American declaration of war against Germany.
April 4, 1917	The Senate votes for war, 82-6.
April 6, 1917	The House of Representatives votes for war, 373-50.
April 14, 1917	The Committee on Public Information is established by executive order; it is charged with rallying American public opinion behind the war.
April 24, 1917	Wilson signs the Liberty Loan Act; Five Liberty Loan drives will eventually net $21.4 billion. American destroyers are dispatched to the war zone.
May 11, 1917	Wilson appoints a commission to travel to Russia to monitor the war effort there; Elihu Root serves as chairman.
May 18, 1917	Wilson signs the Selective Service Act, which has passed both houses of Congress by large majorities.
May 26, 1917	Pershing is selected to head the American Expeditionary Force (AEF); he arrives in Paris on June 14 without an army.
June 5, 1917	National draft registration day is held; more than 10 million men ages twenty-one to thirty register at over four thousand polling places across the country.
June 15, 1917	Congress passes the Espionage Act; the law specifies penalties for spies and people found guilty of aiding the enemy or obstructing conscription or military recruiting. It also empowers the postmaster general to ban from the mail periodicals and other materials deemed subversive.

June 26, 1917	First American troops arrive in France.
July 2, 1917	Pershing requests that the United States raise an army of 1 million soldiers; a few days later he increases his request to 3 million.
July 19, 1917	The German Reichstag passes a resolution calling for peace without annexations or indemnities.
July 20, 1917	The first of a series of draft lotteries is conducted by the War Department.
July 28, 1917	The War Industries Board is established by the Council of National Defense to replace the General Munitions Board.
August 1, 1917	Pope Benedict XV makes a plea for peace based on no annexations or indemnities; Wilson rejects the peace proposal on August 28.
August 10, 1917	Congress passes the Lever Food and Fuel Control Act; Herbert Hoover is appointed food administrator by Wilson.
September 8, 1917	The use of edible grains for distilled alcoholic drinks is prohibited to conserve food for the war effort.
October 3, 1917	Congress passes the War Revenue Act, authorizing a graduated income tax that is to be the chief source of government revenue during the war.
October 6, 1917	Congress passes the Trading with the Enemy Act, giving the federal government control over all foreign trade.
November 7, 1917	The Bolsheviks, led by Lenin and Leon Trotsky, seize power in Russia and declare for peace.
December 7, 1917	The United States declares war on Austria-Hungary.
December 26, 1917	In its most extreme single wartime mobilization action, the federal government takes over management of the nation's railways.
January 18, 1918	Wilson delivers his "Fourteen Points" address to a joint session of Congress, describing his vision of an American peace program.
March 3, 1918	Russia (now the Soviet Union) and the Central Powers sign the Treaty of Brest-Litovsk, ending their state of war.
March 4, 1918	Bernard Baruch is appointed head of the War Industries Board.
March 21, 1918	Reinforced by troops from the east, Germany launches a massive attack on the western front.
April 8, 1918	The National War Labor Board is created to mediate labor conflicts in the United States.

April 14, 1918	General Ferdinand Foch of France is made supreme commander of the Allied forces, including the Americans; he makes a special plea to Wilson for quick deployment of American troops to Europe.
May 16, 1918	Congress passes the Sedition Act, which amends and strengthens the Espionage Act.
May 20, 1918	Congress passes the Overman Act, giving the president greater discretionary authority to reorganize executive agencies.
May 25, 1918	German submarines appear in U.S. waters for the first time.
May 28, 1918	In their first important attack, American troops help win the Battle of Cantigny.
June/July 1918	American soldiers engage in their first major battles at Belleau Wood and Château-Thierry.
June 29, 1918	Socialist leader Eugene V. Debs is indicted for violating the Espionage Act based on an antiwar speech he gave in Canton, Ohio. He is the most prominent of hundreds of war opponents to be arrested, tried, and imprisoned.
Summer 1918	Race riots plague major American cities, including Chicago, where thirty-eight people are killed.
July 1918	The AEF plays a major role in the Second Battle of the Marne; Wilson agrees to a maximum of eighty American divisions for the war effort. (The AEF will stand at forty-two divisions at the time of the November 11, 1918, armistice.)
September 1918	A deadly influenza epidemic strikes the United States; 300,000 die within the next eight weeks.
September 12, 1918	American soldiers launch the St. Mihiel offensive; they take fifteen thousand German prisoners.
September 26, 1918	The final Allied offensive of the war, and the one in which Americans see the most action, begins; the Meuse-Argonne offensive will continue until the war ends in November.
October 6, 1918	Germany and Austria-Hungary send notes to President Wilson requesting an armistice.
October 21, 1918	Germany unilaterally ends unrestricted submarine warfare.
November 3, 1918	American and French forces clear the Argonne forest.
November 5, 1918	Midterm elections give Republicans control of Congress.
November 9, 1918	Kaiser Wilhelm II of Germany abdicates and flees to Holland.

November 11, 1918	An armistice ending the fighting of World War I is reached after Germany asks for peace on the basis of Wilson's Fourteen Points.
December 13, 1918	Wilson arrives in France as head of the American peace delegation.
January 1919	By a vote of 309-1, Congress refuses to seat Wisconsin representative Victor Berger, an avowedly antiwar Socialist.
January 18, 1919	The Paris Peace Conference begins without representatives from the Central Powers.
January 25, 1919	Delegates to the conference formally approve Wilson's request that the League of Nations be made an integral part of the peace treaty.
March 4, 1919	While Wilson is back in the United States for a brief visit, Senator Henry Cabot Lodge circulates a list of objections to the treaty and its proposed League of Nations. Thirty-nine senators and senators-elect—enough to block ratification—sign the Lodge statement.
March 10, 1919	In *Schenk vs. United States*, the Supreme Court upholds the constitutionality of the Espionage Act, under which antiwar critics such as Socialist leader Eugene Debs have been imprisoned for interfering with military conscription and the general war effort.
March 15, 1919	The American Legion is founded in Paris by veterans of the AEF.
May 7, 1919	The Treaty of Versailles is submitted to the German delegation.
June 4, 1919	Congress passes a constitutional amendment to enfranchise women, pending ratification by the states.
June 28, 1919	The Treaty of Versailles is signed by Germany and the Allies. The treaty, which features the creation of the League of Nations as its centerpiece, needs Senate ratification to take effect in the United States.
September 3, 1919	Wilson embarks on a nationwide tour to gain support for the Treaty of Versailles and for the League of Nations.
September 25, 1919	An exhausted Wilson cancels the remainder of his tour; soon after he suffers a debilitating stroke.
November 19, 1919	Henry Cabot Lodge attaches fourteen reservations to the Treaty of Versailles and submits it to the Senate for ratification. By a vote of 55-39, the Senate rejects the treaty.
March 1, 1920	The American railway system, nationalized during the war, is returned to private hands.

March 19, 1920	The Senate holds two final votes on the Treaty of Versailles, one with and one without the Lodge reservations. Both fall short of ratification.
May 1920	Congress passes a joint resolution formally declaring an end to hostilities with Germany and Austria-Hungary; the resolution is vetoed by Wilson.
July 1920	The Democrats nominate James Cox of Ohio and Franklin Roosevelt of New York for president and vice president on a platform calling for the election to be a "solemn referendum" on the treaty and the League.
August 26, 1920	The Nineteenth Amendment, granting women the right to vote, is ratified.
November 2, 1920	Republican Warren G. Harding is elected president; his election signals a rejection of "Wilsonian" dreams of a new international order.
July 2, 1921	Harding signs a congressional joint resolution declaring an end to war with Germany.

Annotated Bibliography

James L. Abrahamson. *America Arms for a New Century: The Making of a Great Military Power.* New York: Macmillan, 1981. A history of the evolution of American military thinking and planning between 1880 and 1920 with an emphasis on key figures, including General John J. Pershing.

Lloyd Ambrosius. *Woodrow Wilson and the American Diplomatic Tradition: The Treaty Fight in Perspective.* New York: Cambridge University Press, 1987. A major reinterpretation of Woodrow Wilson's leadership and the reasons for his failure to implement his vision of a new world order at the Paris Peace Conference.

Tony Ashworth. *Trench Warfare, 1914–1918: The Live and Let Live System.* New York: Holmes and Meier, 1980. A military and social history of trench warfare and trench life, which included unofficial truces that "broke out" along the various fronts.

Robert B. Asprey. *At Belleau Wood.* New York: Putnam, 1965. A solid history of the first major military action involving U.S. troops in World War I.

Arthur Barbeau and Florette Henri. *The Unknown Soldiers: Black American Troops in World War I.* Philadelphia: Temple University Press, 1974. A thoroughly researched account of African American soldiers, whose activities had been previously neglected by historians.

Daniel R. Beaver. *Newton D. Baker and the American War Effort, 1917–1919.* Lincoln: University of Nebraska Press, 1966. A sympathetic study of Woodrow Wilson's wartime secretary of war.

George T. Blakey. *Historians on the Homefront: American Propagandists for the Great War.* Lexington: University of Kentucky Press, 1970. An examination of the motives and work of professional historians on behalf of the American war effort.

John Morton Blum. *Woodrow Wilson and the Politics of Morality.* Boston: Little, Brown, 1956. A biography of Wilson that stresses the significance of his often unyielding morality in his policy making.

William J. Breen. *Uncle Sam at Home: Civilian Mobilization, Wartime Federalism, and the Council of National Defense, 1917–1919.* Westport, CT: Greenwood Press, 1984. A study of wartime mobilization that concentrates on state governments, thereby providing a regional look at this process.

Edward H. Buehrig. *Woodrow Wilson and the Balance of Power*. Gloucester, MA: Peter Smith, 1968. A study of Wilsonian diplomacy contending that though national security concerns did play a role in the president's thinking, his idealism was the primary factor in making decisions.

Frederick S. Calhoun. *Power and Principle: Armed Intervention in Wilsonian Foreign Policy*. Kent, OH: Kent State University Press, 1986. A systematic account of the relationship between national interest, American power, and Wilsonian idealism in the making of American foreign policy.

Richard D. Challener. *Admirals, Generals, and American Foreign Policy, 1898–1914*. Princeton, NJ: Princeton University Press, 1973. An important study of the influence of the American military on American foreign policy just prior to the onset of World War I.

John Whiteclay Chambers II. *To Raise an Army: The Draft Comes to Modern America*. New York: Free Press, 1987. The best account of the background to and implementation of conscription during World War I.

Allen Churchill. *Over Here! An Informal Re-Creation of the Home Front in World War I*. New York: Dodd, Mead, 1968. A readable introductory history of the American home front.

Bruce Clayton. *Forgotten Prophet: The Life of Randolph Bourne*. Baton Rouge: Louisiana State University Press, 1984. The sympathetic biography of an important opponent of American entry into World War I.

Kendrick A. Clements. *Woodrow Wilson: World Statesman*. Boston: Twayne, 1987. A positive assessment of the character and political career of the U.S. president.

J. Garry Clifford. *The Citizen Soldiers: The Plattsburg Training Camp Movement, 1913–1920*. Lexington: University of Kentucky Press, 1972. A solid study focusing on the efforts of Grenville Clark and Leonard Wood to promote military training and create a new kind of "citizen soldier."

Edward M. Coffman. *The War to End All Wars: The American Military Experience in World War I*. New York: Oxford University Press, 1968. A brilliant description of the war as it was experienced by American soldiers and generals in the training camps, the trenches, and War Department headquarters.

Paolo E. Coletta. *Admiral Bradley A. Fiske and the American Navy*. Lawrence: Regents Press of Kansas, 1979. This history of the American navy before and during World War I contends that excessive civilian interference left it ill prepared to fight that conflict.

Benjamin F. Cooling, ed. *War, Business, and American Society: Historical Perspectives on the Military-Industrial Complex*. Port Washington, NY: Kennikat Press, 1977. A collection of important articles on the early development of ties between the military and American business.

John Milton Cooper. *The Vanity of Power: American Isolationism and the First World War, 1914–1917*. Westport, CT: Greenwood Press, 1969. A study of the politics and role of key isolationists in Congress during the debate over American entry into World War I.

John Milton Cooper. *The Warrior and the Priest: Woodrow Wilson and Theodore Roosevelt.* Cambridge, MA: Belknap Press of Harvard University Press, 1983. An inventive dual biography of two dominant political leaders in the United States during World War I: the "warrior," Theodore Roosevelt, and the "priest," Woodrow Wilson.

John Milton Cooper, ed. *Causes and Consequences of World War I.* New York: Quadrangle, 1972. A collection of essays by distinguished historians dealing with World War I.

Stanley Cooperman. *World War I and the American Novel.* Baltimore: Johns Hopkins University Press, 1967. A comprehensive literary history tracing the profound influence of World War I on a generation of American writers.

Patrick Devlin. *Too Proud to Fight: Woodrow Wilson's Neutrality.* New York: Oxford University Press, 1975. A sympathetic portrait of Woodrow Wilson written by a British historian and jurist who concludes that Wilson entered the war primarily to have a voice in postwar diplomacy.

Edward Robb Ellis. *Echoes of Distant Thunder: Life in the United States, 1914–1918.* New York: Kodansha International, 1996. A compelling and informative social history of the United States during World War I.

Robert H. Ferrell. *Woodrow Wilson and World War I, 1917–1921.* New York: Harper & Row, 1985. A solid single-volume account of Wilson and the war that combines diplomatic, military, and social history.

John P. Finnegan. *Against the Specter of a Dragon: The Campaign for American Military Preparedness, 1914–1917.* Westport, CT: Greenwood Press, 1974. A thorough history of the preparedness movement in America, whose goals were widely adopted only after the decision to enter the war.

Marvin Fletcher. *The Black Soldier and Officer in the U.S. Army, 1891–1917.* Columbia: University of Missouri Press, 1974. Both a history of the black soldier and an examination of the racial views of American army leaders prior to and during World War I.

Charles Forcey. *The Crossroads of Liberalism: Croly, Weyl, Lippmann, and the Progressive Era, 1900–1925.* New York: Oxford University Press, 1961. An intellectual history of leading progressives who supported the war that examines the impact of the war on their thinking.

Frank Freidel. *Over There: The Story of America's First Great Overseas Crusade.* Boston: Little, Brown, 1964. A solid general overview, highlighted by excellent photographs and extracts from the diaries and letters of major and minor participants in the conflict.

Paul Fussell. *The Great War and Modern Memory.* New York: Oxford University Press, 1975. A masterful analysis of the western front as expressed by novelists and poets, concentrating on the British experience.

Charles Gilbert. *American Financing of World War I*. Westport, CT: Greenwood, 1970. A study of Wilson administration financial policies during the war.

Martin Gilbert. *The First World War: A Complete History*. New York: Henry Holt, 1994. An excellent recent military history of World War I.

Aaron A. Godfrey. *Government Operation of the Railroads, 1918–1920: Its Necessity, Success, and Consequences*. Austin, TX: Jenkins, 1974. A well-researched study of the process by which the federal government took control of and ran the American railroad system during the war.

Edwyn Gray. *The Killing Time: The U-Boat War, 1914–1918*. New York: Scribner, 1972. A popular narrative of Germany's efforts to wage submarine warfare that makes effective use of interviews with former submarine captains.

Maurine Weiner Greenwald. *Women, War, and Work: The Impact of World War I on Women Workers in the United States*. Westport, CT: Greenwood Press, 1980. A thorough account of women workers that concludes the war provided significant opportunities for women to advance economically.

Carol S. Gruber. *Mars and Minerva: World War I and the Uses of the Higher Learning in America*. Baton Rouge: Louisiana State University Press, 1975. A highly critical account of the activities and ideas of college professors and others in higher education during World War I.

Oron J. Hale. *The Great Illusion, 1900–1914*. New York: Harper & Row, 1971. A brilliant synthesis of European politics, society, culture, and economics on the eve of the Great War.

Ellis W. Hawley. *The Great War and the Search for a Modern Order: A History of the American People and Their Institutions, 1917–1933*. New York: St. Martin's Press, 1979. A history of the evolution of bureaucracy in America, with an emphasis on the impact of the World War I experience.

Derek Heater. *National Self-Determination: Woodrow Wilson and His Legacy*. New York: St. Martin's Press, 1994. A study of Wilson's foreign policy ideas and their impact on the postwar peace process.

August Heckscher. *Woodrow Wilson*. New York: Scribner, 1991. A recent and comprehensive biography of America's president during World War I.

Linda L. Hewitt. *Women Marines in World War I*. Washington, DC: History and Museums Division, U.S. Marine Corps, 1974. The official history of the role of women in the U.S. Marines during World War I.

Henry J. James. *German Submarines in Yankee Waters: The First World War*. New York: Gotham House, 1940. An older but still quite valuable history of the U.S. Navy's war against German submarines that ventured into American waters.

Donald Johnson. *Challenge to American Freedoms: World War I and the Rise of the American Civil Liberties Union.* Lexington: University of Kentucky Press, 1963. A history of the origins of the American Civil Liberties Union that argues that a genuine civil liberties movement in America was first made possible because of World War I hysteria.

David M. Kennedy. *Over Here: The First World War and American Society.* New York: Oxford University Press, 1980. An acclaimed account of the impact of the war on American life.

Thomas J. Knock. *To End All Wars: Woodrow Wilson and the Quest for a New World Order.* New York: Oxford University Press, 1992. A study of Woodrow Wilson and the sources of his ideas on war and diplomacy.

Laurence LaFore. *The Long Fuse: An Interpretation of the Origins of World War I.* Philadelphia: Lippincott, 1971. A superbly written, concise overview of the background to World War I that points to Slavic nationalism as a major cause.

Jack C. Lane. *Armed Progressive: A Study of the Military and Public Career of Leonard Wood.* San Rafael, CA: Presidio Press, 1978. A biography with much information on the role Wood played in the preparedness movement prior to 1917.

William L. Langer. *Gas and Flames in World War I.* New York: Knopf, 1965. An account of chemical warfare during World War I written by a distinguished scholar of diplomatic history.

Earl Latham, ed. *The Philosophy and Policies of Woodrow Wilson.* Chicago: University of Chicago Press, 1958. A collection of scholarly essays on various aspects of Wilson's presidency, including the road to World War I and the treaty-making process.

Eric J. Leed. *No Man's Land: Combat & Identity in World War I.* New York: Cambridge University Press, 1979. A social and cultural history of World War I as seen through the eyes of those who participated in it.

N. Gordon Levin. *Woodrow Wilson and World Politics: America's Response to War and Revolution.* New York: Oxford University Press, 1968. An examination of Wilson's foreign policy that argues that the president sought to make the world safe for liberal capitalism, thereby making him an opponent of both traditional imperialism and revolutionary socialism.

Arthur Link. *Wilson the Diplomatist: A Look at His Major Foreign Policies.* Baltimore: Johns Hopkins University Press, 1957. A collection of lectures and essays concerning various aspects of Wilsonian foreign policy, including American neutrality, the decision for war, and his peace program.

Seward Livermore. *Politics Is Adjourned: Woodrow Wilson and the War Congress, 1916–1918.* Middletown, CT: Wesleyan University Press, 1966. A revisionist history that questions the extent of bipartisan cooperation during World War I, arguing that Republican Party leaders worked behind the scenes to undermine the president's policies.

Frederick Luebke. *Bonds of Loyalty: German-Americans and World War I*. De Kalb: Northern Illinois University Press, 1974. A compelling study of the plight of German Americans whose "bonds of loyalty" cut two ways during World War I.

C. Roland Marchand. *The American Peace Movement and Social Reform, 1898–1918*. Princeton, NJ: Princeton University Press, 1973. A study of the peace movement in the United States both before and during World War I.

Herbert F. Margulies. *Reconciliation and Revival: James R. Mann and the House Republicans in the Wilson Era*. Westport, CT: Greenwood Press, 1996. A political history of Republican members of Congress during the presidency of Woodrow Wilson.

Ernest R. May. *The World War and American Isolationism, 1914–1917*. Cambridge, MA: Harvard University Press, 1959. A history of American diplomacy during the period of official American neutrality that seeks to capture the drama of an essentially peace-minded president leading his country to war.

Henry F. May. *The End of American Innocence: A Study of the First Years of Our Own Time, 1917–1919*. New York: Knopf, 1959. A cultural and intellectual history that analyzes how World War I affected American thought.

Arno J. Mayer. *The Politics and Diplomacy of Peacemaking: Containment and Counterrevolution at Versailles, 1918–1919*. New York: Knopf, 1967. An exhaustive study of the peace negotiations at Versailles that emphasizes the eventual decision of Woodrow Wilson to align himself with the "forces of order" and against the Soviet Union's Bolshevik revolutionary regime.

Lyn McDonald. *Voices and Images of the Great War, 1914–1918*. London: Michael Joseph, 1988. A compelling collection of primary sources that offer a vivid glimpse into the experiences of ordinary soldiers.

William D. Miller. *Pretty Bubbles in the Air: America in 1919*. Urbana: University of Illinois Press, 1991. A social history of the immediate postwar era that relies heavily on American newspaper accounts.

Paul L. Murphy. *World War I and the Origin of Civil Liberties in the United States*. New York: W.W. Norton, 1979. A history of the federal government's violations of civil liberties during World War I that examines how the government's actions sparked a movement to protect civil liberties.

Aaron Norman. *The Great War: The Men, the Planes, the Saga of Military Aviation, 1914–1918*. New York: Macmillan, 1968. A comprehensive history of the air war, including the role of the Americans.

Gerald W. Patton. *War and Race: The Black Officer in the American Military, 1915–1941*. Westport, CT: Greenwood Press, 1981. A study of black officers and the difficulties they faced in the American military.

John J. Pershing. *My Experiences in the World War*. New York: Frederick A. Stokes, 1931. The memoirs, in two volumes, of the iron-willed head of the American Expeditionary Force (AEF) and his battles with both the Allies and his own War Department.

Horace C. Peterson and Gilbert C. Fite. *Opponents of War, 1917–1918*. Madison: University of Wisconsin Press, 1957. An older but still very serviceable account of World War I–era dissenters and how they were treated.

Richard Polenberg. *Fighting Faiths: The Abrams Case, the Supreme Court, and Free Speech*. New York: Viking Press, 1987. A detailed history of what proved to be a pathbreaking Supreme Court case on civil liberties during wartime.

James Oliver Robertson. *No Third Choice: Progressives in Republican Politics, 1916–1921*. New York: Garland Press, 1983. An account of the decline and fall of the Progressive Party as an alternative to the two major parties during and after World War I.

Stuart I. Rochester. *American Liberal Disillusionment: In the Wake of World War I*. University Park: Pennsylvania State University Press, 1977. An intellectual history of the impact of World War I on American social and political thought.

Elliott M. Rudwick. *Race Riot at East St. Louis, July 2, 1917*. Carbondale: Southern Illinois University Press, 1964. A richly detailed study of a major race riot in the context of the American entry into World War I.

Ronald Schaffer. *America in the Great War: The Rise of the War Welfare State*. New York: Oxford University Press, 1991. An inventive study of the wartime home front which focuses on the efforts of the government to manage the American people.

Daniel M. Smith. *The Great Departure: The United States and World War I, 1914–1920*. New York: Wiley, 1965. A valuable general overview of American neutrality, belligerency, and peacemaking that is essentially sympathetic to Woodrow Wilson's ideas and efforts.

Daniel M. Smith. *Robert Lansing and American Neutrality, 1914–1917*. Berkeley and Los Angeles: University of California Press, 1958. A well-documented study that concentrates on the differences between President Woodrow Wilson and his second secretary of state, Robert Lansing, who viewed American entry into the war as necessary long before Wilson did.

Laurence Stallings. *The Doughboys: The Story of the AEF, 1917–1918*. New York: Harper & Row, 1963. An account of the war written by an American marine who was wounded at Belleau Wood.

Barbara J. Steinson. *American Women's Activism in World War I*. New York: Garland, 1982. An examination of the various activities of American women in World War I, including relief work and political lobbying.

Ralph Stone. *The Irreconcilables: The Fight Against the League of Nations*. Lexington: University of Kentucky Press, 1970. Brief biographical sketches of the dozen senators who opposed the League of Nations in any form and their successful fight to block ratification of the Versailles treaty.

A.J.P. Taylor. *The Struggle for Mastery in Europe, 1848–1918*. Oxford: Clarendon Press, 1960. A broad history of events leading to World War I that challenges those who seek to excuse Germany from major responsibility for the war.

John Terraine. *The Western Front, 1914–1918*. Philadelphia: Lippincott, 1965. A thought-provoking collection of essays on various aspects of the war on the western front.

John A. Thompson. *Reformers and War: American Progressive Publicists and the First World War*. New York: Cambridge University Press, 1987. An intellectual history of leading progressive reformers and the impact of World War I on their thinking and behavior.

John Toland. *No Man's Land: 1918 — The Last Year of the Great War*. Garden City, NY: Doubleday, 1980. A highly detailed history that makes effective use of firsthand recollections of soldiers.

David Trask. *Captains & Cabinets: Anglo-American Naval Relations, 1917–1918*. Columbia: University of Missouri Press, 1972. A comparative history of naval policy on both sides of the Atlantic during World War I.

David Trask. *The United States in the Supreme War Council: American War Aims and Inter-Allied Strategy, 1917–1918*. Middletown, CT: Wesleyan University Press, 1961. A study of American war aims and of joint British-French-American strategizing during World War I.

David Trask, ed. *World War I at Home: Readings on American Life, 1914–1920*. New York: Wiley, 1970. A collection of important primary sources concerning the debate over American entry into the war, wartime mobilization issues, civil liberties, and peacemaking.

Barbara Tuchman. *The Guns of August*. New York: Macmillan, 1962. A colorful account of the early maneuverings and opening battles of World War I.

Melvin I. Urofsky. *Big Steel and the Wilson Administration: A Study in Business-Government Relations*. Columbus: Ohio State University Press, 1969. An examination of wartime and postwar policy involving the efforts of the Wilson administration to bring a major American industry under its control.

Stephen Vaughn. *Holding Fast the Inner Lines: Democracy, Nationalism, and the Committee on Public Information*. Chapel Hill: University of North Carolina Press, 1980. A study of the Committee on Public Information, otherwise known as the Creel Committee, and its efforts to garner support for the American war effort.

Larry Wayne Ward. *The Motion Picture Goes to War: The U.S. Government Film Effort During World War I*. Ann Arbor, MI: UMI Research Press, 1985. A study of the efforts of both the Committee on Public Information and the film industry to influence American thinking on participation in World War I.

Edward A. Weinstein. *Woodrow Wilson: A Medical and Psychological Biography*. Princeton, NJ: Princeton University Press, 1981. A thought-provoking study that seeks to make connections between the president's policy making, medical history, and character.

James Weinstein. *The Corporate Ideal in the Liberal State, 1900–1918*. Boston: Beacon Press, 1968. A study of the evolution of progressive thought and action, culminating in the close relationship between business and government during World War I.

Rachel West. *The Department of State on the Eve of the First World War*. Athens: University of Georgia Press, 1978. A highly critical study of both President Woodrow Wilson and Secretary of State William Jennings Bryan and their failure to prepare the country to face the impending conflict in Europe.

Index

and credit for Allies, 173
and problem of inflation, 180-81
from taxation on large companies, 175-79
War Industries Board, 235
War of 1812, 30, 95
Washington, George, 27, 35, 71, 98, 210
Watson, Tom, 152
Watterson, Henry, 77
weapons, 29
  manufacturers of, 37
  munitions factories, 58
Weyl, Walter, 116
White, William Allen, 195
Wilhelm II of Germany, 78, 222
  see also Hohenzollern family
Wilson, Woodrow, 63, 71, 85, 94-95, 199
  on American neutrality, 65, 233-34
  call for increased taxation, 177
  call for military expansion, 32
  on cause of organized labor, 103
  leadership of, 120-22, 123
  member of Council of Four, 192
  patience of, 106
  and political opposition, 186, 206-207
  response to *Lusitania* incident, 77

and support for League of Nations, 199
  on vote for women, 138
Wisconsin, 154, 156
Wisconsin brigade, 30
Woman's Peace Party, 141, 142, 143, 144
women
  as pacifists, 141, 142-43
    international gathering of, 144
    practical program of, 145-46
  and suffrage, 138, 139, 145
  and support of war, 132, 133
    through care of men, 134
    in industry, 136
    through paid work, 134-35
    professions, 137
    service to nation, 140
Women's Land Army, 132
Wood, Leonard, 26, 166
World War I
  number of men lost, 230
  unprecedented nature of, 64
  as war of commercialism, 95, 96, 113, 117, 125
  see also commerce